IMAGES of America
SANDUSKY
OHIO

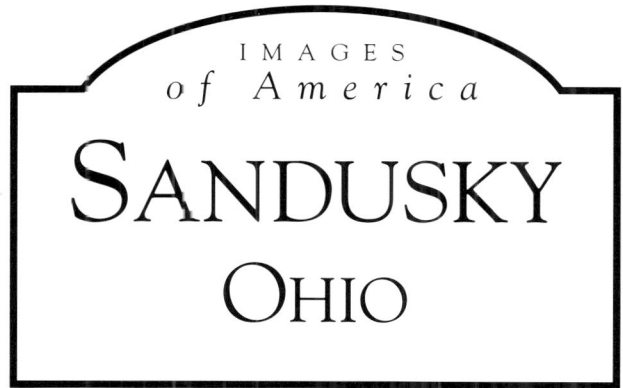

IMAGES of America

SANDUSKY
OHIO

Ron Davidson

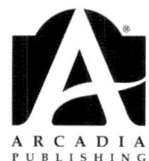

Copyright © 2002 by Ron Davidson
ISBN 978-0-7385-2030-8

Published by Arcadia Publishing
Charleston SC, Chicago IL, Portsmouth NH, San Francisco CA

Printed in the United States of America

Library of Congress Catalog Card Number: 2002112089

For all general information contact Arcadia Publishing at:
Telephone 843-853-2070
Fax 843-853-0044
E-mail sales@arcadiapublishing.com
For customer service and orders:
Toll-Free 1-888-313-2665

Visit us on the Internet at www.arcadiapublishing.com

Contents

Acknowledgments 6

Introduction 7

1. Early Sandusky 9

2. Development of the City:
   Institutions, Industries, Interurbans 29

3. Modern Times 83

Acknowledgments

Thanks first should go to Julie Brooks, director of the Sandusky Library, and to the library board, for allowing me the opportunity to put this book together as a library project; and to my supervisors, Terri Estel and Dennis McMullen, for giving me the time to work on this project. Thanks also to the Sandusky Library reference staff for taking some of the pressure off of my reference duties. I also must recognize the library staff whose important work contributed to the success of this project: those who did much (if not most) of the research and gathering for this book, particularly Michelle Wardle, Sean Templeton, Sue Reardon, Dorene Paul; Maggie Marconi, who offered many good suggestions and helped with fact-gathering; Barbara Bishop, who helped select the cover image and is helping to promote the book in the community; and all other staff, who offered suggestions and words of support. My most heartfelt gratitude is reserved for Terri Light, whose love, support, and encouragement has helped me in so many ways.

Most importantly, we must thank all the people who have contributed to preserving the history of the community. Many of these people are long gone, but they and their actions are not forgotten. We are of course very grateful for all the donors of historical materials to the Sandusky Library and Follett House Museum over the past hundred-plus years; this book is a product of those contributions. From the earliest contributors, such as Mrs. L.S. Johnson (in 1902), to the most recent, including Jackie Mayer Townsend (whose support for this project is particularly appreciated), each donor has made an important contribution to the community.

Charles Frohman must be acknowledged because of the vastness of his contribution to the community memory. He was a tireless chronicler of the history of Sandusky; much of the information in this book, including some of the images, is derived from sources he collected and produced.

Finally, we need to reserve special thanks to two of the most important promoters of Sandusky's history: Helen Hansen and Virginia Steinemann, who worked at the Follett House Museum for many years and wrote books and articles on the history of their community; their contributions are innumerable. Much of the information in this book was first researched and reported by them. It is fair to say that the community owes a great debt to Mrs. Hansen and Mrs. Steinemann for their work in preserving and promoting its history.

INTRODUCTION

From the earliest known times, the place we now call Sandusky was dominated by trade and transportation. The Erie were probably the first people to occupy the region at the mouth of the Sandusky Bay, a convenient location for travel by water. After the Erie were gone, the Ottawa and the Wyandot used the area as a portage and encampment site in their travels from the land that is now Michigan. The area was briefly known as Ogontz Place, named after an Ottawa chief who lived on the site. The French and the British each operated trading posts in the area during the 18th century—both called Fort Sandusky.

As with these earlier settlements, the city of Sandusky came about primarily because its location made it a good site for trade and travel. Today when many think of Sandusky, they think of a different sort of trade and travel—trade in souvenirs and travel on roller coasters! But the history of Sandusky is more than amusement parks. It is a story of conquering adversity and building a community.

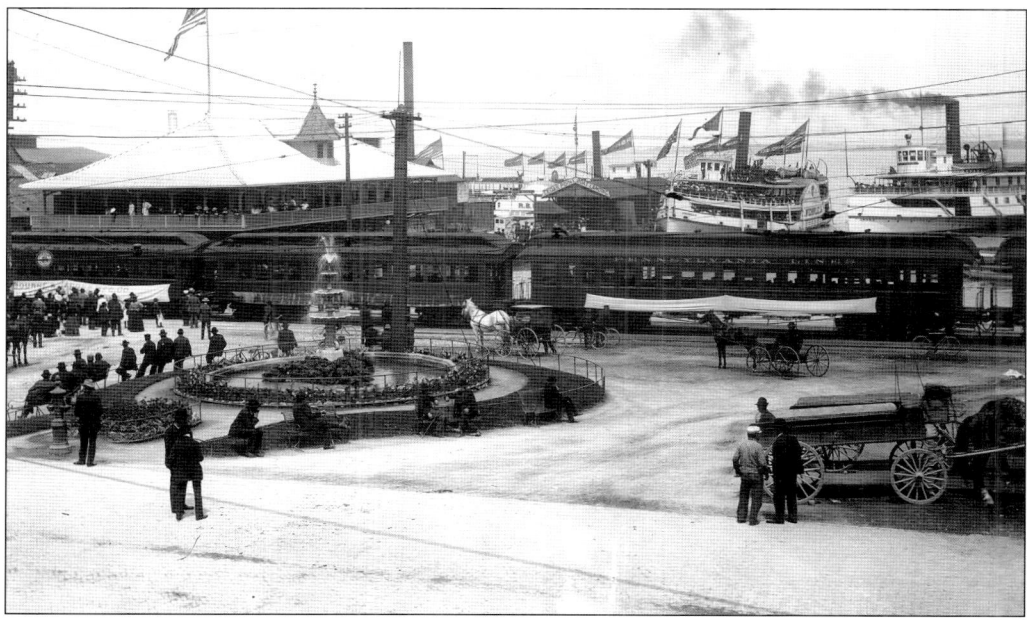

One

Early Sandusky

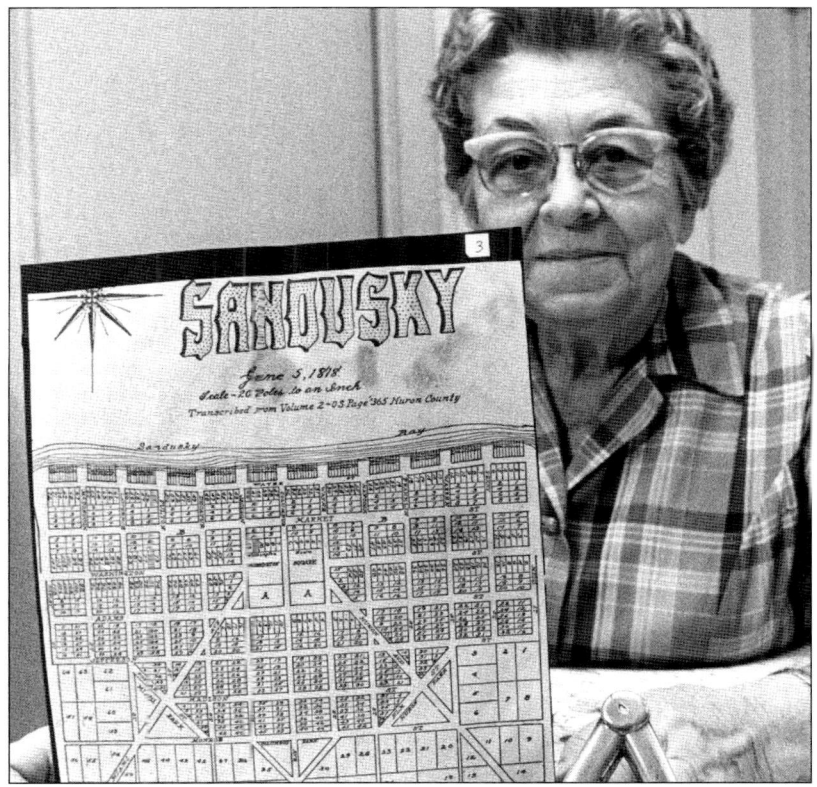

The town of Portland was founded in the spring of 1817, when Zalman Wildman of Danbury, Connecticut, began laying out a settlement on land along the Sandusky Bay. Later that year, Isaac Mills of New Haven, Connecticut, made a land claim overlapping Wildman's territory. Eventually they, together with George Hoadley, reached a compromise and joined their tracts, creating "Sandusky City" in the spring of 1818. Hector Kilbourne, a Mason, surveyed and platted the land, using the Masonic emblem of a square and compass as inspiration for the diagonal roads on the street grid. Helen Hansen, former curator of the Follett House Museum in Sandusky (who celebrated her 100th birthday in 2002), is holding a copy of one of the first maps of Sandusky City, as it was then called.

Although a co-founder of the city, Isaac Mills never established permanent residence in Sandusky. He kept his home in Connecticut while continuing his land speculation in Ohio. His son, however, was a Sanduskian.

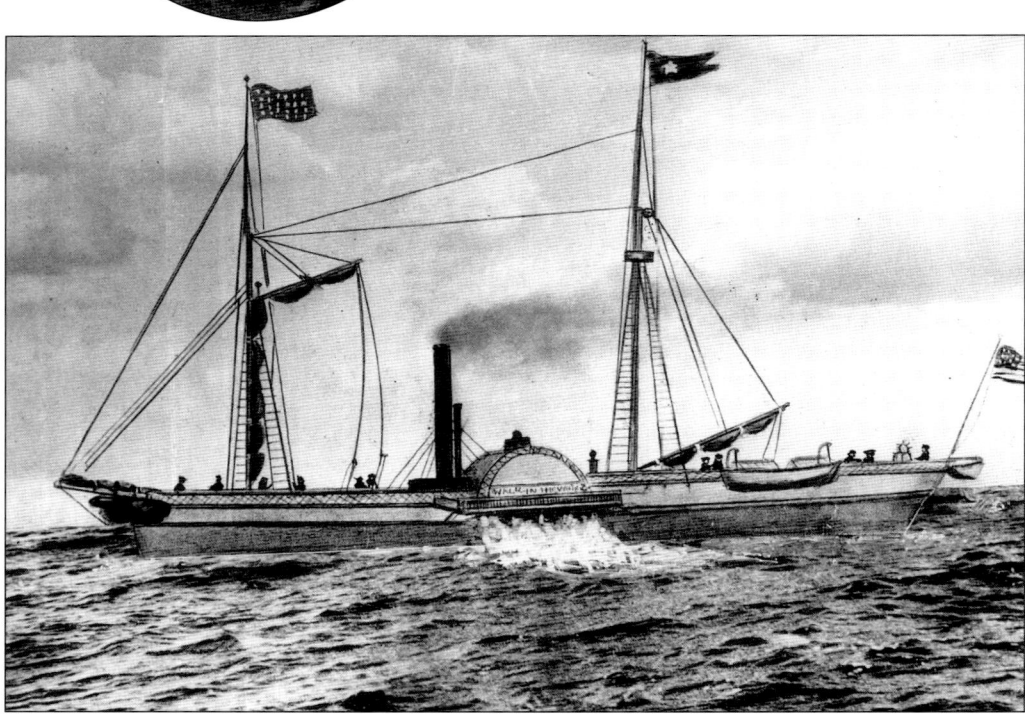

Soon after it was settled, Sandusky became an important transportation terminus on Lake Erie. Steamships soon became the major means of navigation on the lakes. The *Walk-in-the-Water* was the first steamship to travel on Lake Erie. Built in Buffalo in 1818, it operated between Buffalo and Detroit, making occasional stops in and around Sandusky. It sailed until the fall of 1821, when it was wrecked in a storm near Buffalo.

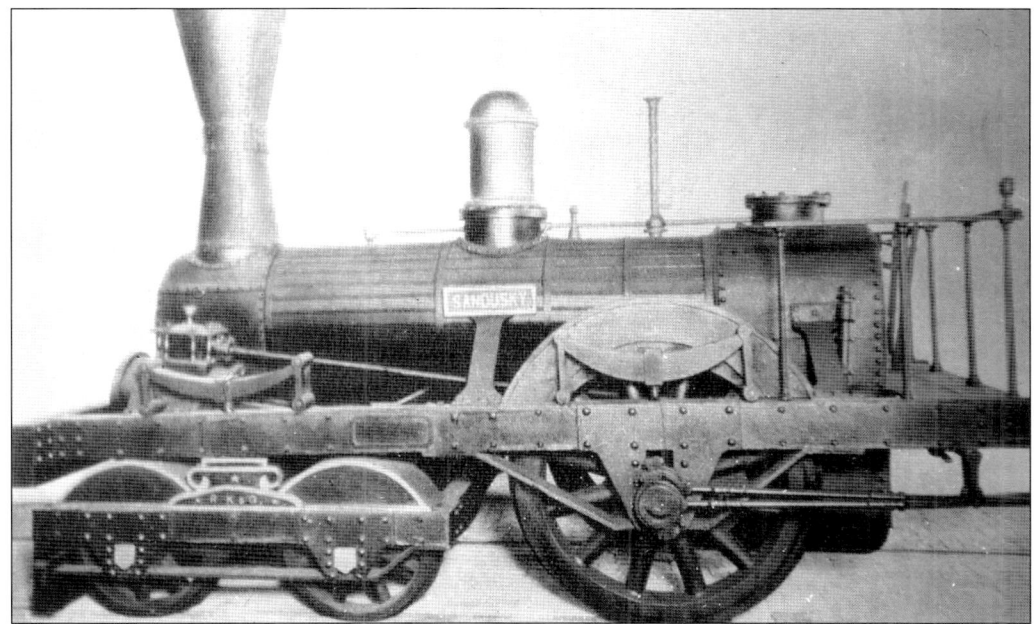

Around the same time that steamships came to dominate lake transportation, railroads arrived to facilitate overland travel to the west and the south. In 1826, the Ohio legislature granted a charter establishing the Mad River and Lake Erie Railroad to operate between Dayton and Sandusky. Beginning operation in 1832, it was one of the earliest railroads west of the Appalachians. The *Sandusky* was the first locomotive put into service on that line. Built in Paterson, New Jersey, in 1837, it was shipped to Sandusky via the Erie Canal and a Lake Erie schooner (also called the *Sandusky*). It was also the first locomotive to use a steam whistle.

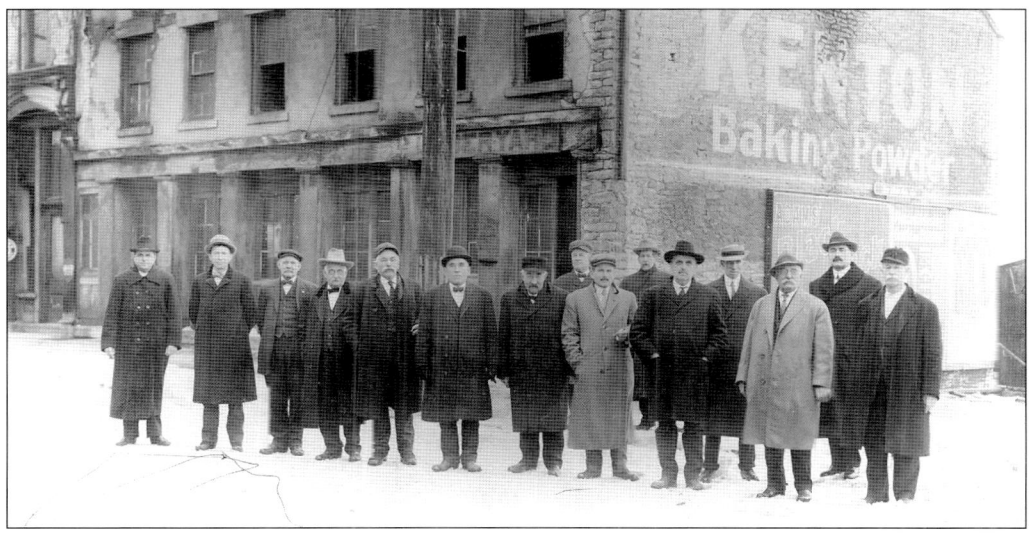

The Mad River passenger depot was built in 1838 on the northwest corner of Jackson and Water Streets. The image shows the building long after it stopped being used as a train station. The reason this photograph was taken is a mystery; the identities of the men are unknown. Perhaps they were affiliated with the Gilcher and Schuck Lumber Company, which owned the building after the railroad company.

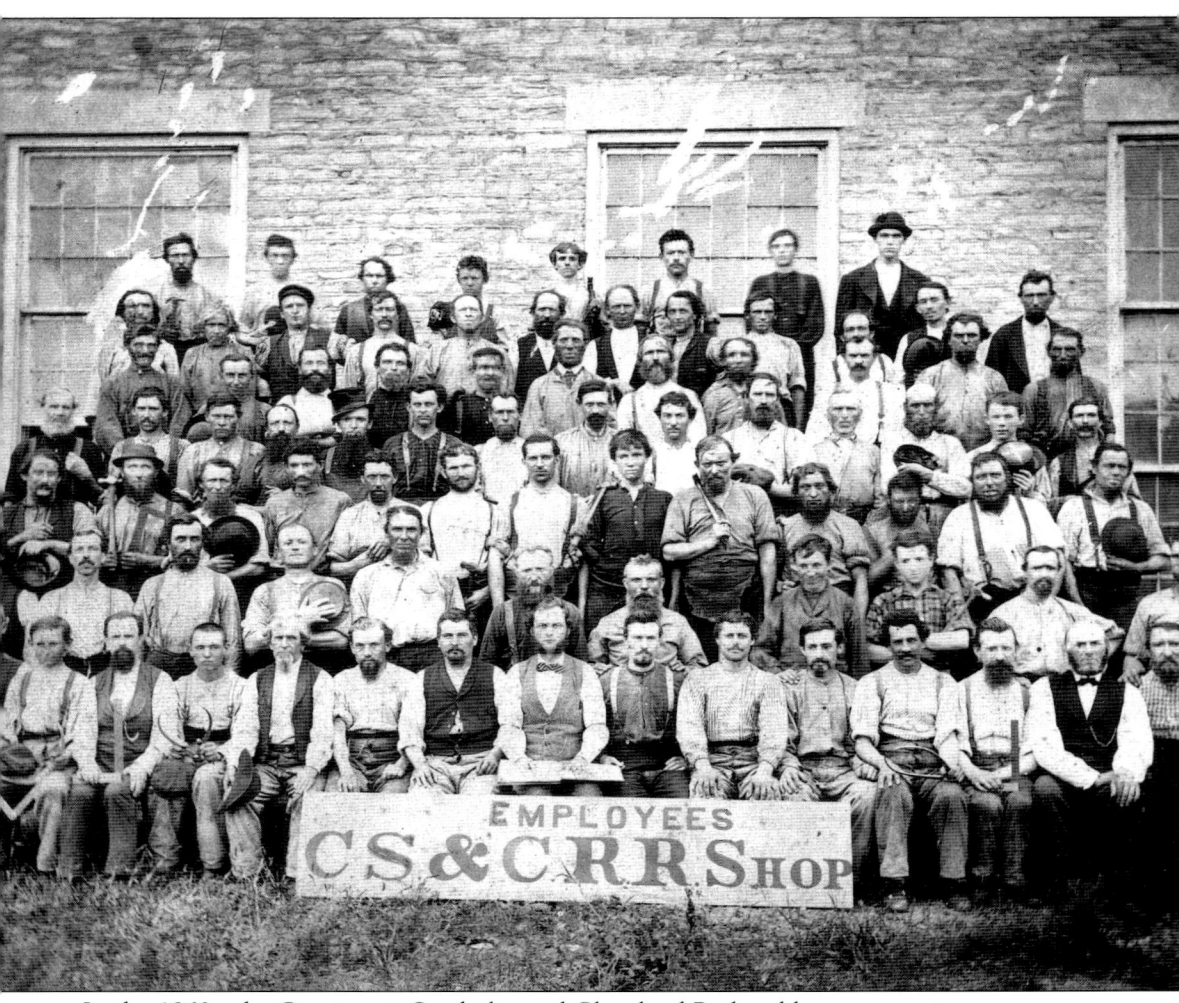

In the 1860s, the Cincinnati, Sandusky, and Cleveland Railroad began operation as successor to the Sandusky Dayton and Cincinnati Railroad (the name adopted by the Mad River and Lake Erie in 1858). The crew of the Sandusky shop is seen in this image. Judging from the tools held and the dress of the men, they appear to be both office workers and road crew.

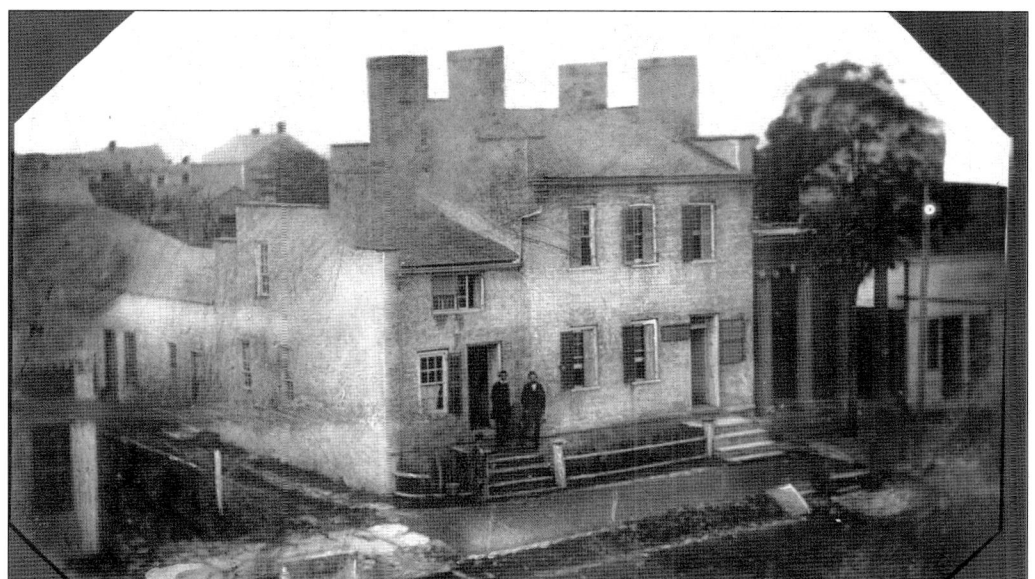

Eleutheros Cooke, the first lawyer in Sandusky, helped to secure the charter from the Ohio legislature to establish the Mad River and Lake Erie Railroad. He also served in the Ohio House of Representatives and was a representative in the United States Congress. His first home in Sandusky, seen here, is said to be the first house in the city built of native limestone. This image of that house is from a daguerreotype, probably taken around 1852—long after Cooke had sold the house to John Beatty, mayor of Sandusky from 1834 to 1836. After Beatty died in 1845, the house again changed ownership, ultimately being razed in 1854.

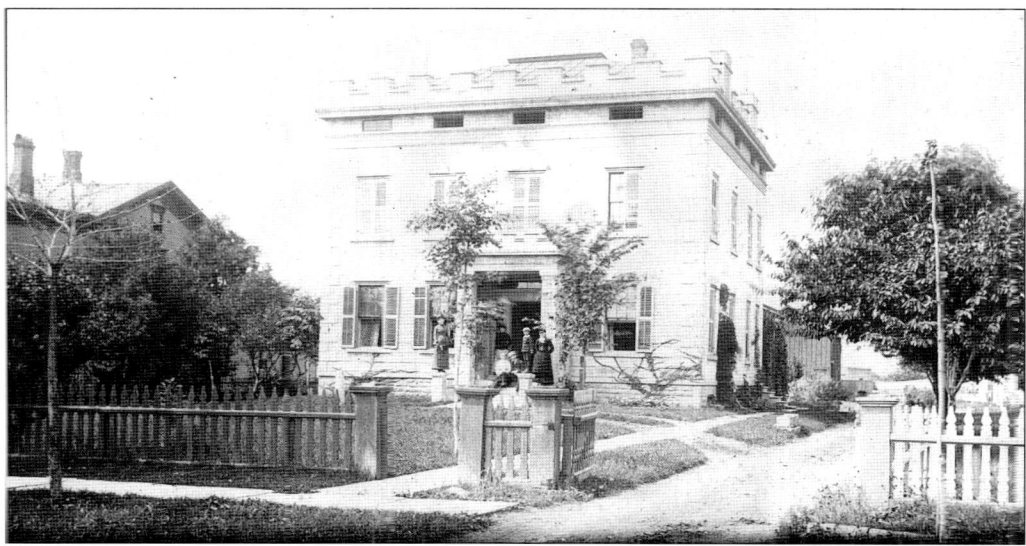

Although the original Cooke house no longer exists, his later home, pictured here, still stands—but not where it was built. The Eleutheros Cooke House was built in 1843–1844 at the corner of Columbus Avenue and Washington Row, where Cooke lived until his death in 1864. In 1879, the house was dismantled and reassembled about a mile south on Columbus Avenue. The Cooke House is now a museum, managed by the Old House Guild of Sandusky for the Ohio Historical Society.

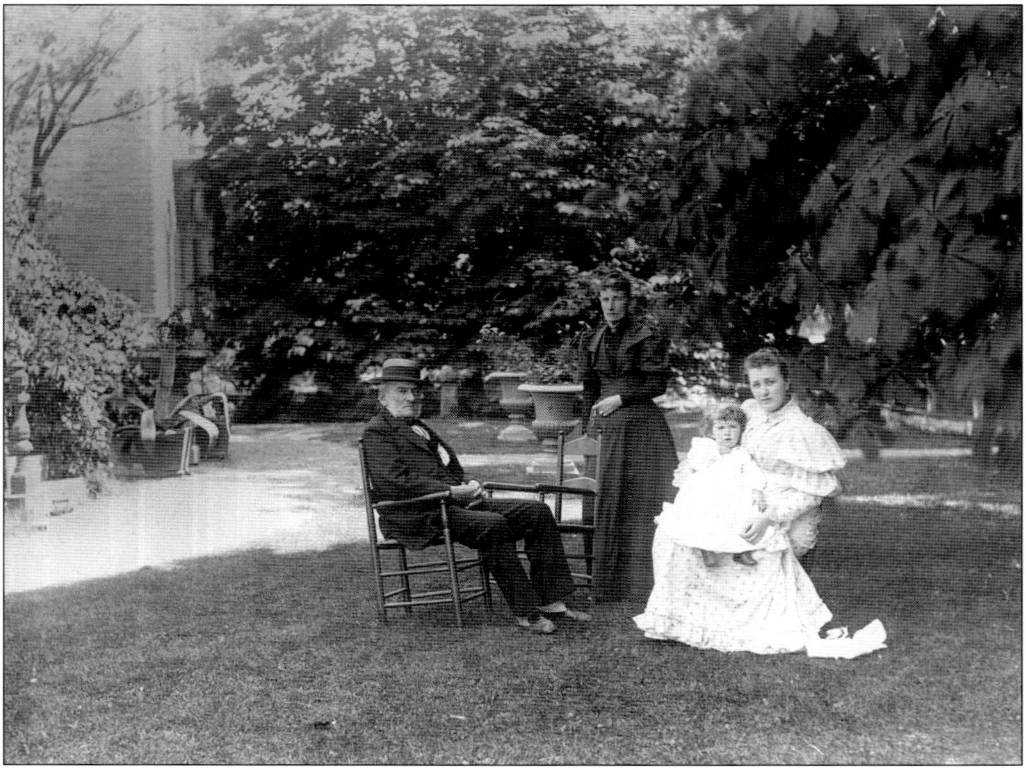

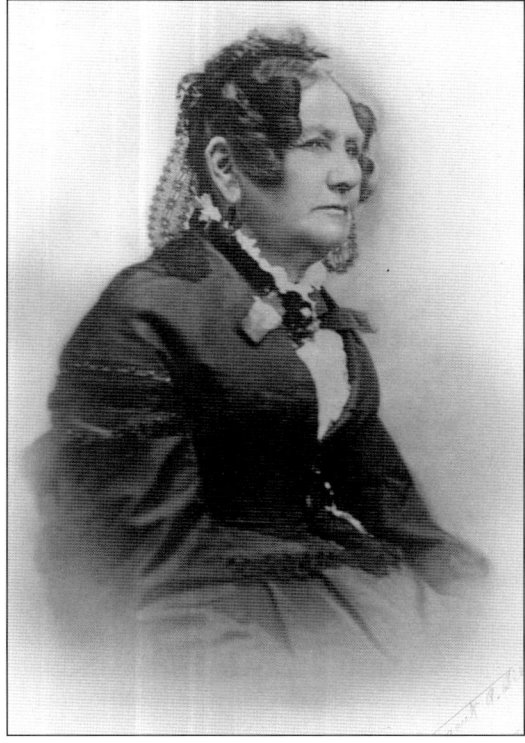

Oran Follett played a prominent role in the affairs of early Sandusky. His influence went beyond Sandusky as well. Among his many activities, he served as editor of the Columbus newspaper, the *Ohio State Journal*, was president of the Sandusky, Dayton, and Cincinnati Railroad, and was active in the Republican Party. Here he is seen in the yard of his home, in his nineties, with his daughter, granddaughter, and great-granddaughter, c. 1893.

Eliza Follett, wife of Oran, was influential in her own right. She was involved in many charitable activities and was a participant in the abolitionist cause. She also helped nurse the sick during the cholera outbreaks of the 1840s and 1850s. The Sandusky Library archives holds a letter describing her role in bringing Thanksgiving dinner to the Union troops on Johnson's Island during the Civil War. She was so admired in the community that the day of her funeral was a citywide day of mourning.

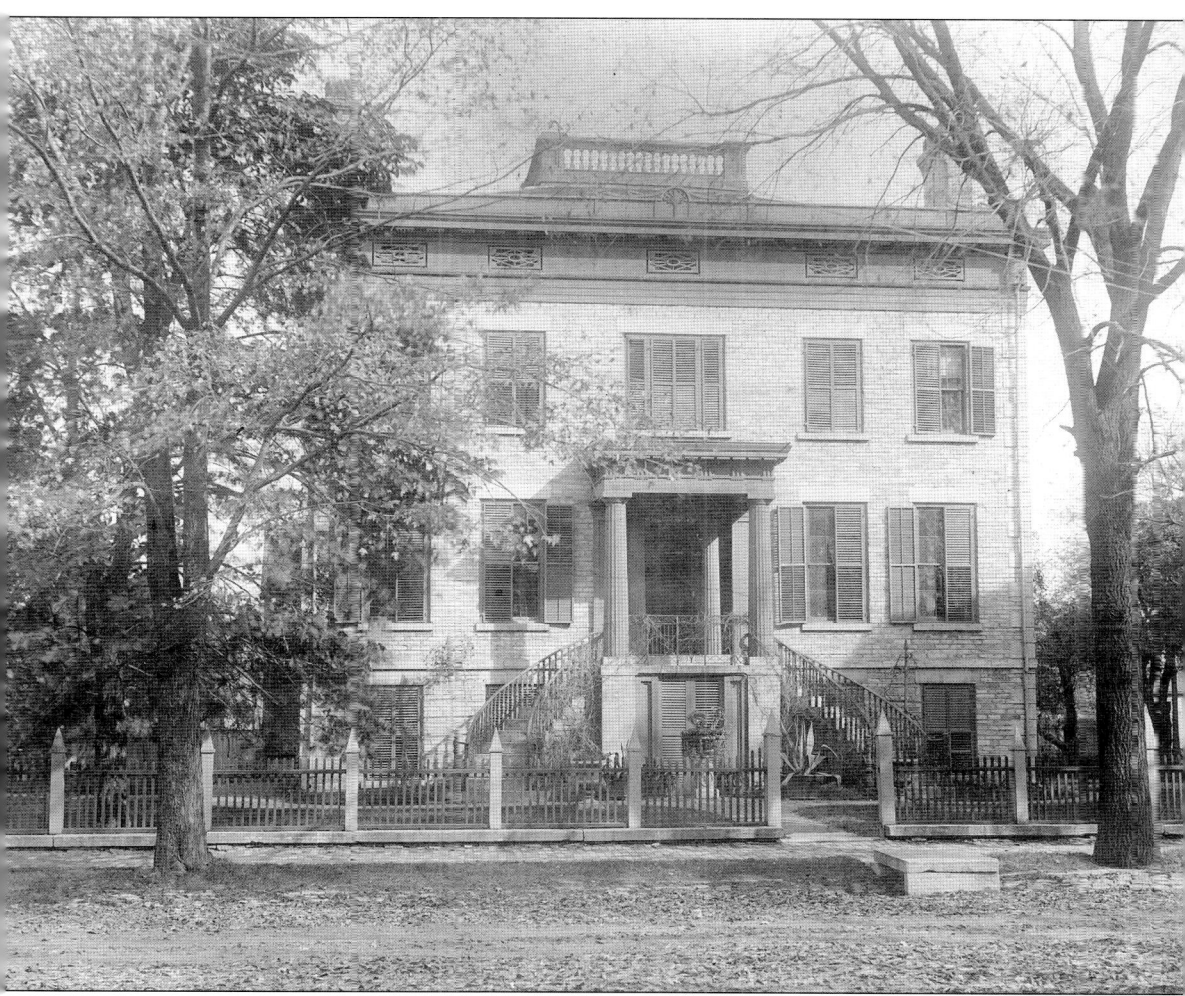

The Follett family home, on the corner of Wayne and Adams Streets, was built in the 1830s, shortly after Oran Follett moved to Sandusky from Buffalo, New York. It was built from limestone quarried from a lot across Adams Street. Oran Follett lived in the house until his death in 1894, at age 95. In the 20th century, the house was used as an office for the Depression-era federal Works Progress Administration; later, the Sandusky High School used the house as a classroom for teaching home economics. Today, it is the Follett House Museum, a branch of the Sandusky Library.

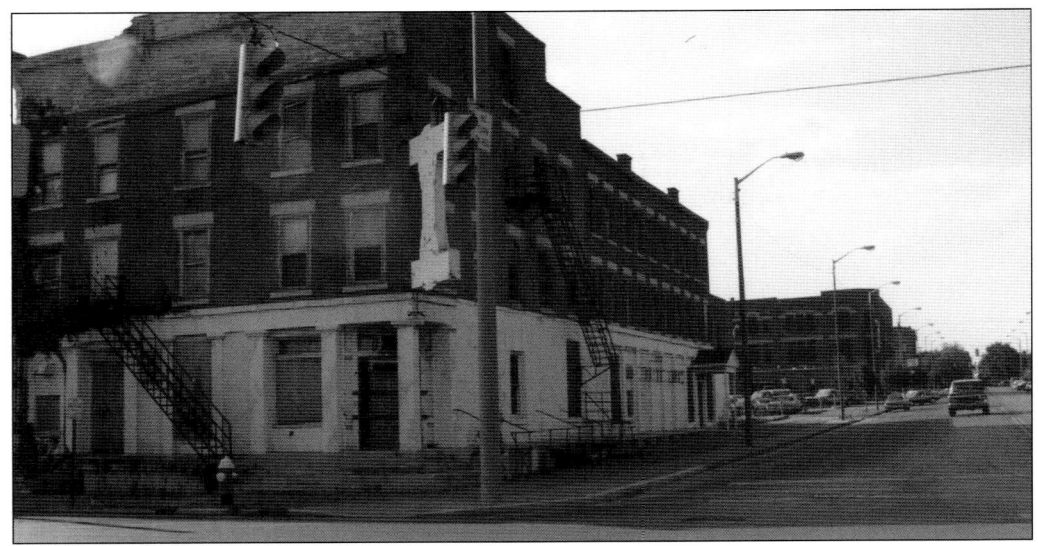

Because of its position as a junction of railroad and lake port, Sandusky was a transportation hub of sorts in its early years. During his travels through America in 1842, the English author Charles Dickens briefly visited Sandusky, spending a night at the Colt's Exchange (later called the Porterhouse) Hotel at Water and Wayne Streets, while he awaited steamship passage to Buffalo. He wrote about this experience in his book, *American Notes*. It might be fair to say that his feelings toward Sandusky were mixed. Although he described the city as "sluggish and uninteresting enough . . . something like the back of an English watering-place out of the season," he was pleased with the informal hospitality offered him and his wife. The building where Dickens slept stood for nearly 150 years, until it was demolished in 1985. This image was taken shortly before the building was razed.

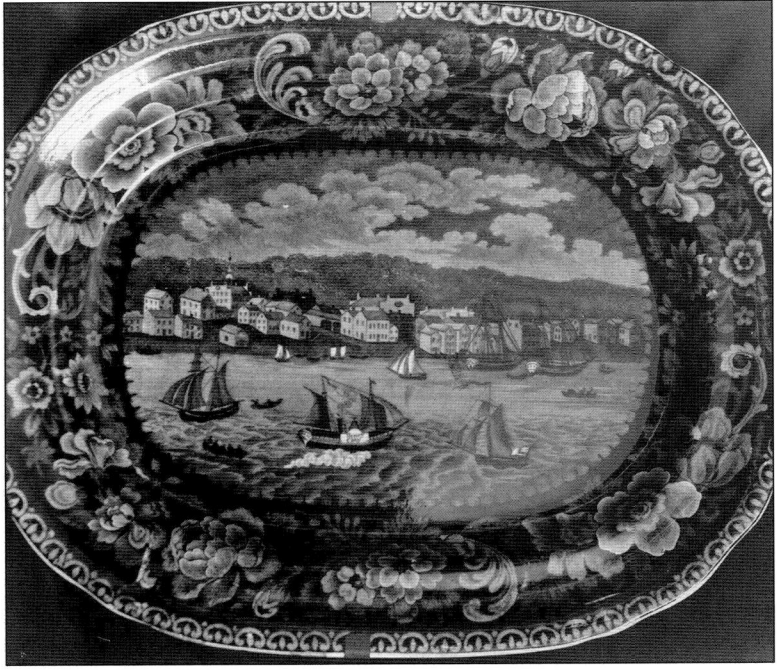

To Dickens, Sandusky probably appeared similar to how it was portrayed on the Sandusky Platter. Designed in the late 1830s, the Sandusky Platter may have been part of an "American Series" of city platters done by the maker J&R Clews. This platter is exhibited in the Follett House Museum in Sandusky. The Colt's Exchange, where Dickens stayed, is not portrayed on the platter, however.

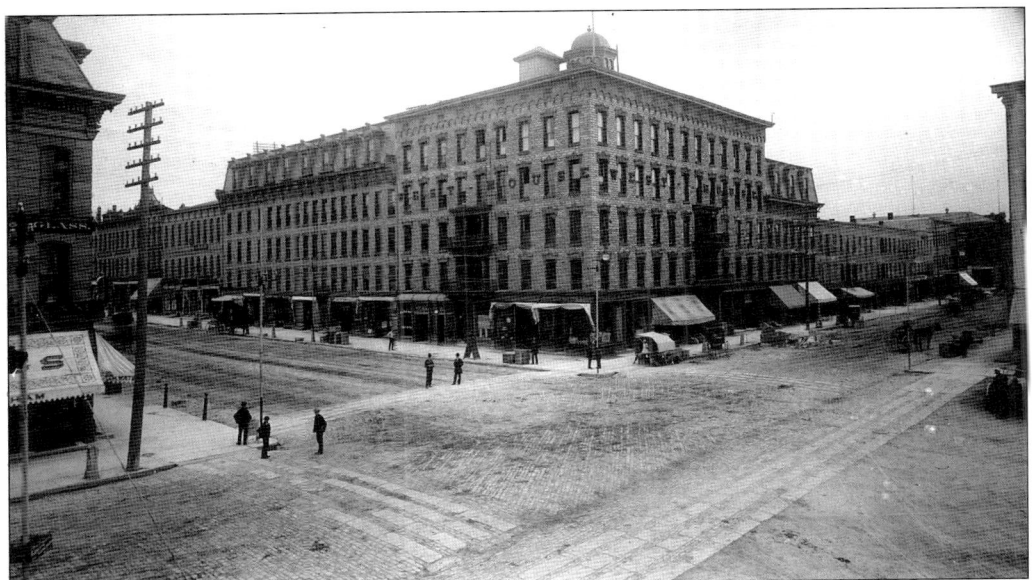

The West House was the first "high-rise" hotel in Sandusky. It opened in 1858 under the proprietorship of W.T. and A.K. West. Its location at the corner of Columbus Avenue and Water Street made it popular with steamship travelers who landed at the docks only a few feet away. The luxury accommodations and the attractive views of the bay added to its appeal. The building was torn down in 1919.

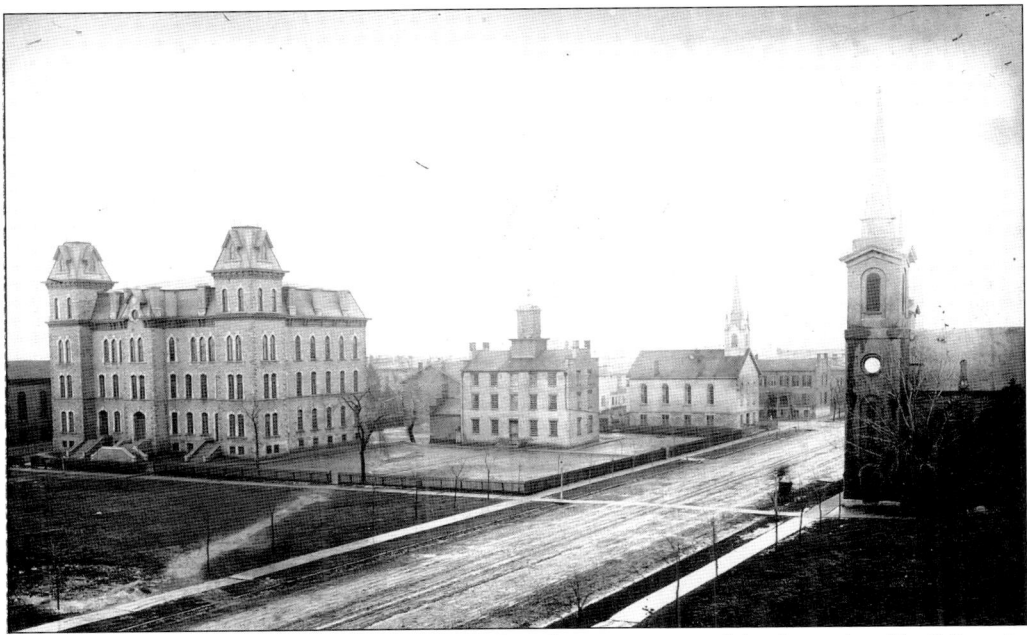

The academy building, seen in the center of this photo, was one of the first school buildings in the city. (The High School is on the left; Emmanuel Church and the Congregational Church on the square are to the right.) It was built in 1828 for school purposes, but in 1838 it became the courthouse for the newly-created Erie County, serving in the role until the new courthouse was opened in 1874. It returned to school use until 1886, when it was torn down.

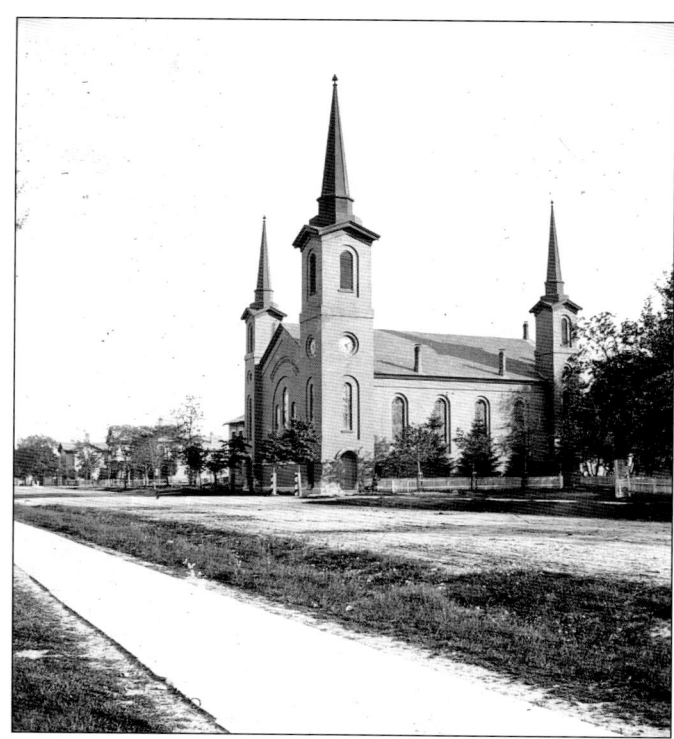

From the earliest days after settlement, churches have held a prominent place in the architectural and cultural landscape of the city. The first Congregational church building was constructed on the city square in 1835. The congregation was organized in 1819. The present church, on Columbus Avenue and Jefferson Street, was dedicated in 1896.

The Grace Episcopal Church, one of two churches remaining on the city square, is the oldest church building in continual use in the city. The cornerstone of the building was laid in 1835.

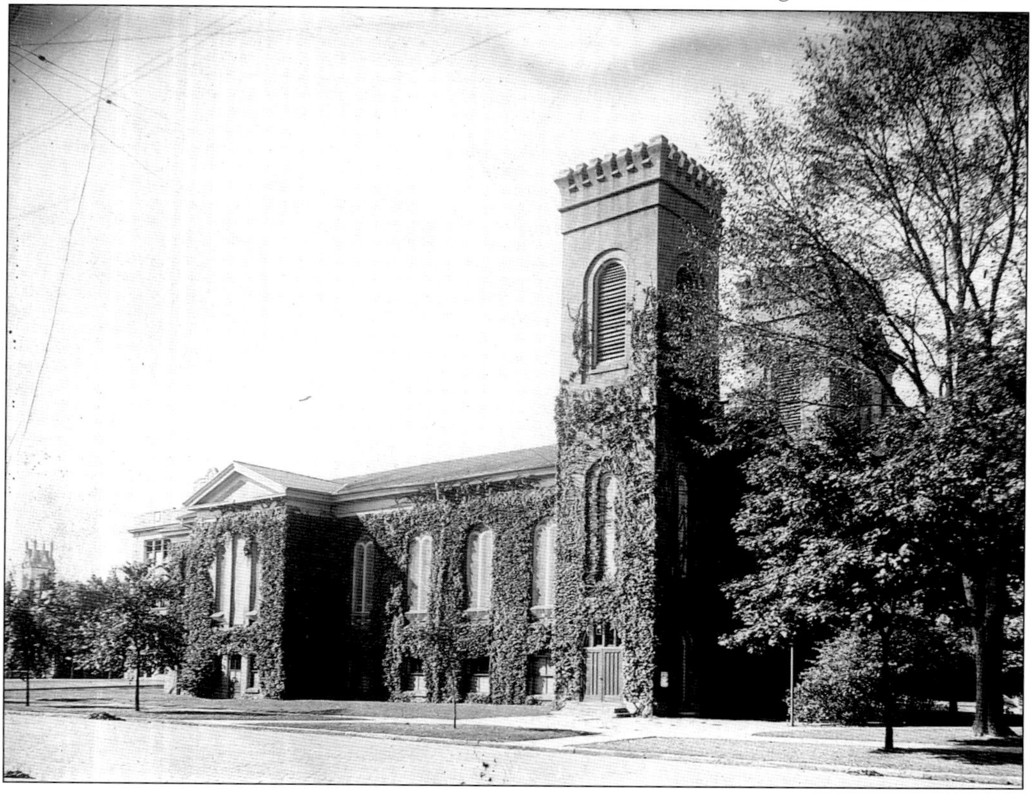

The First Reformed Church, home of a German congregation, was built in 1854 at the corner of Hancock and Jefferson Streets. There was a sizable German population in the city during the 19th century, enough to support several churches.

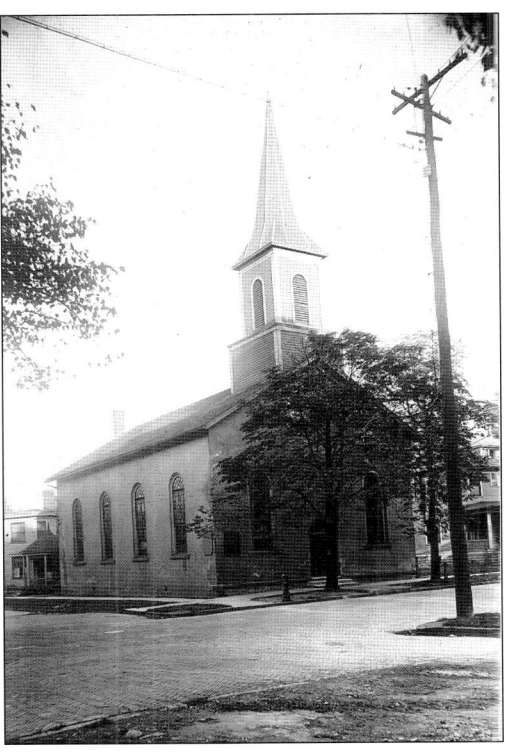

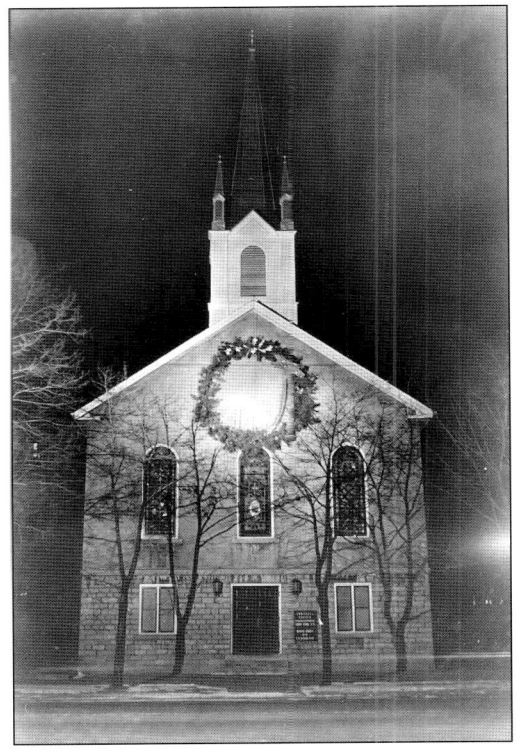

The Emmanuel Evangelical Church is the other church building still on the city square. It was built in 1866 for a congregation formed in 1844, and expanded in 1958. Here we see the church decorated for Christmas in 1939.

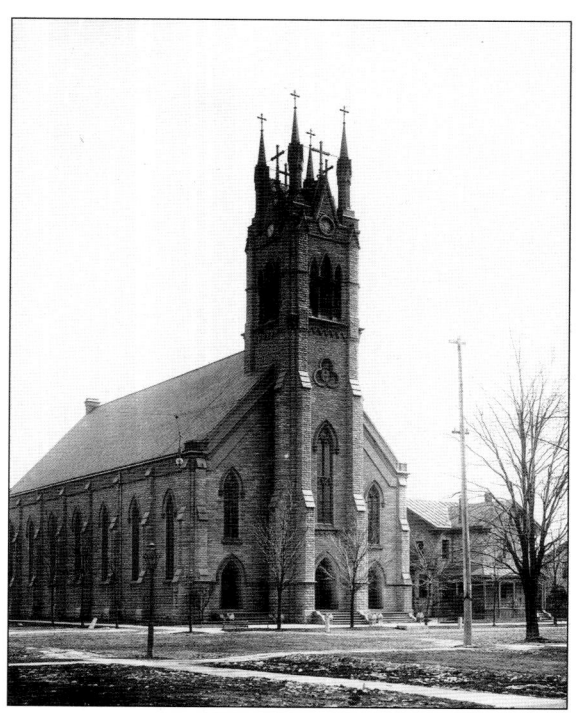

Saints Peter and Paul Roman Catholic Church was dedicated in 1872. This image is probably from around 1890. It is one of three churches now at the interesection of Columbus Avenue and Jefferson Street. (Zion Luthern and the First Congregational Church are the others.)

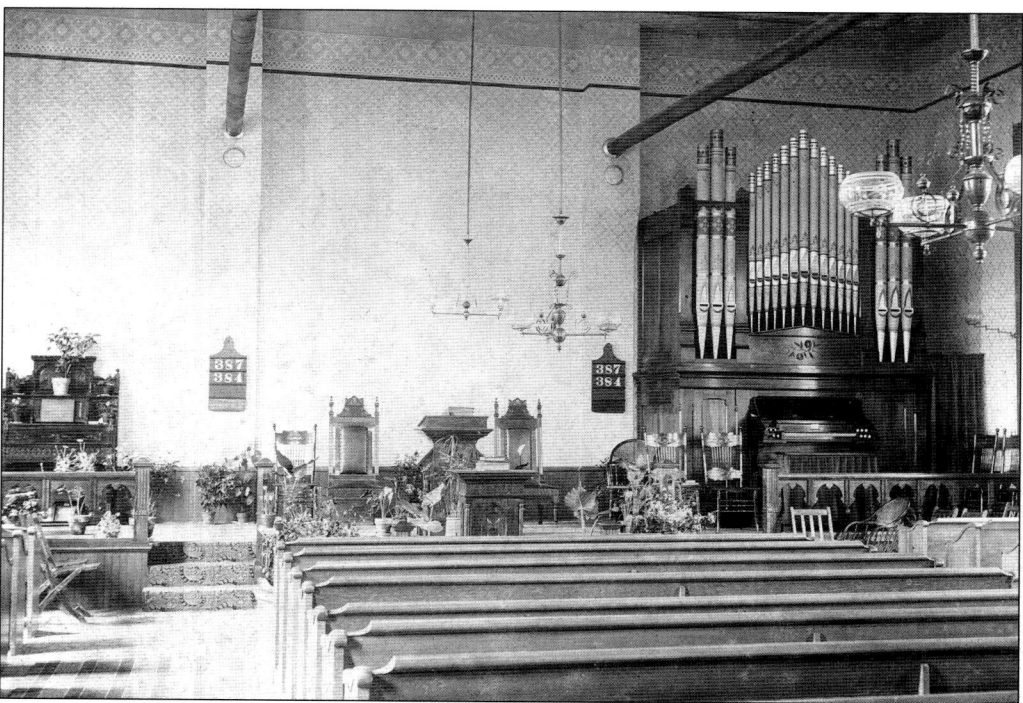

Pictured is the interior of St. Stephen German Evangelical Church, c.1900, when it was at the corner of Jefferson and Lawrence Streets. The congregation was founded by Dr. Ernst Von Schulenberg, who is perhaps best known today for having written a history of Sandusky in German in 1889.

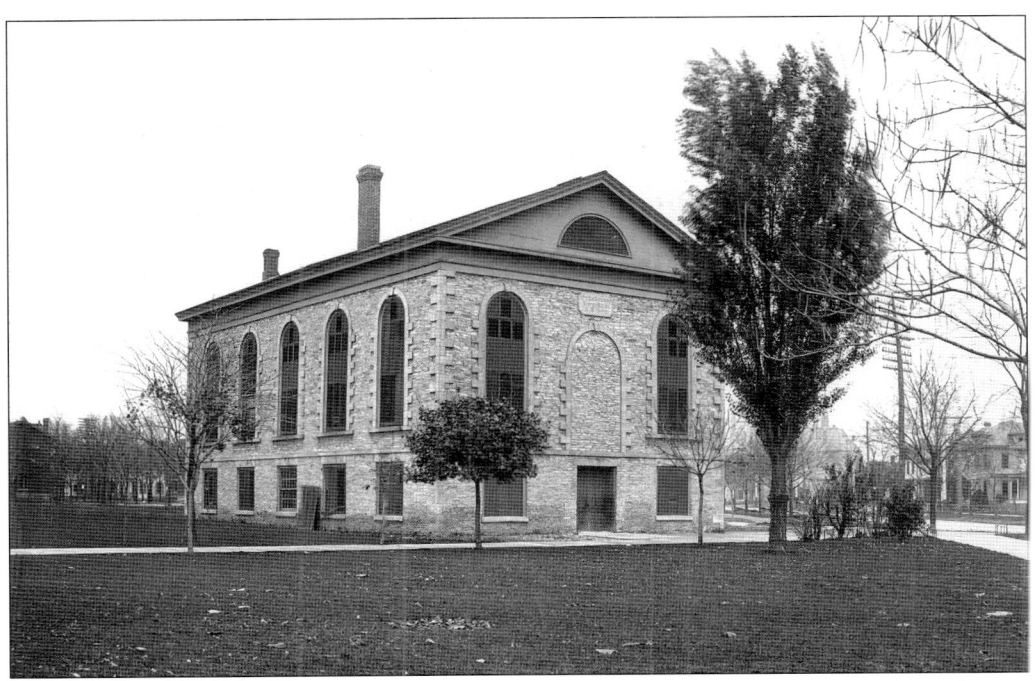

A Lutheran congregation in Sandusky was organized in 1852. Their church was built on the city square in 1882. It served until 1899, when the present Zion Lutheran Church was dedicated.

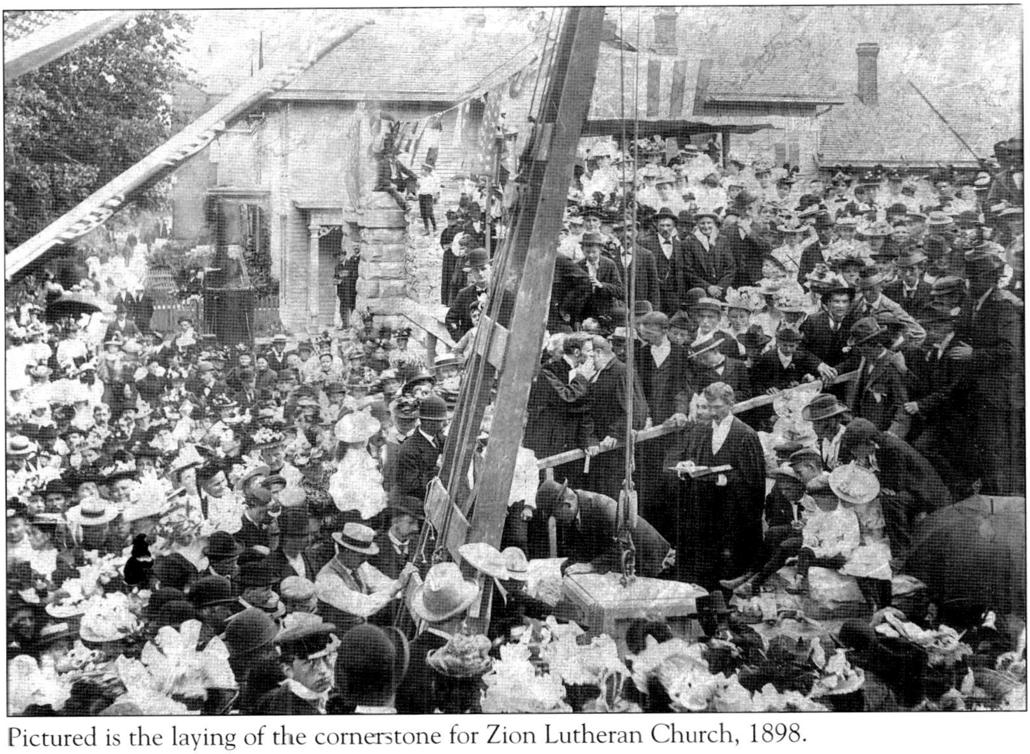

Pictured is the laying of the cornerstone for Zion Lutheran Church, 1898.

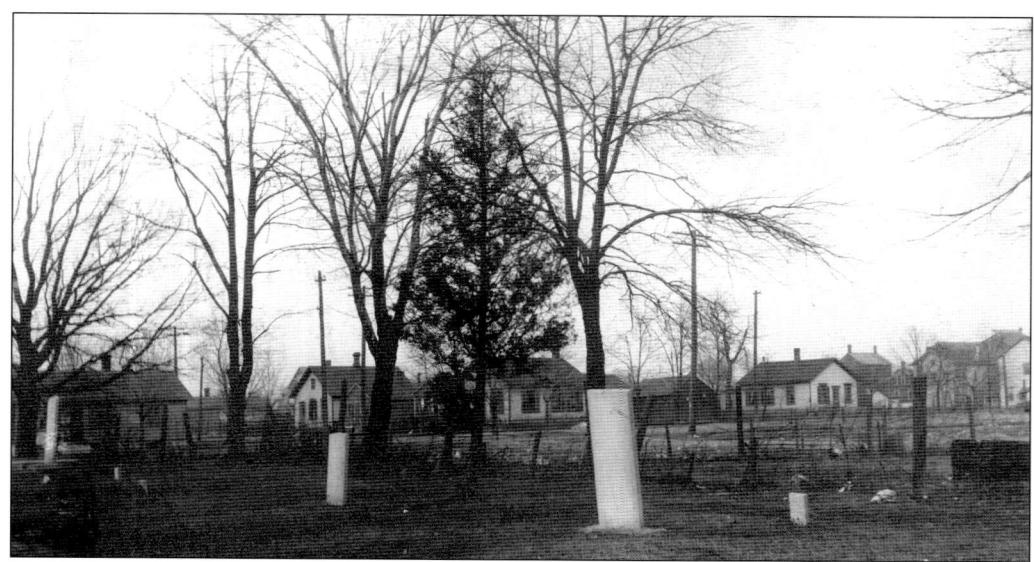

Despite the level of commercial activity in the early years of the 19th century, it was far from certain that the city of Sandusky would survive into the 20th century. Its commercially beneficial location on a solid rock foundation, with an abundant natural supply of water, arguably contributed to the city's first major crises—the cholera outbreaks.

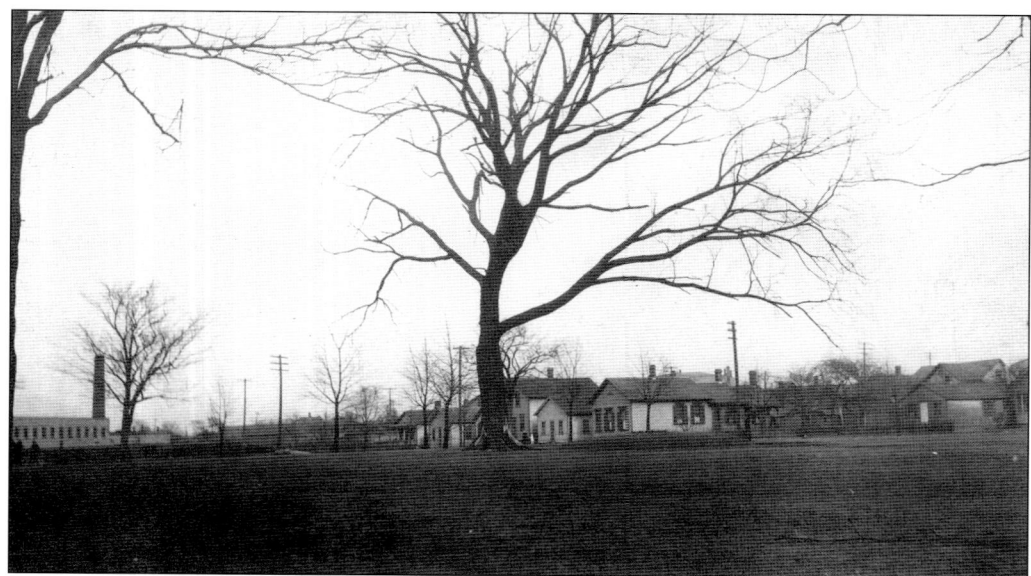

Cholera struck Sandusky several times in its first decades, most likely spawned by contaminated ground water trapped close to the surface of the land. The worst attacks struck in 1849 and 1852. The cholera cemetery on Harrison Street, shown here in these photos from 1916, was founded during the outbreak of 1849.

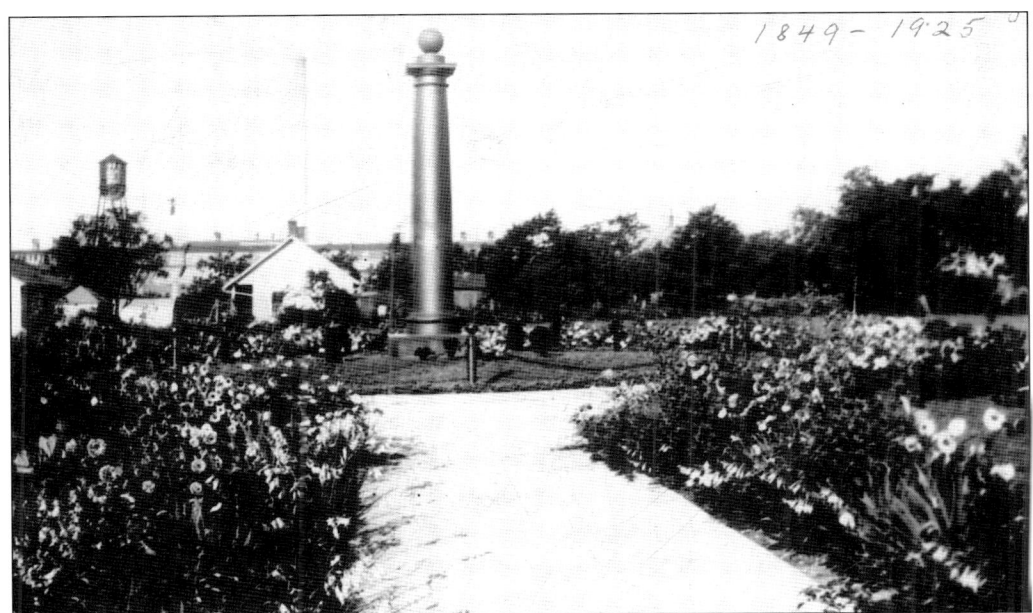

Although initially neglected (perhaps from an unconscious desire to forget a horrible time) the cholera cemetery was restored and rededicated as a local memorial site in 1924, when this monument was constructed. It was rededicated again, with a historical marker added, in 1965. The 1849 cholera outbreak in Sandusky was horrific, with roughly 400 people (of a population of about 5,000) killed by the disease; nearly half the remaining population fled in fear. Despite this devastation, Sandusky proved its resilience in the succeeding decades: the city's growth rate from 1850 to 1890 was the highest in its history.

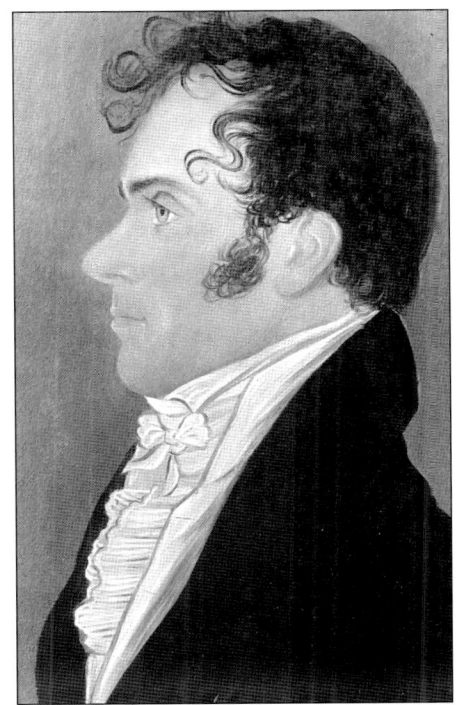

George Anderson, Sandusky's first physician and a prominent civic leader, was among the earliest victims of the cholera. He was fatally stricken while treating victims of the city's first major cholera outbreak in 1832.

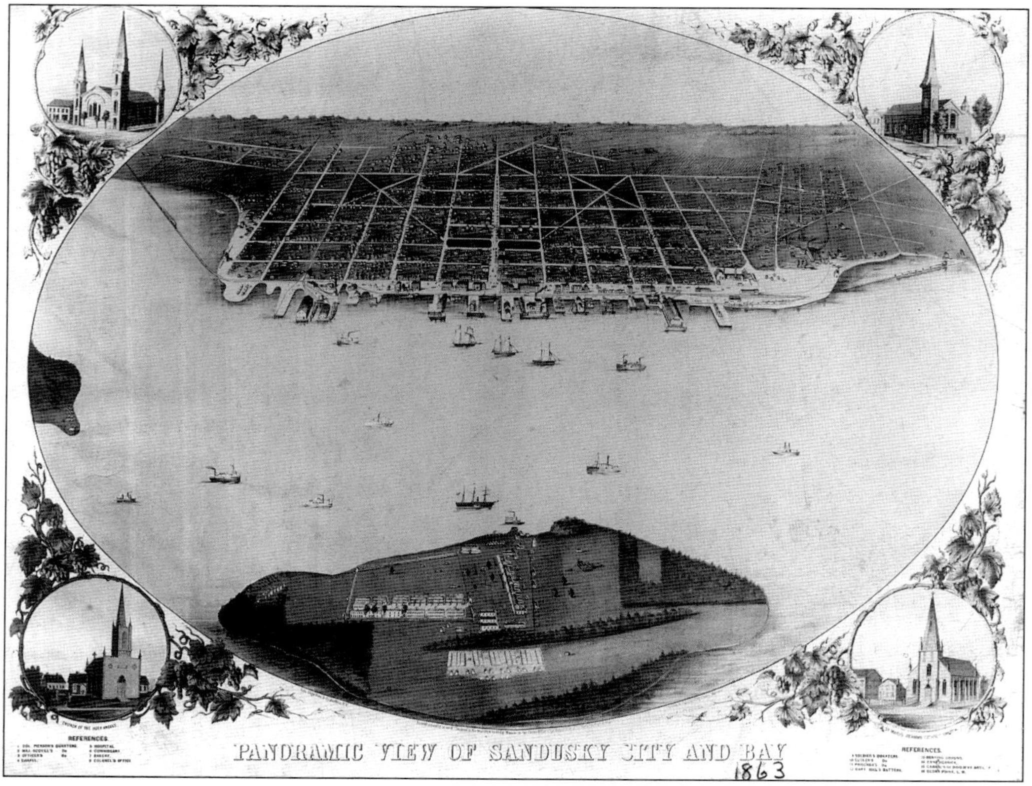

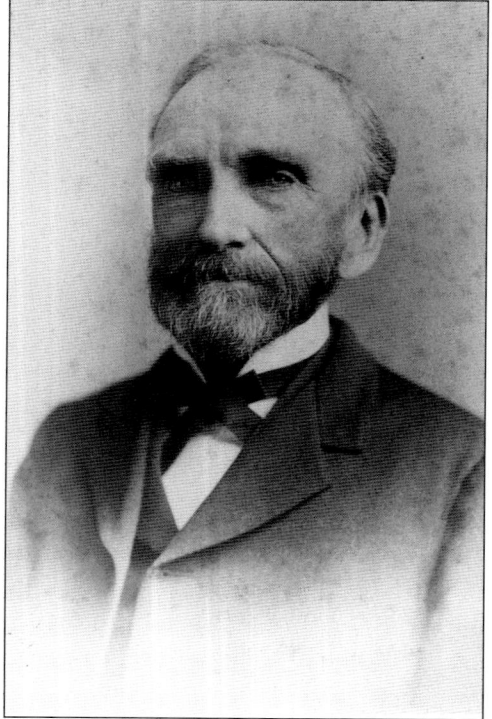

Despite its distance from the front line of the Civil War (or, perhaps, because of it), Sandusky played a major role for the Union during the war. Johnson's Island in Sandusky Bay, seen here in the foreground of this 1863 drawing, served as the site of a prisoner-of-war camp for Confederate soldiers captured by Union troops.

Leonard B. Johnson purchased Bull's Island in Sandusky Bay in 1852, renaming it Johnson's Island. In 1862, he leased the island to the United States government for use as a prison camp for Confederate soldiers. The Army decommissioned the camp and returned control of the island to Johnson by 1866. He still owned a majority of the island upon his death at age 90 in 1898.

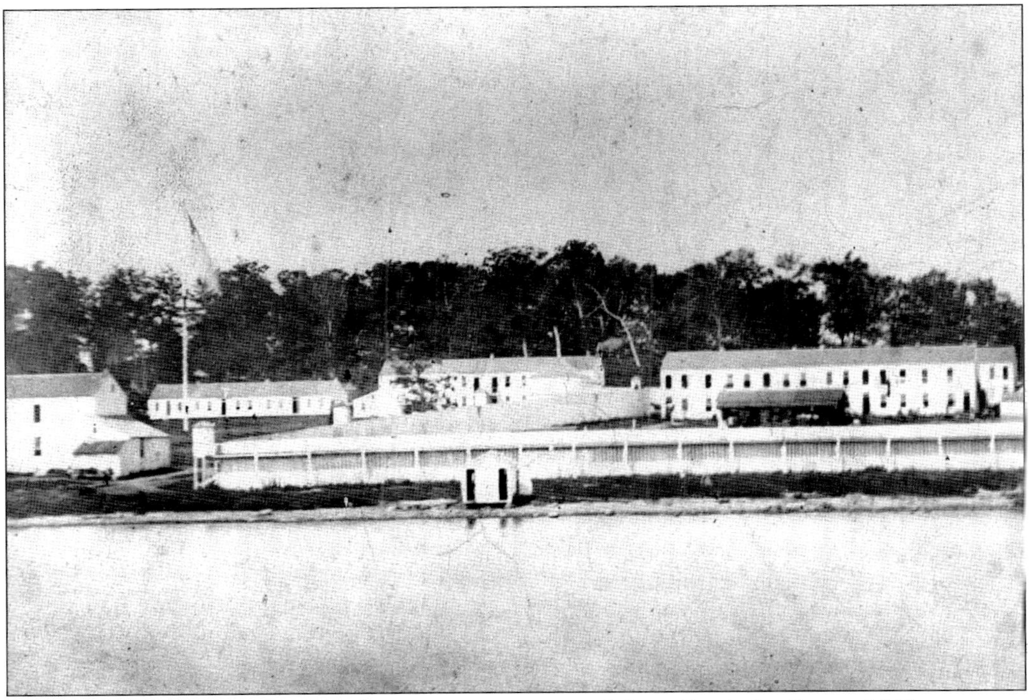

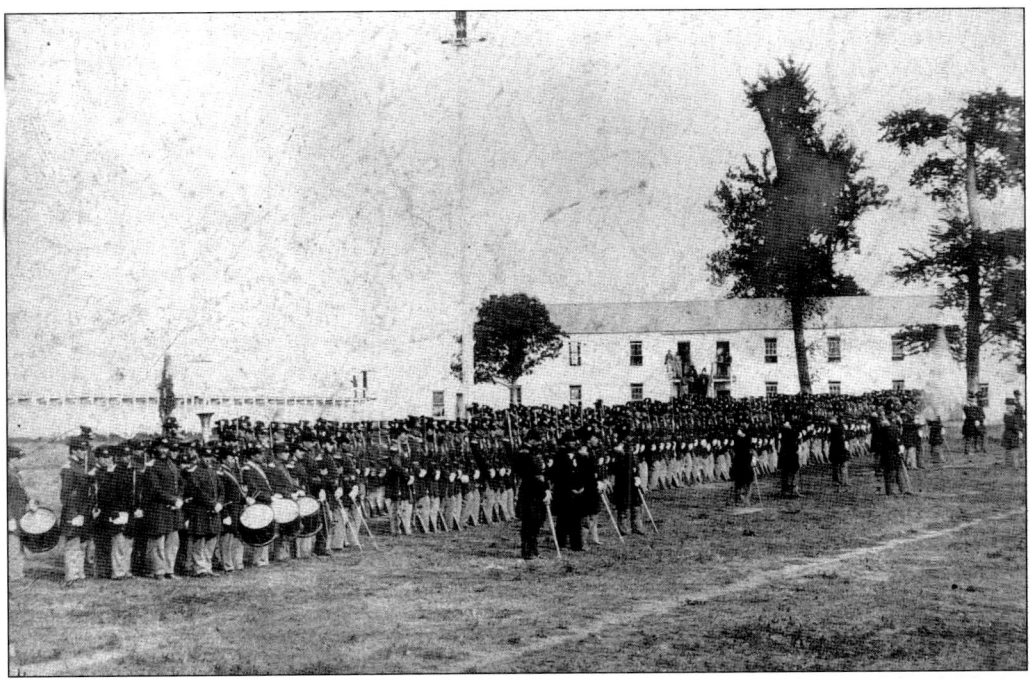

A portion of the Johnson's Island prison camp is viewed from Sandusky Bay, c. 1863.

The Hoffman Battalion, part of the 128th Ohio Volunteer Infantry, at Johnson's Island. Under the command of Lt. Col. William Hoffman, these men served as the guard force for the prison camp during the war.

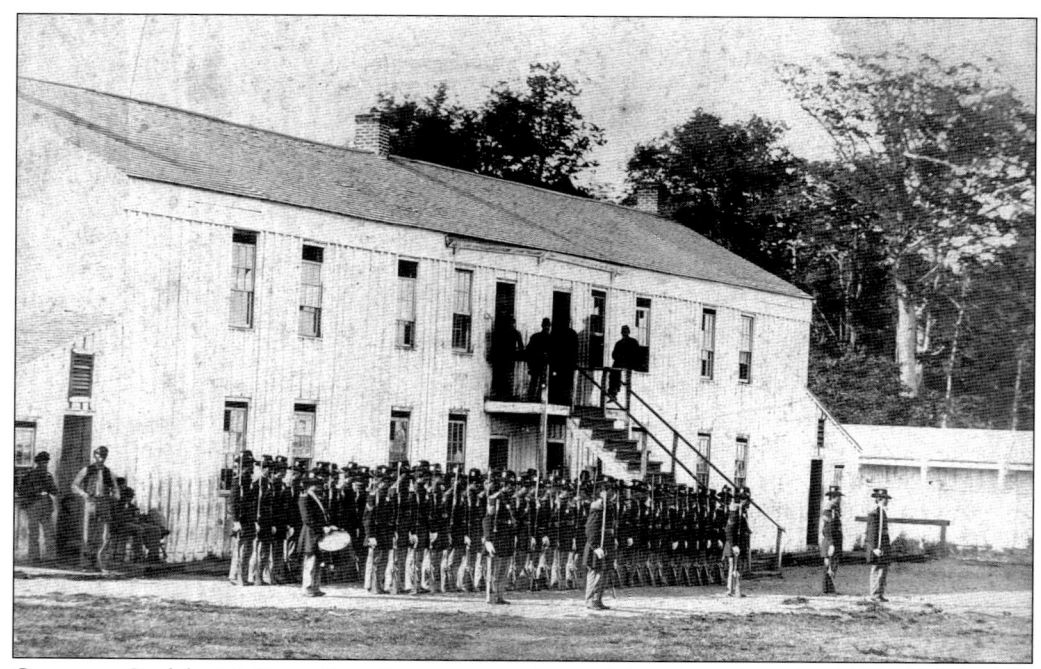

Company C of the Hoffman Battalion stands in front of their barracks. Most of the buildings of the camp were razed immediately after the war, when the camp was abandoned.

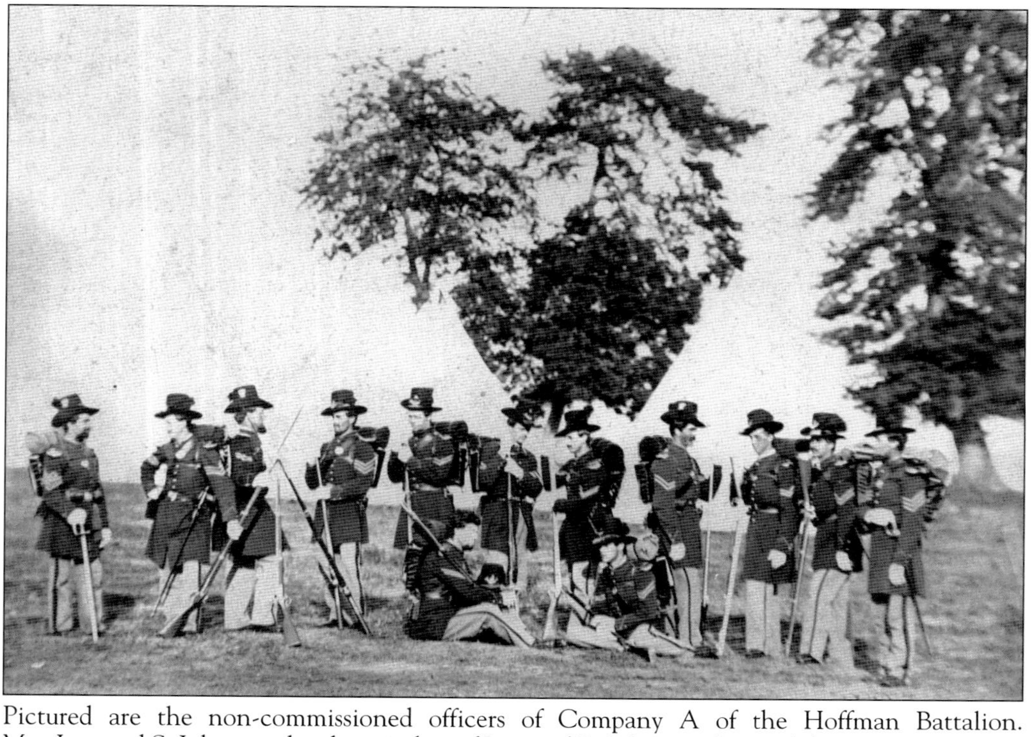

Pictured are the non-commissioned officers of Company A of the Hoffman Battalion. Mrs. Leonard S. Johnson, daughter-in-law of Leonard B. Johnson, donated this image and many other Johnson's Island photographs to the Sandusky Library.

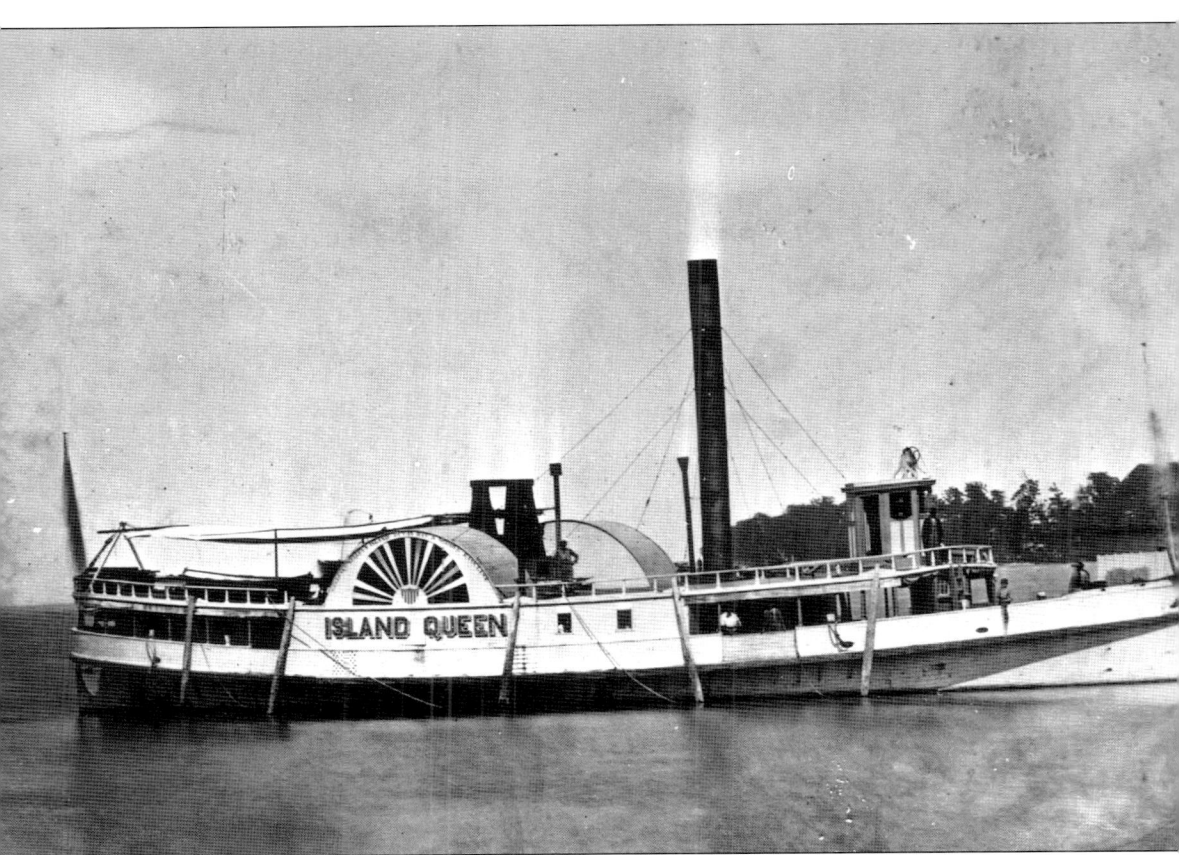

The *Island Queen* steamship was one of the few victims of the "Johnson's Island Conspiracy." Confederate agent and guerrilla John Yates Beall plotted a raid against the prison to free the Confederate soldiers held there. Beall and his co-conspirators, operating from Canada, hijacked the Detroit-based ship *Philo Parsons* at Kelleys Island on September 19, 1864, after boarding the ship in Canada as passengers. The *Island Queen* had the misfortune of arriving at Kellys Island just as the plot was taking place, and was thereupon hijacked and scuttled to prevent escape. The conspiracy ultimately failed when most of Bealls' men panicked and refused to go through with the attack. Several months later, Bealls was captured and executed as a Confederate spy.

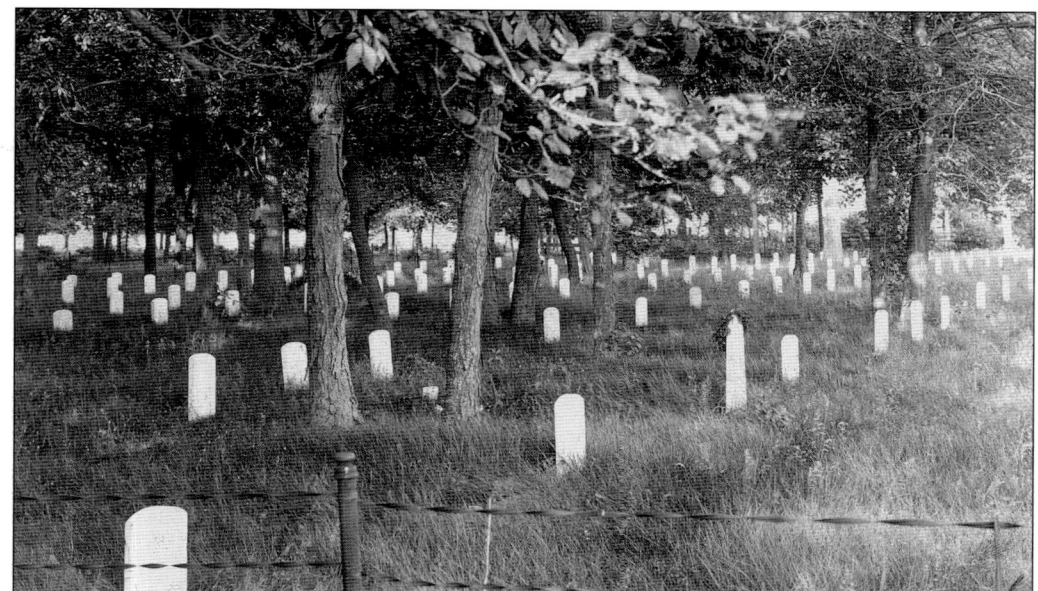

Today, the only visible evidence of the Civil War prison on Johnson's Island is the prisoner's cemetery. There are 206 Confederate soldiers buried in the cemetery, seen here in 1898.

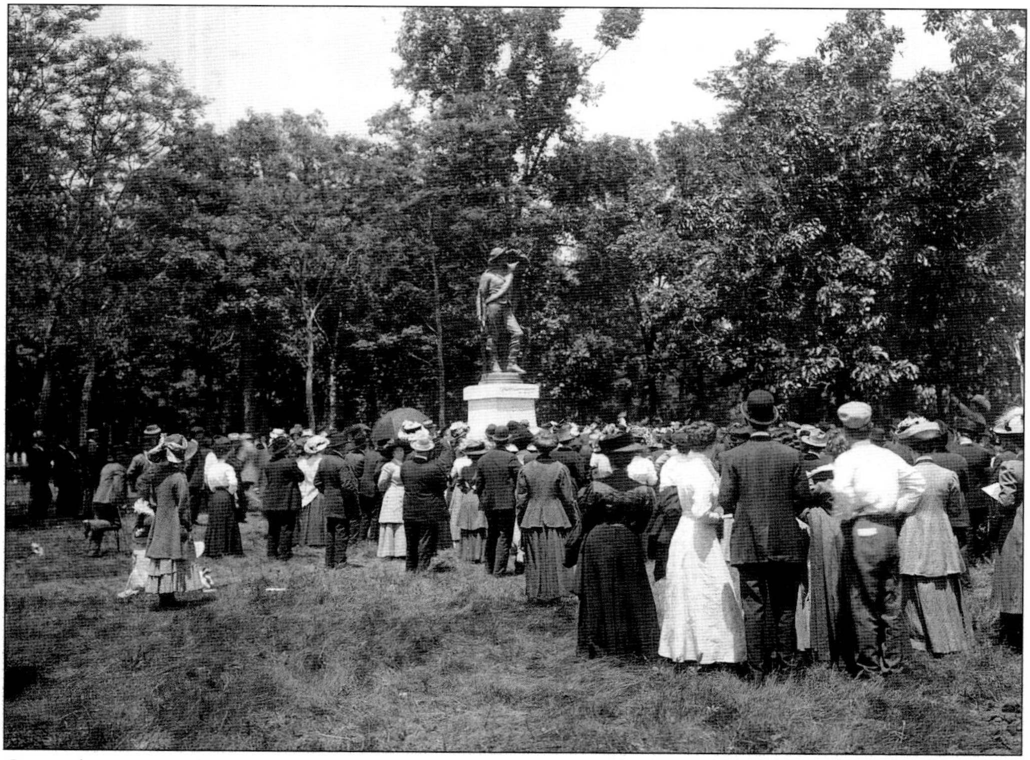

Over the years, the cemetery has been preserved and maintained by the Daughters of the Confederacy and other groups and individuals. Marble headstones were erected on the graves in 1890. The dedication of a memorial statue of a Confederate soldier, seen here, occurred in 1910.

Two

DEVELOPMENT OF THE CITY
INSTITUTIONS, INDUSTRIES, INTERURBANS

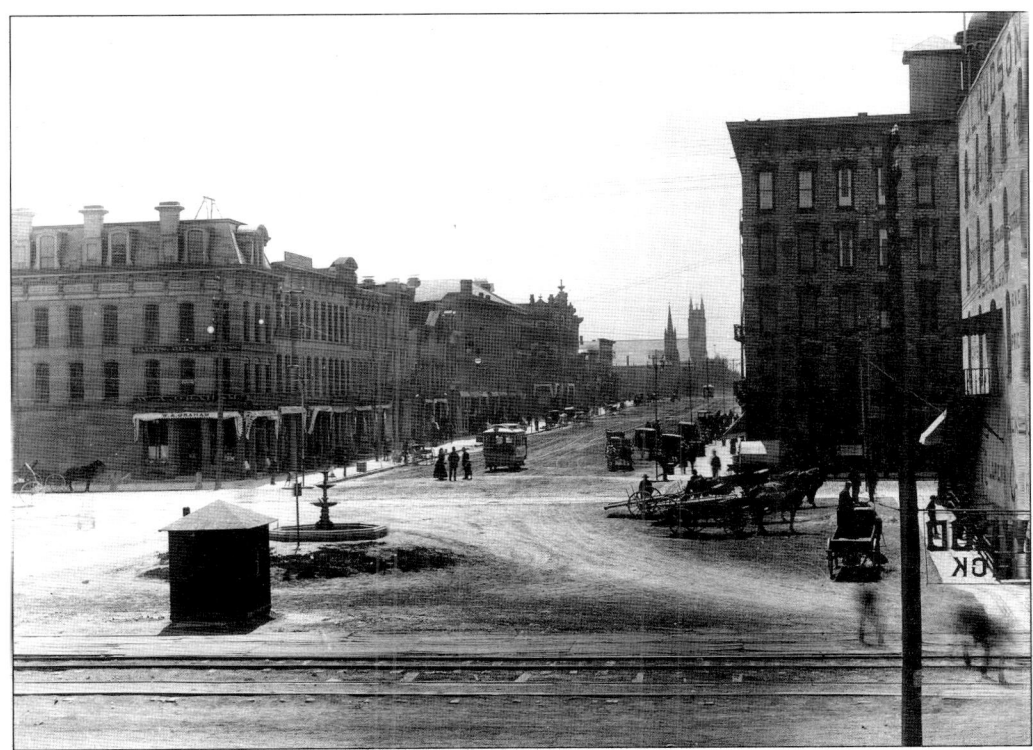

After the turmoil and "growing pains" of the first 50 years, the citizens of Sandusky were ready to make their town a city. During these second 50 years, the people built the institutions and infrastructure that help to define Sandusky today. Columbus Avenue, seen here looking south from Railroad Street, was the heart of a growing community.

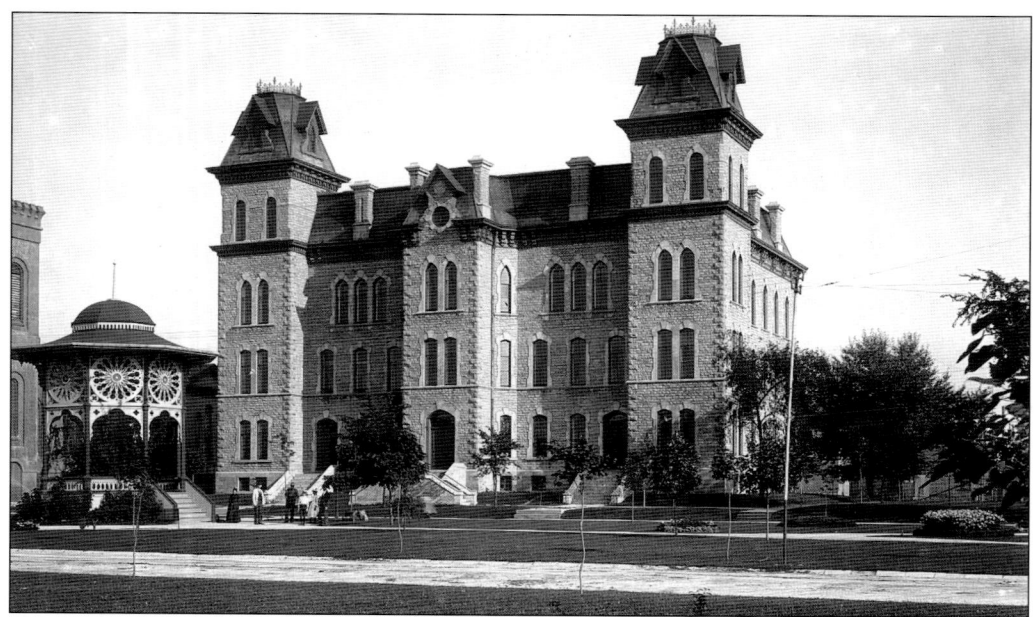

Construction of the Sandusky High School, pictured here, was begun in 1866. The school opened to students in 1869. The building (modified and expanded) still operates as Adams Junior High School.

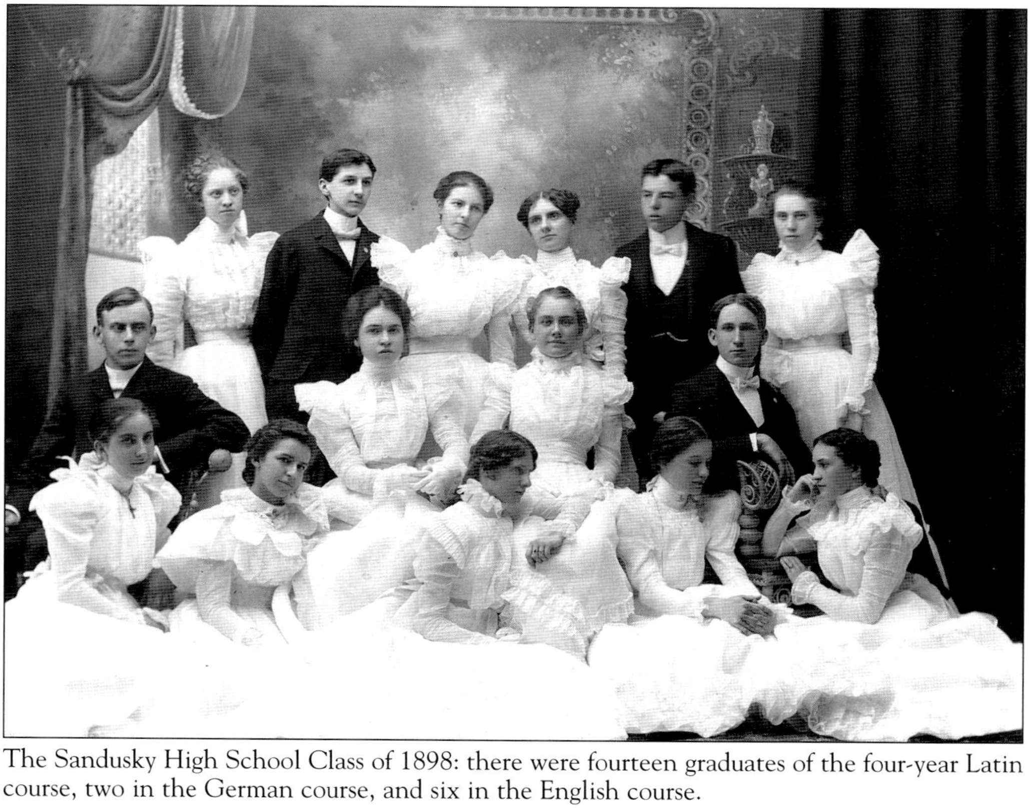

The Sandusky High School Class of 1898: there were fourteen graduates of the four-year Latin course, two in the German course, and six in the English course.

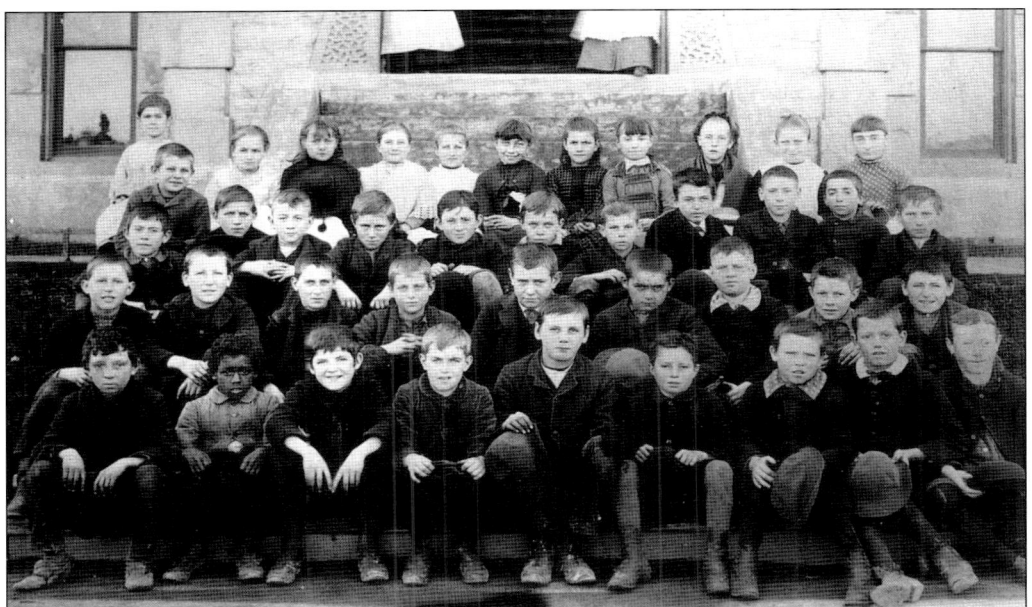

The Eighth Ward (Campbell) School was built in 1885. The photo shows a class from that school in October of 1888.

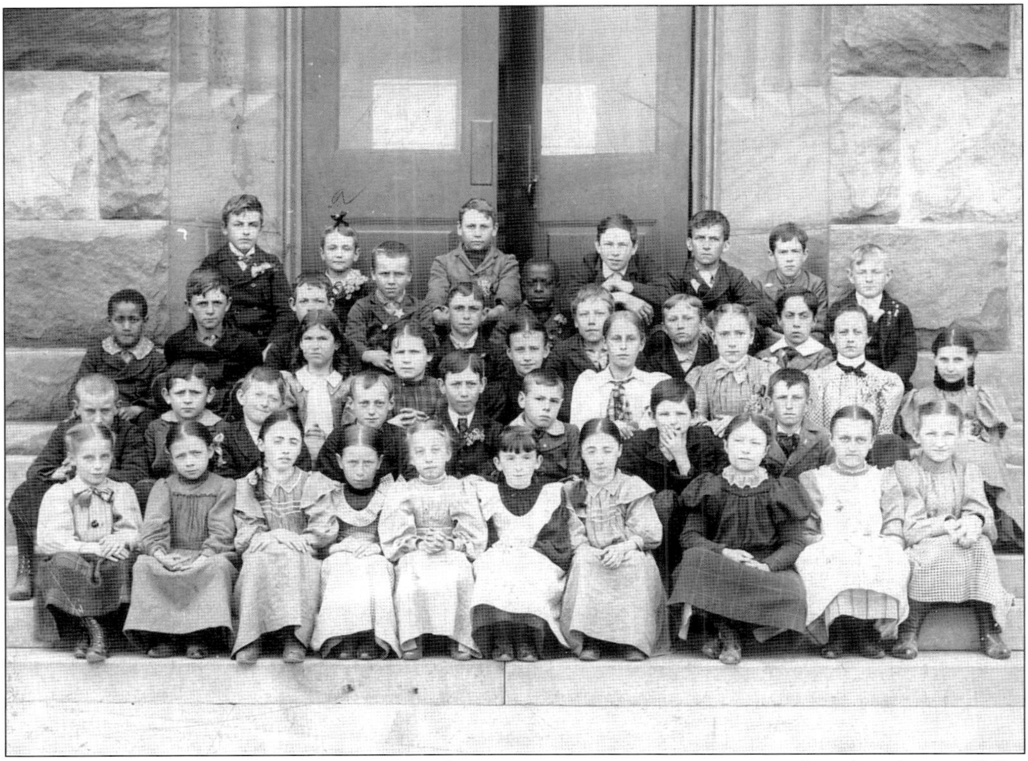

The Ninth Ward (Monroe) School opened in 1894. It is interesting to note that this class, and the class in the previous picture, was integrated—a progressive notion for that time in the nation.

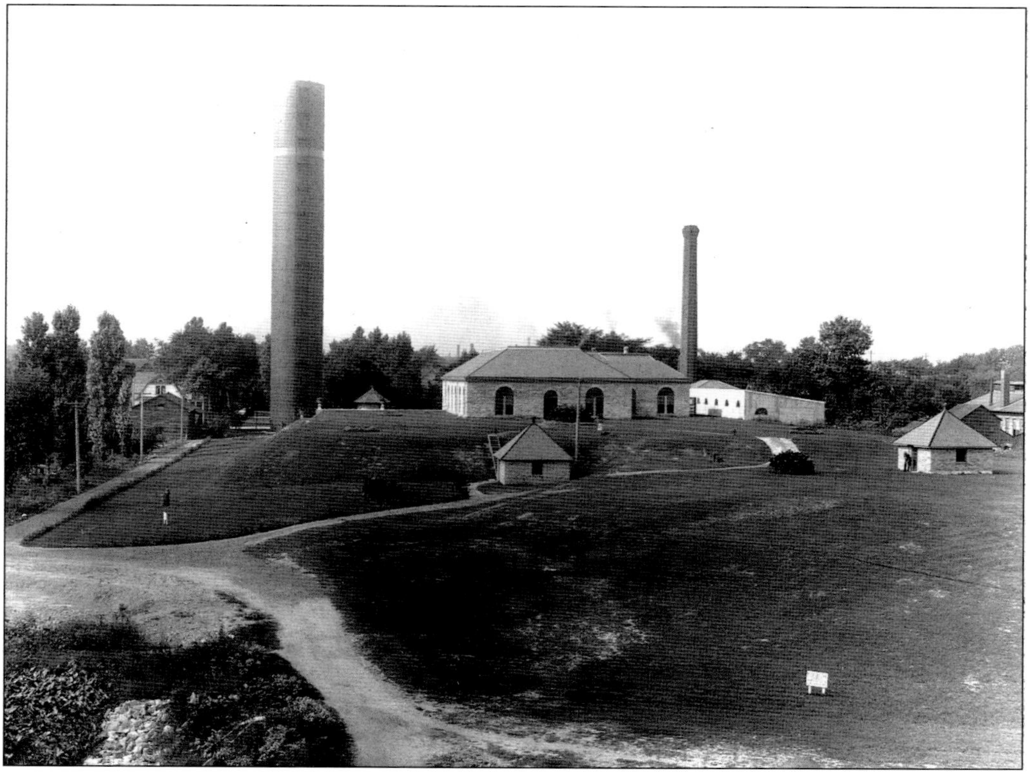

Perhaps the most important public institution created during this era was the Sandusky Water Works, on Meigs Street. Water from contaminated wells was a major factor in the city's cholera outbreaks—the solid limestone foundation on which Sandusky is built prevented contaminants from filtering out of the groundwater. After many years of debate and delay (it was first proposed in 1852, the year of the last major cholera outbreak in the city), creation of the municipal water works was approved in a public referendum in 1875. It began operation in 1876, pumping water from Lake Erie into most homes and businesses in the city.

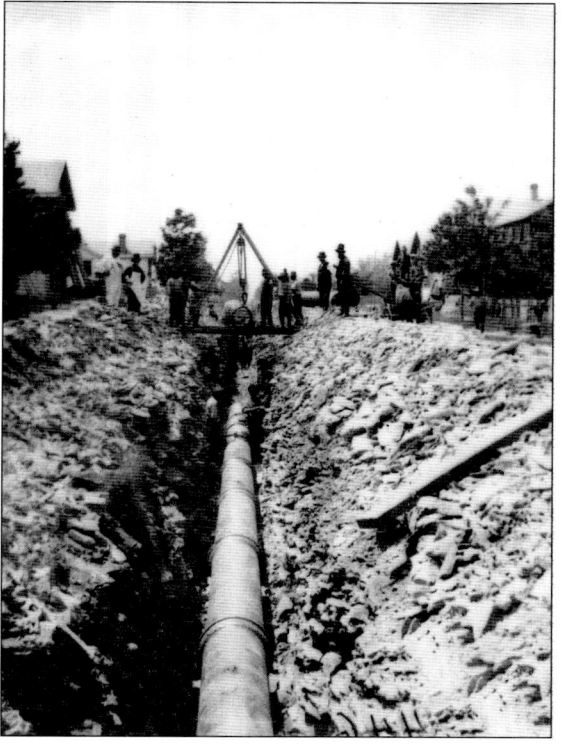

Workers are laying some of the first water pipes in the city, 1875. Notice how shallow the pipes are laid—because of the solid rock foundation on which Sandusky rests.

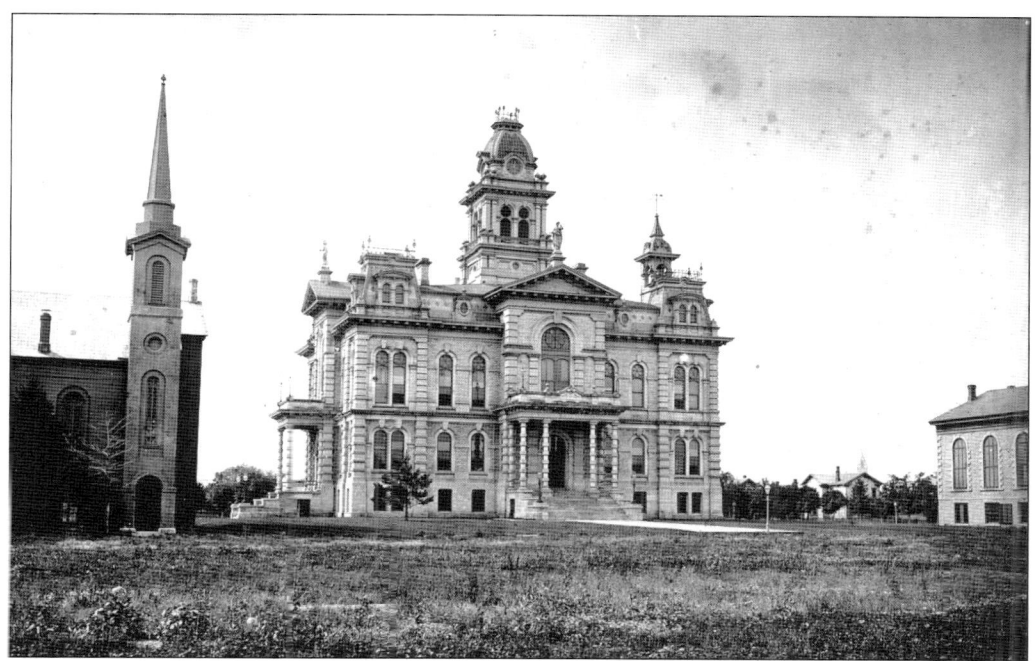

The Erie County Courthouse replaced the academy building as the judicial seat of Erie County in 1874. It was built of limestone and sandstone in the Second Empire style, with Mansard roofs and ornate design—a popular architectural style of the period. The Congregational church is on the left; the Lutheran church is on the right. (Neither church building is standing today.) The courthouse was completely remodeled in an Art Deco style in the 1930s.

"The Bar of Erie County" poses for a photograph inside the newly built county courthouse in 1875. Judge William G. Lane is seated at the bench, with a fresco of Justice behind him. From left to right, Judge E.B. Sadler, Judge S.F. Taylor, and Sheriff Merrill Starr are seated in front of the bench, with attorneys and court officers.

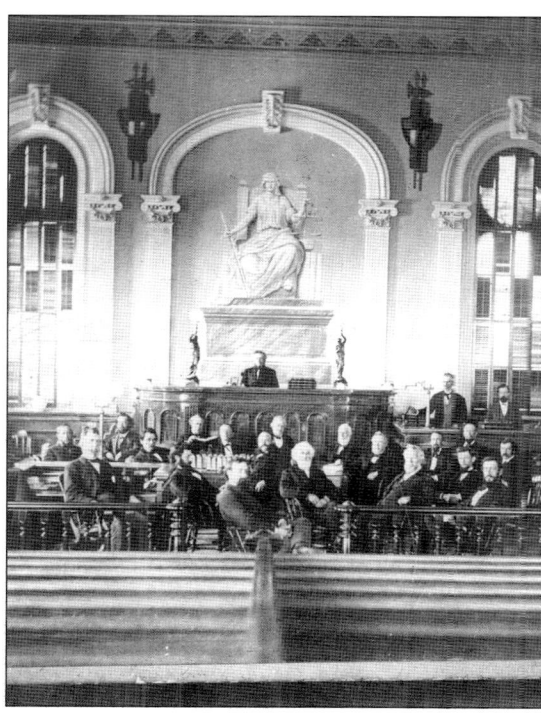

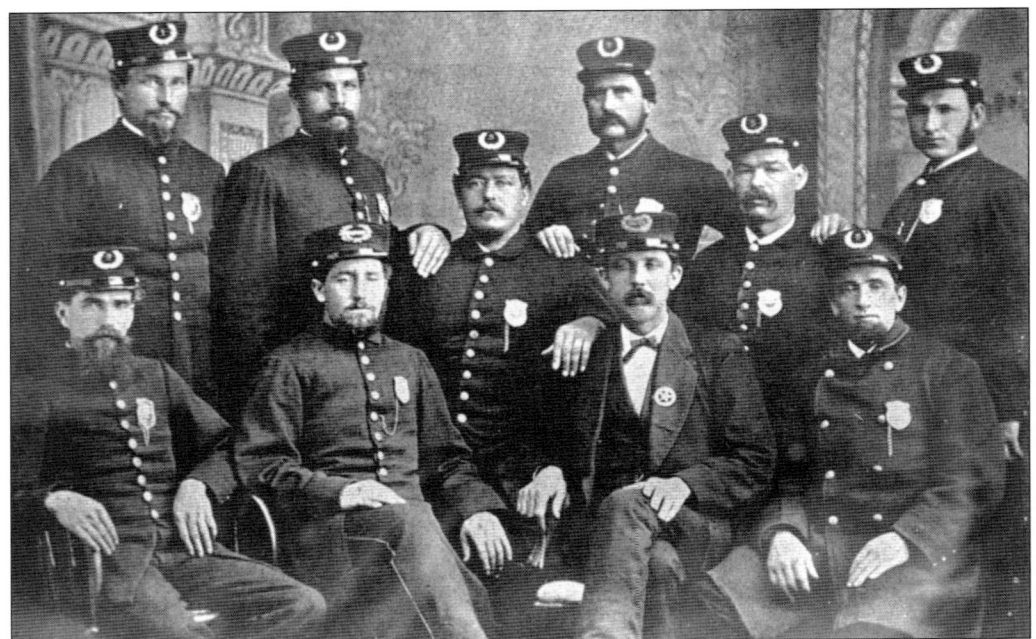

Sandusky's first law enforcement officer was the town marshal, Lemuel Robinson, in 1825. The first regular police force began in 1870, when the city council passed an ordinance establishing a staff of police officers and night watchmen. This photo shows the Sandusky police department of 1876.

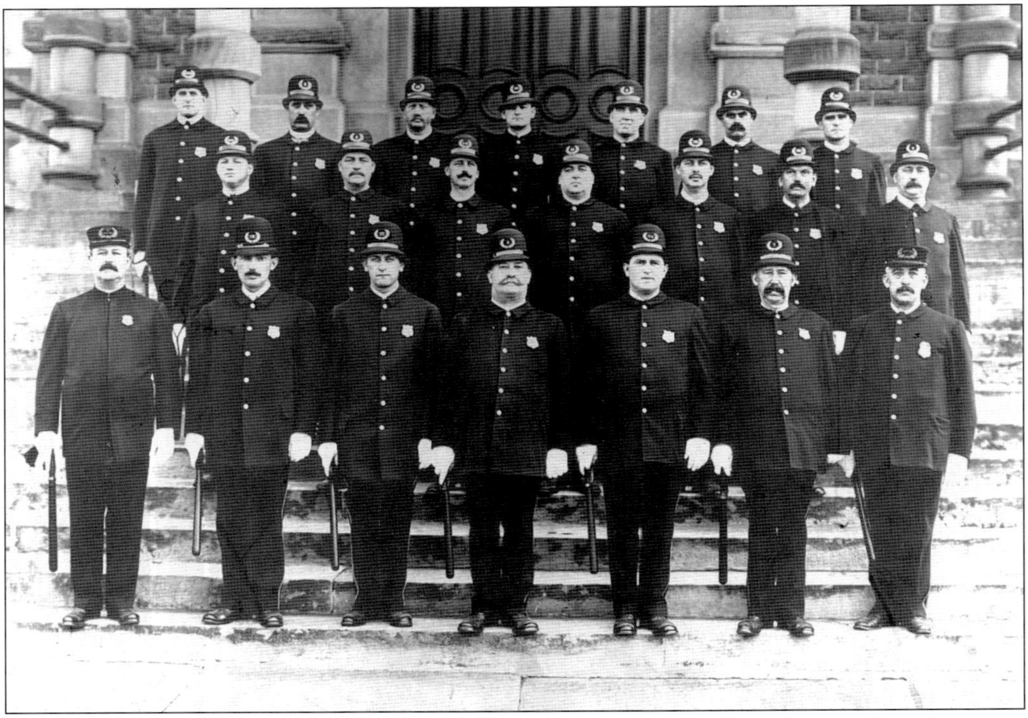

The Sandusky Police Department, pictured on the steps of the Erie County Courthouse in 1909, in the uniform style of the time.

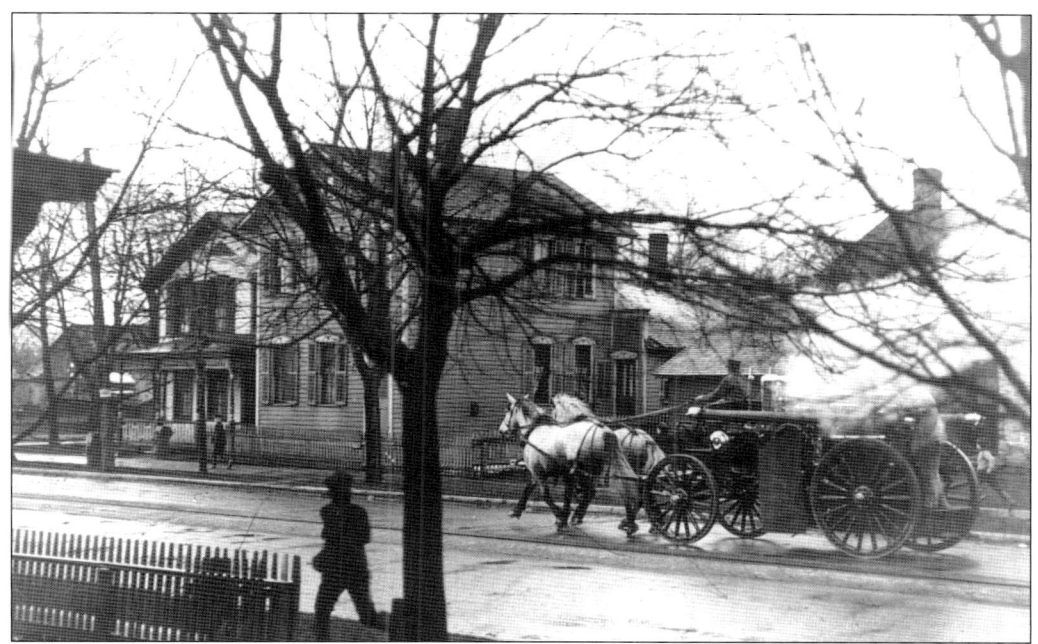
The first professional fire department in Sandusky began operation in 1883, replacing the volunteer companies first organized in 1855. A horse-drawn engine is traveling down Camp Street c. 1900.

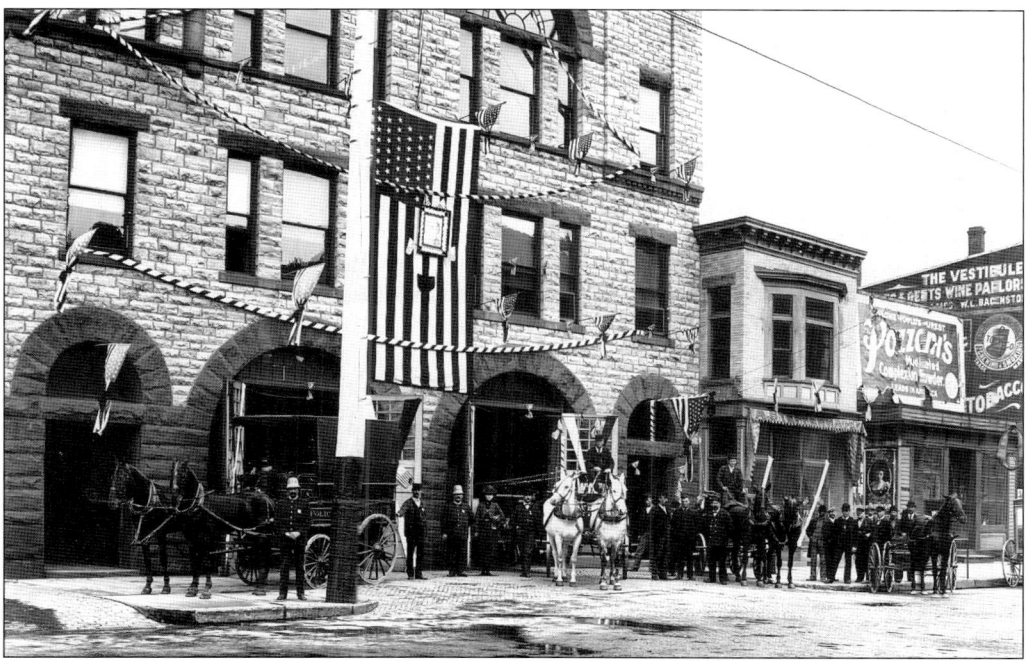
The Central Police and Fire Station was built in 1890. The police and fire departments shared the building until 1957, when the police moved to their new headquarters on Meigs Street. Firefighters and police officers are in front of the building, which is decorated in mourning for the assassinated President McKinley, in 1901.

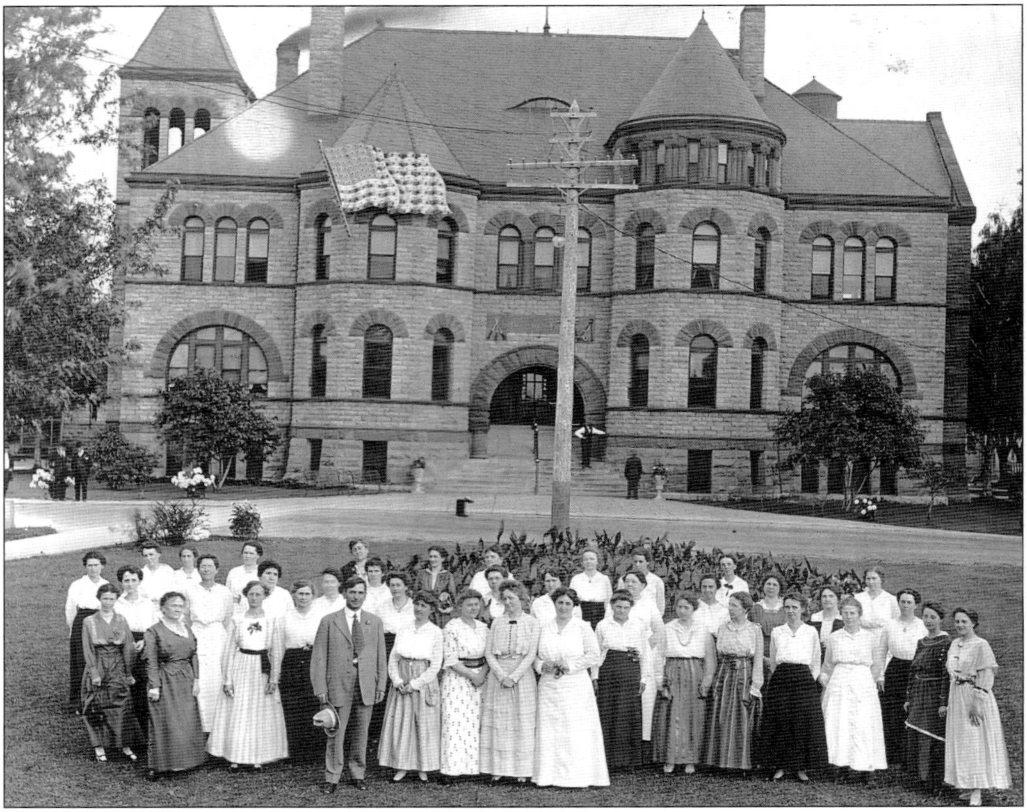

On November 17, 1888, the Ohio Soldiers' and Sailors' Home (now called the Ohio Veterans Home) admitted its first residents—17 veterans of the Grand Army of the Republic. Since that day, the Home has served as the residence for over 50,000 military veterans from Ohio. In this scene, the staff poses in front of the administration building, c.1920.

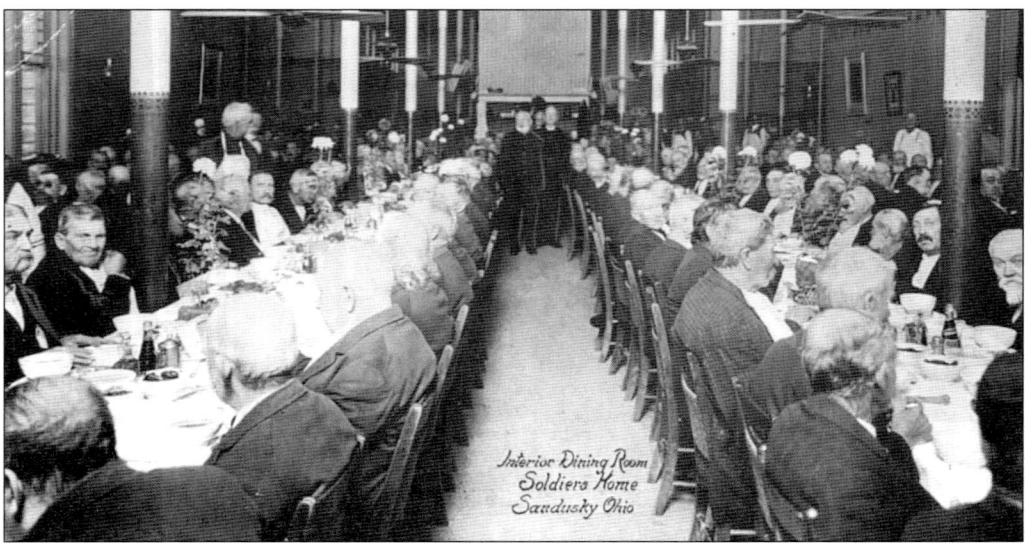

This is a post card view of the dining room of the Soldiers' Home, c. 1900.

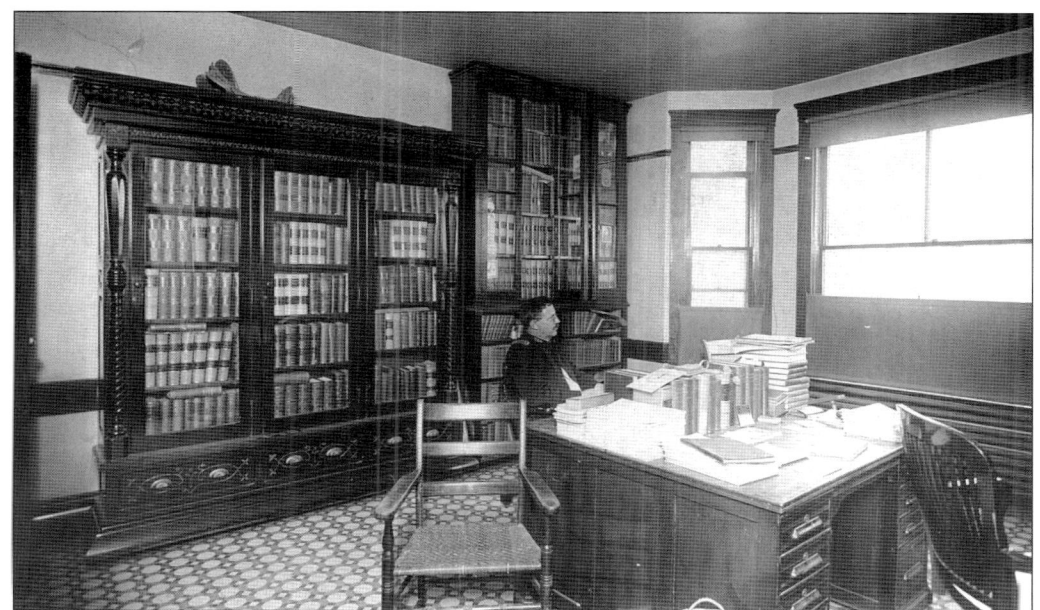

Pictured is the surgeon's office of the Ohio Soldiers' and Sailors' Home, December 1914. Doctor J.T. Haynes is seated at the desk.

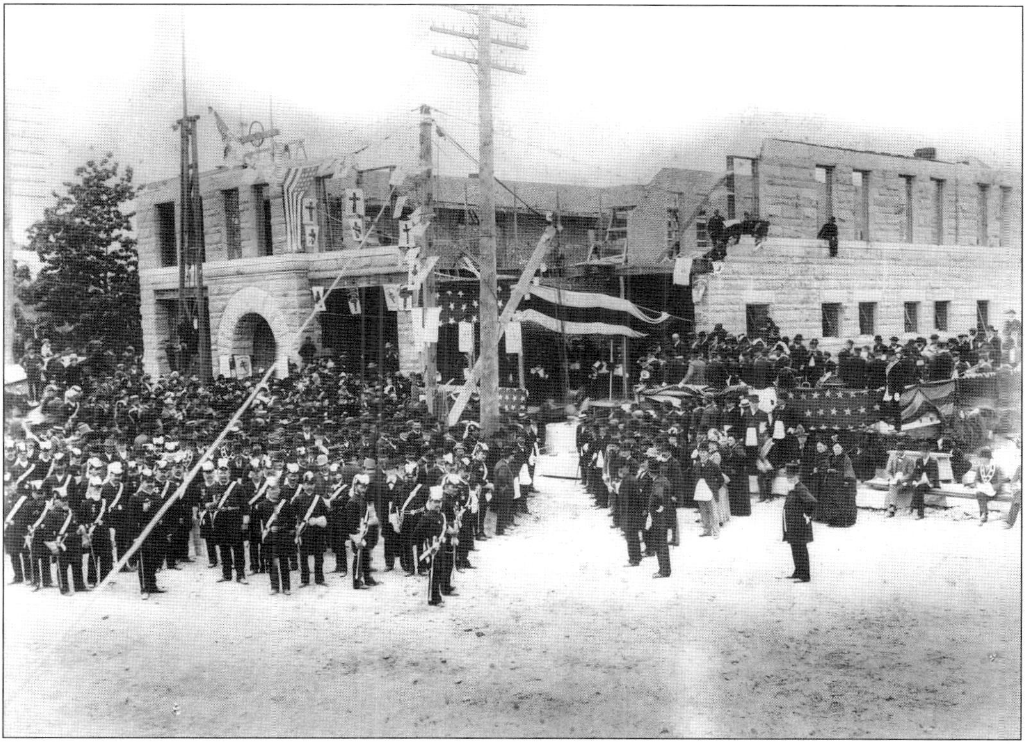

As Sandusky was founded and organized by Masons, it is not surprising that a Masonic Temple was built in the city in 1889. The cornerstone laying ceremony on June 24, 1889, was a prominent event, as can be seen in this view.

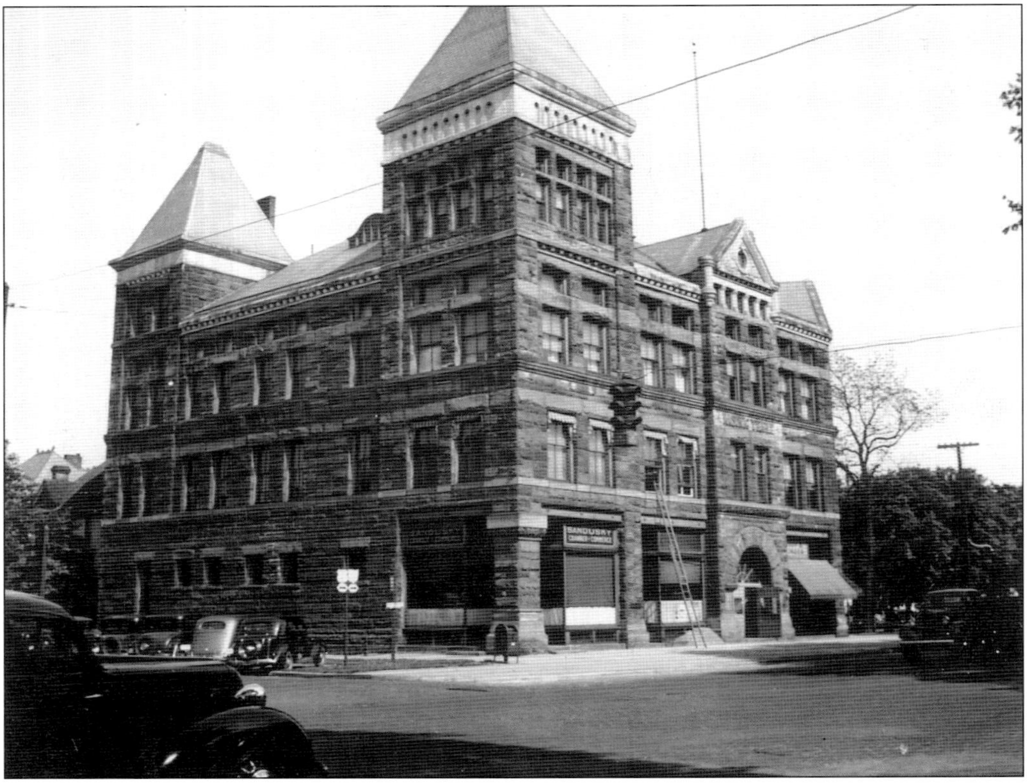

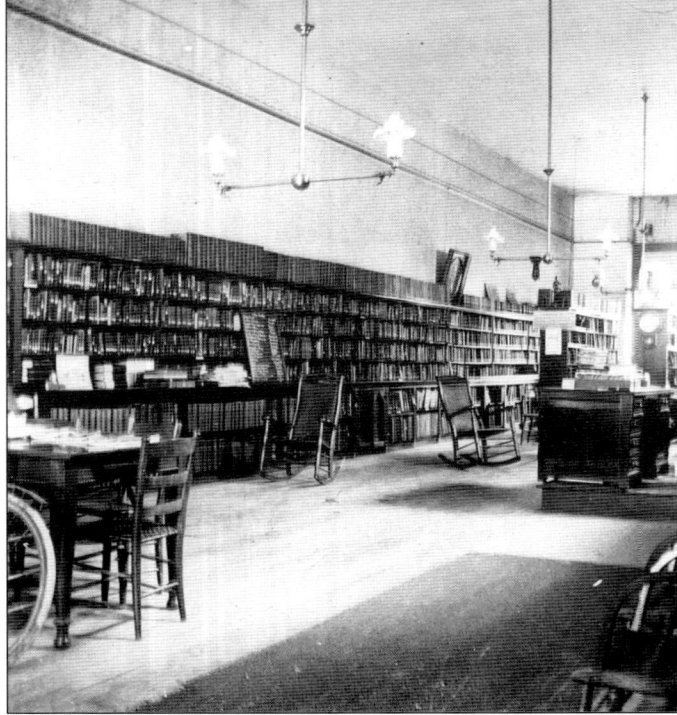

The Masonic Temple was severely damaged in a 1943 fire, but it was rebuilt with significant modification. This is how the building looked shortly before the fire.

The Masonic Temple briefly housed the public library, before the library's Carnegie building was built in 1901. The Library Association was incorporated in 1895, and operated briefly out of the high school. It moved to the Masonic Temple in 1896. Libraries have a long history in Sandusky—the Ladies' Library Association was founded in 1870, but it could trace its roots to the first subscription library in Sandusky, the Portland Library, founded in 1825.

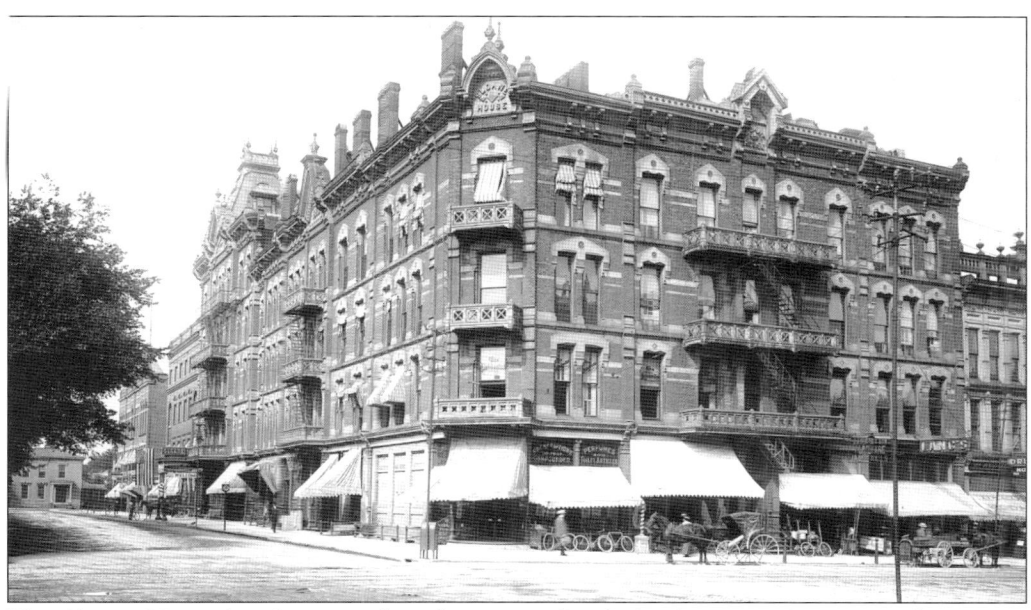

The Sloane House hotel operated in downtown Sandusky for over 75 years. Built in 1880 at the corner of Washington Row and Columbus Avenue, the hotel was named for its first owner, Rush Sloane, a prominent businessman and former mayor. He is perhaps best remembered as an abolitionist, often participating in the activities of the Underground Railroad. The building was razed in 1957.

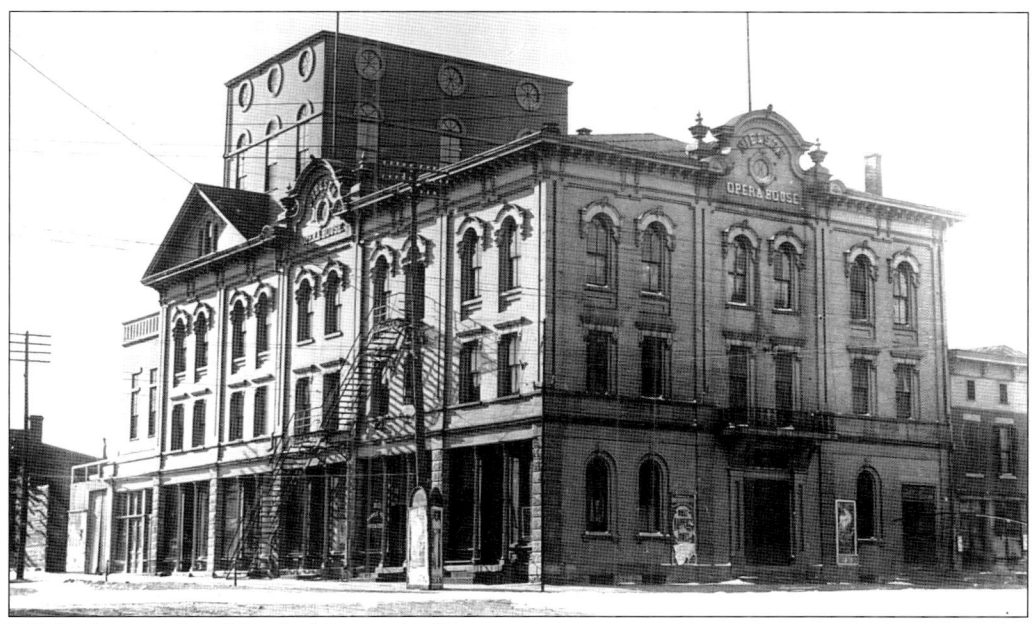

While the people of Sandusky were building a community in the 19th century, they were also building a culture. Institutions of entertainment and recreation arose with vigor. Few people today might realize that Sandusky was the home of an opera house for many years. Built in 1877 on Jackson Street as the Biemiller Opera House, it was later known as the Nielsen Opera House. In 1902, John Himmelein converted the building to a playhouse.

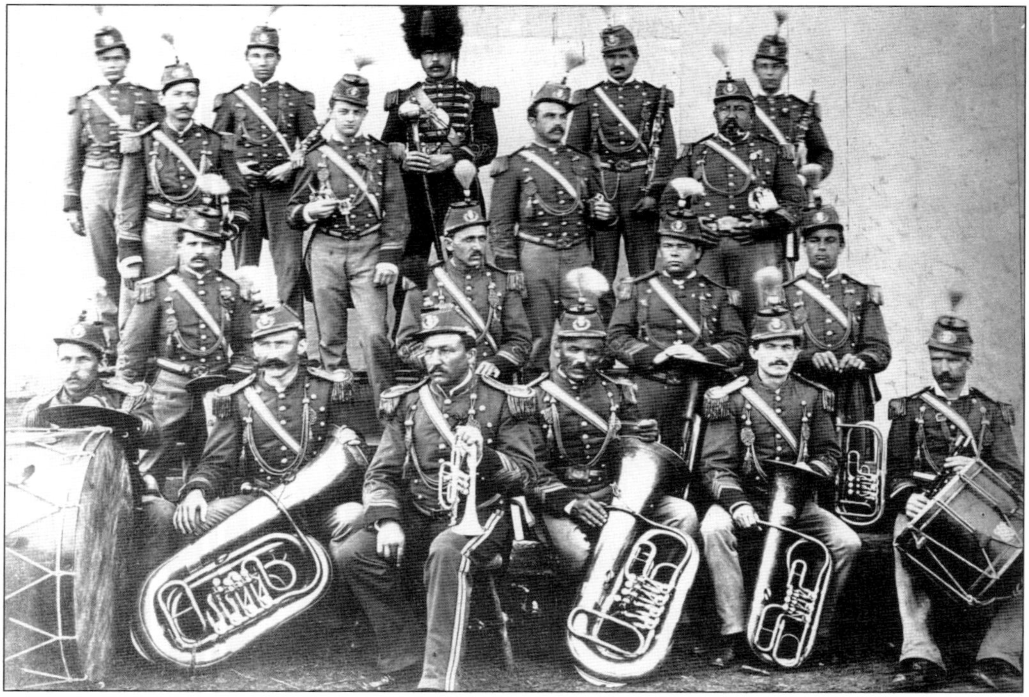

Brass bands were very popular in the days before radio and recorded music. The Great Western Band was among the most popular of these bands. Formed in 1867 from the consolidation of the Jaeger Band (the first organized band in Sandusky) and the Sandusky City Band, the Great Western Band played throughout the Midwest to great acclaim for over 20 years.

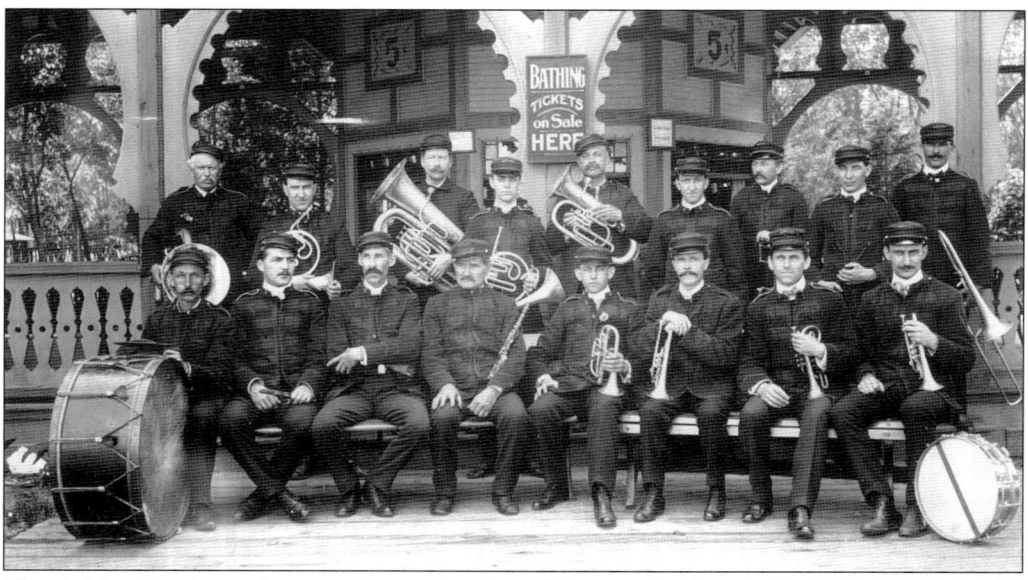

The Ackley Band was the successor to the Great Western Band and one of the most popular bands in Sandusky, beginning in 1893. Eugene B. Ackley, the leader of the band, was considered the "music man" of Sandusky for many years. In addition to his work with bands, he also taught music and led orchestras. The Ackley Band is seen here at Cedar Point, c. 1900.

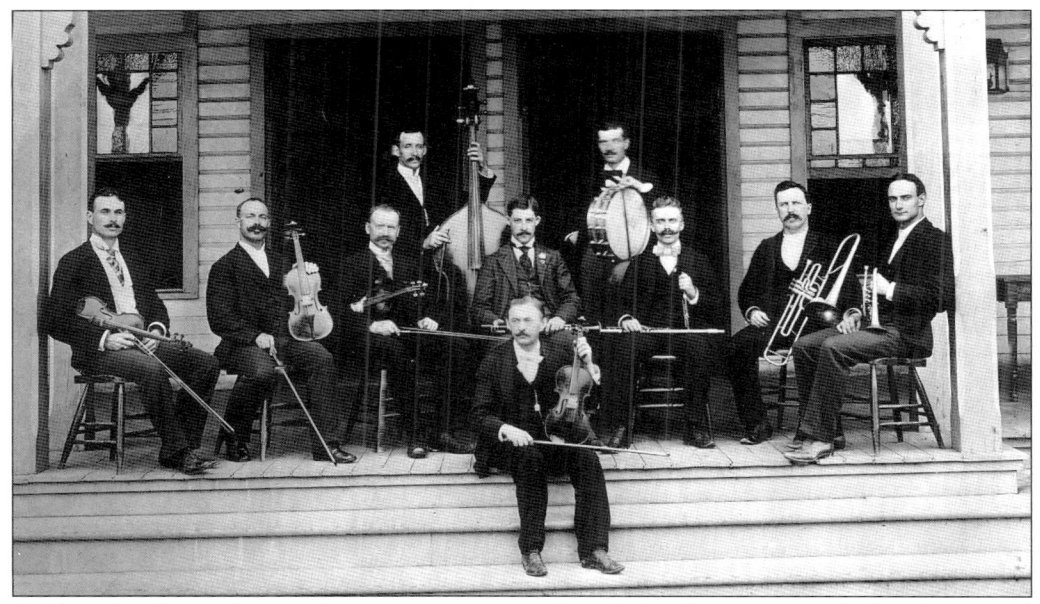

Ackley also directed an orchestra that performed at Cedar Point, primarily for dances and vaudeville acts. Here is the orchestra at Cedar Point in 1900.

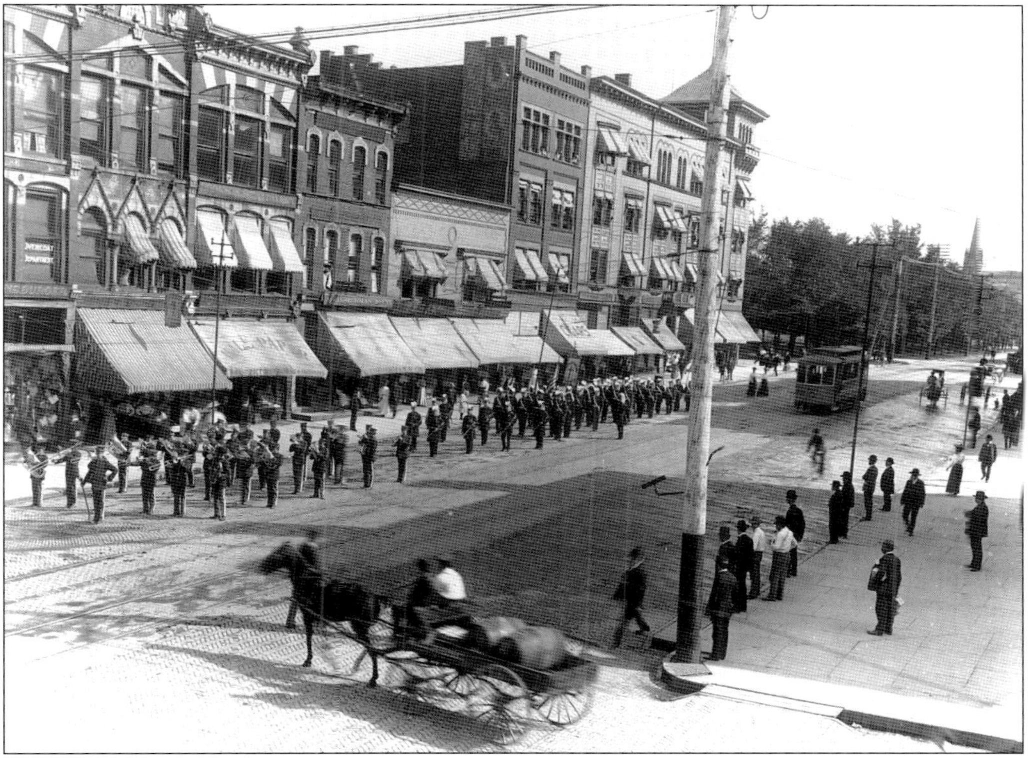

Parades were popular in early Sandusky and bands were usually an important part of these parades. Here we see an unidentified band, possibly Ackley's Band, leading a Knights of St. John parade in 1910.

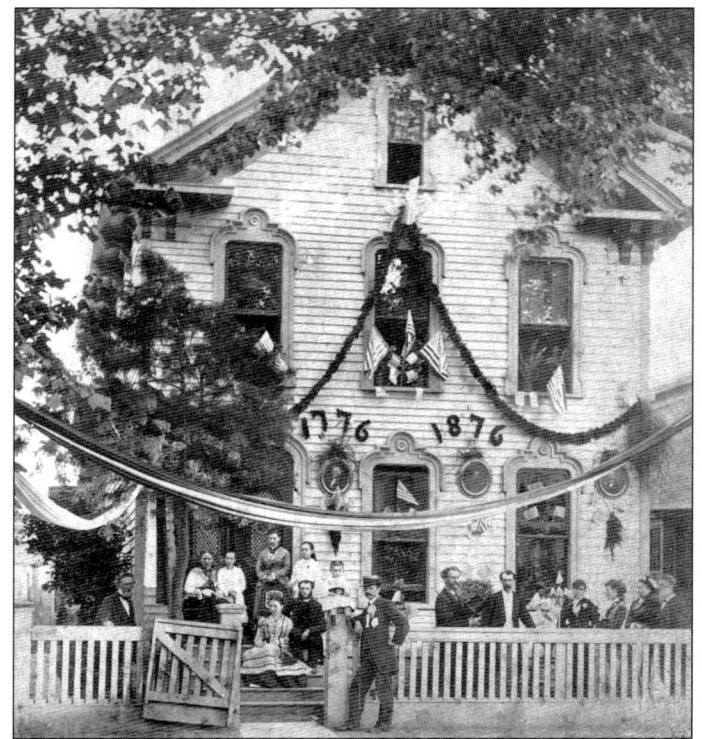

Civic commemorations have brought people out in celebration many times in Sandusky's history. One of the first big events was the national centennial in 1876. Sandusky was bustling with activities that Fourth of July. Some people decorated their houses, as we see in this stereocard image.

Of course, as Sandusky is a maritime city, there had to be maritime activities during the centennial celebration. This image shows a scene from a pound boat regatta in Sandusky Bay. The steamship *B.F. Ferris* is docked in the foreground.

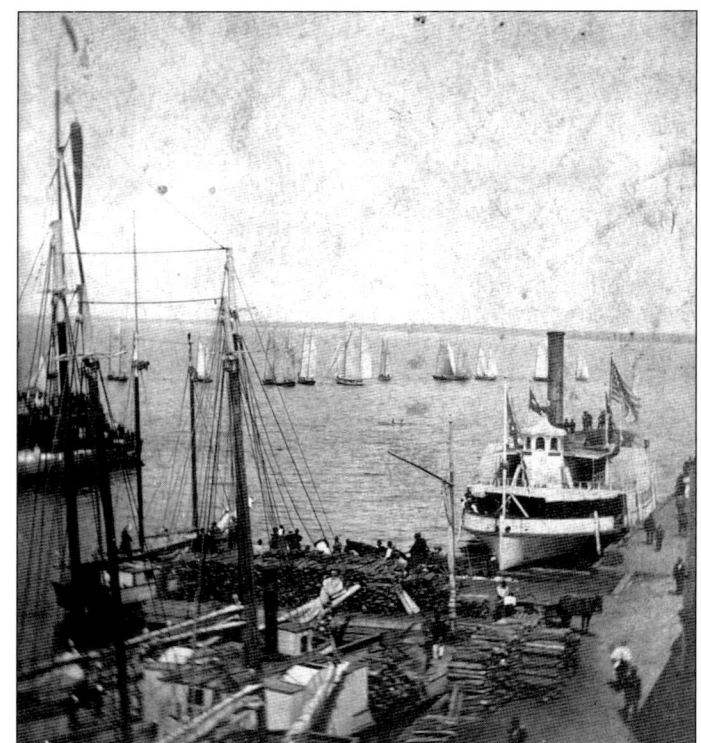

And what is a Fourth of July celebration without a high-wire acrobat? This centennial celebration performance was at the foot of Columbus Avenue, above the present site of the Schade-Mylander Plaza.

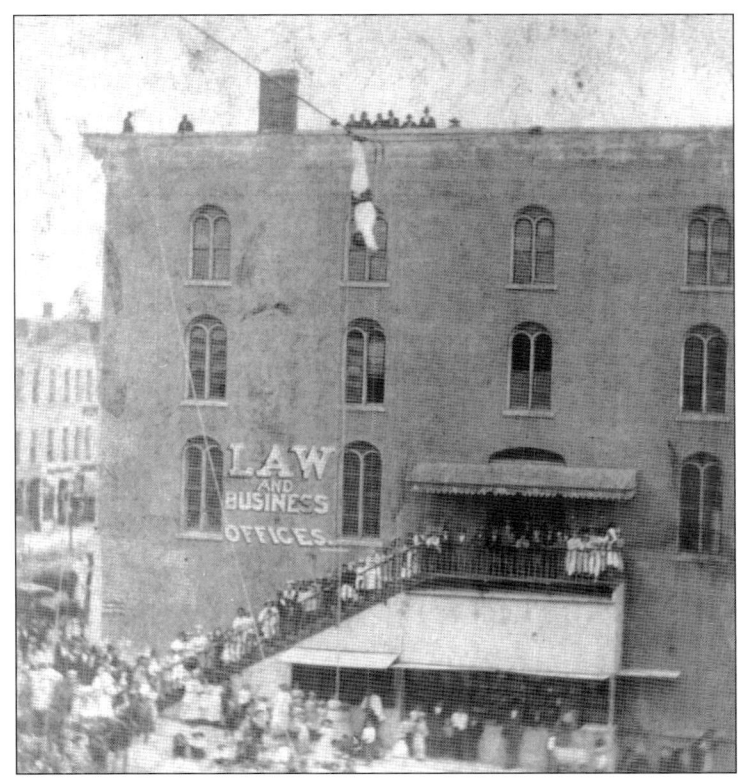

It didn't take a national holiday to get a party going! This photograph is titled "Leap Year Party—Friday, January 21, 1876." The names of these men and the story behind their dress are a mystery, but it is an interesting illustration of social life in the 19th century.

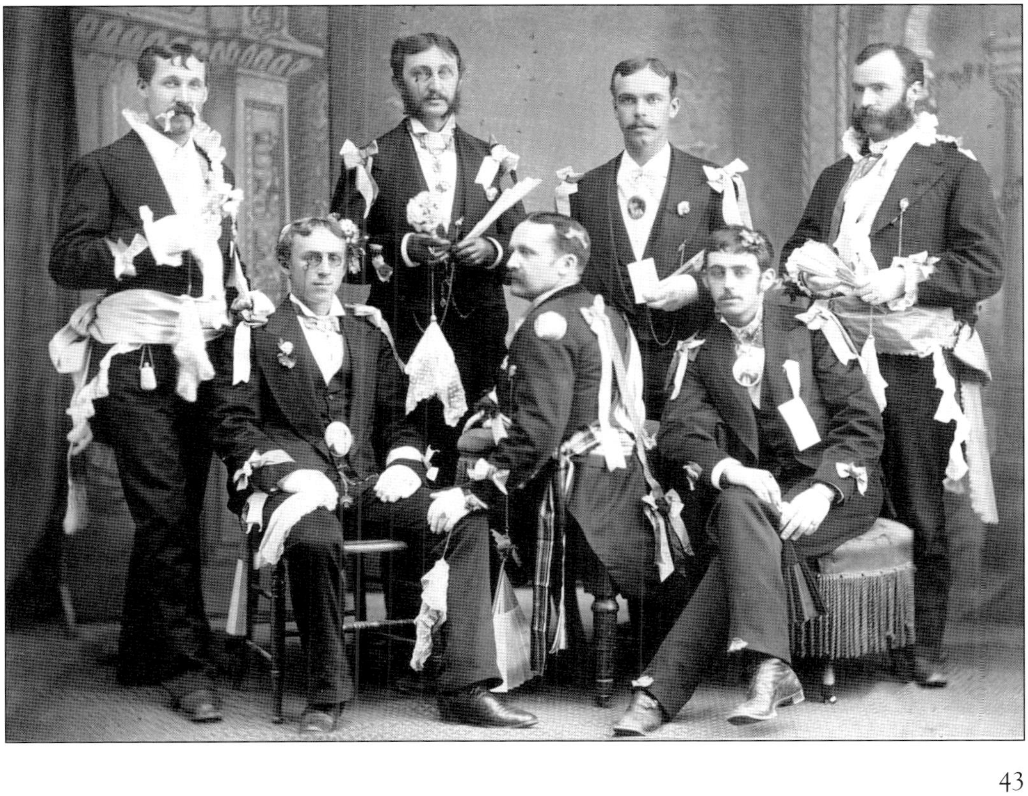

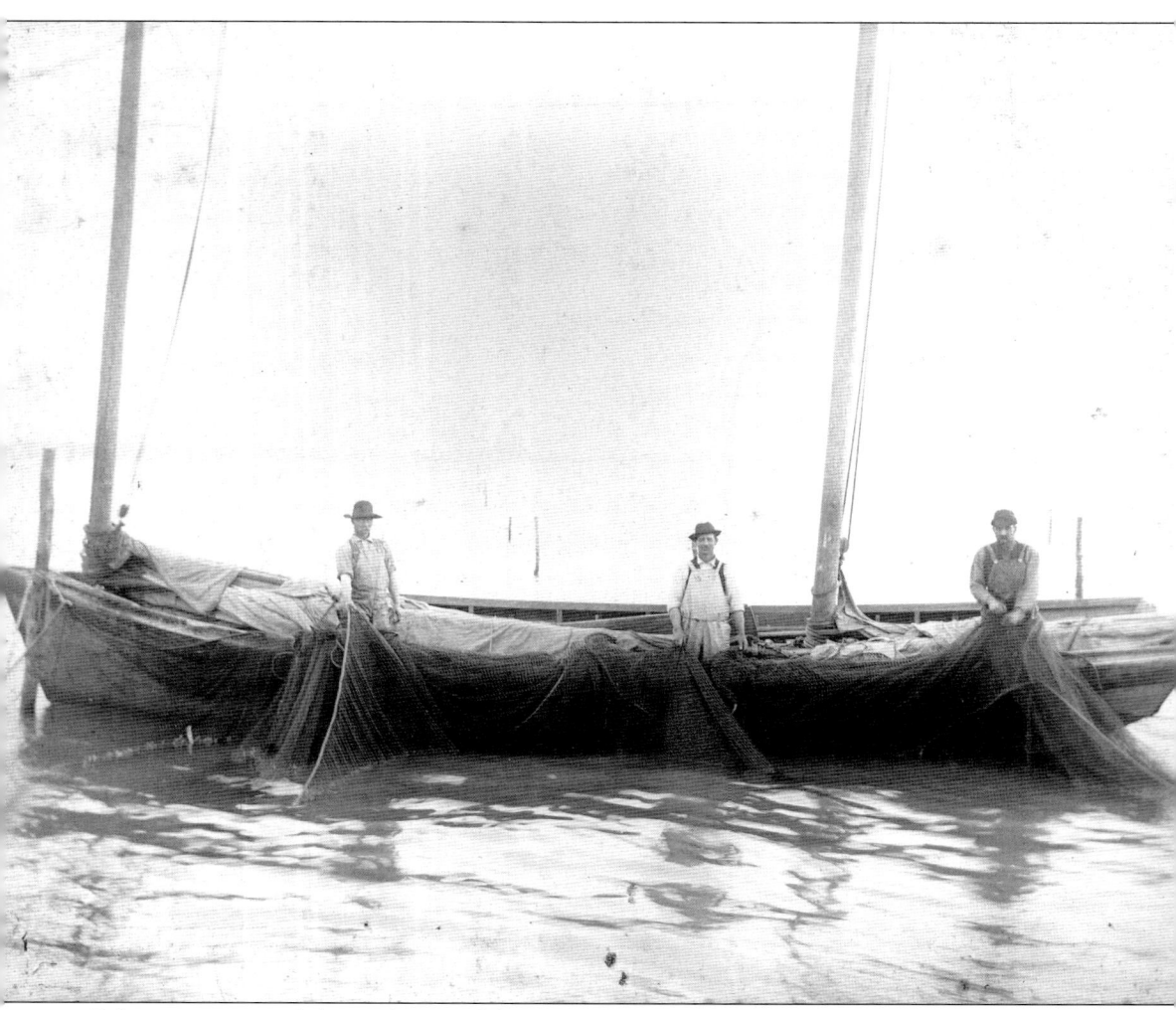

Fishing was one of the earliest and largest industries in Sandusky in the 19th century—at one time Sandusky had one of the largest fresh-water fishing industries worldwide. It became a major industry around 1850, when the use of pound nets began. The men in this image, probably from around 1870, are using pound nets. H.C. Post and Company was the first large fishing firm in the city, beginning operations in 1856. At its peak, the company annually employed over 700 workers.

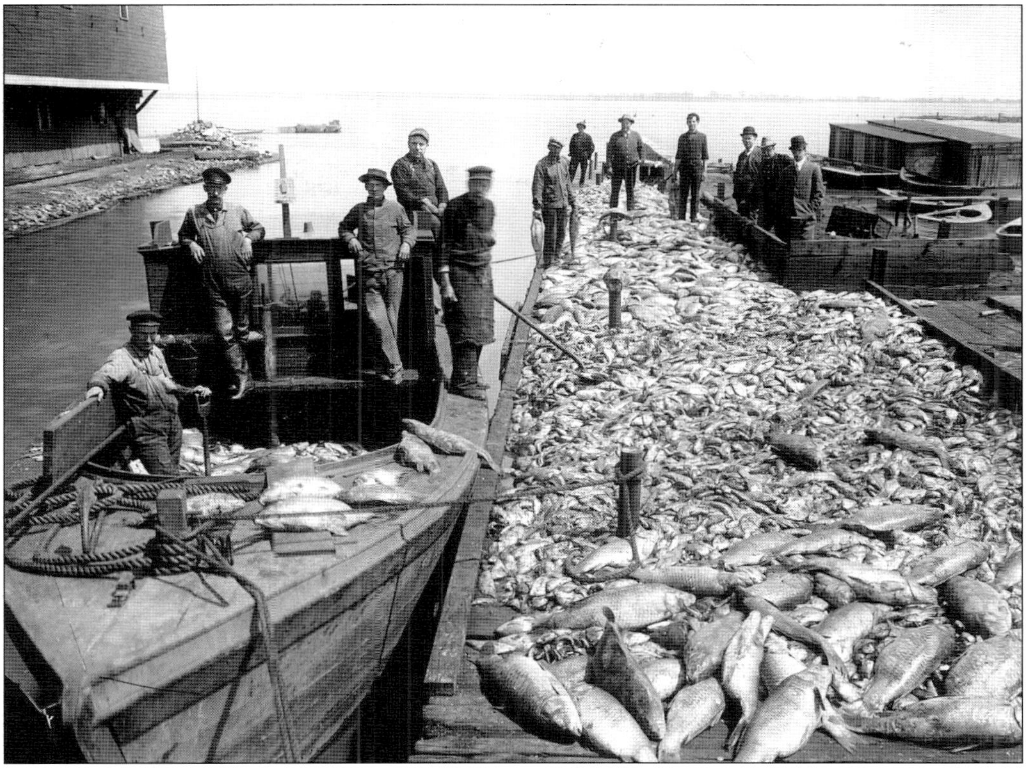

Fish harvests were bountiful in the early years of the industry as the images suggest. Thousands of tons of fish were harvested annually by the many companies operating along the Sandusky shoreline.

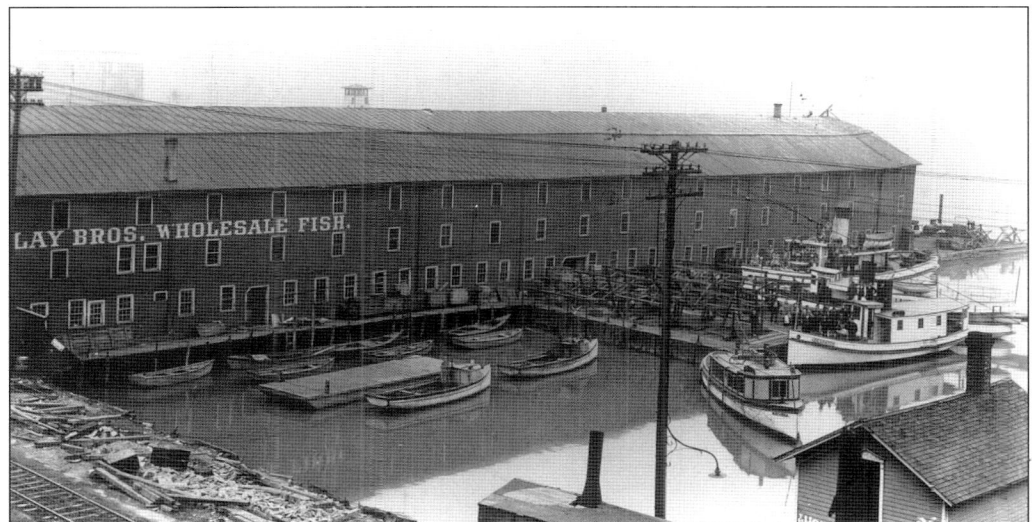

The Lay Brothers Fishery was one of the most successful, and one of the last, commercial fisheries in Sandusky. Founded in 1870, the company operated well into the 20th century. This building, at the foot of Wayne Street, burned in 1932, but the business continued for many more years. Today, there are no commercial fisheries in Sandusky.

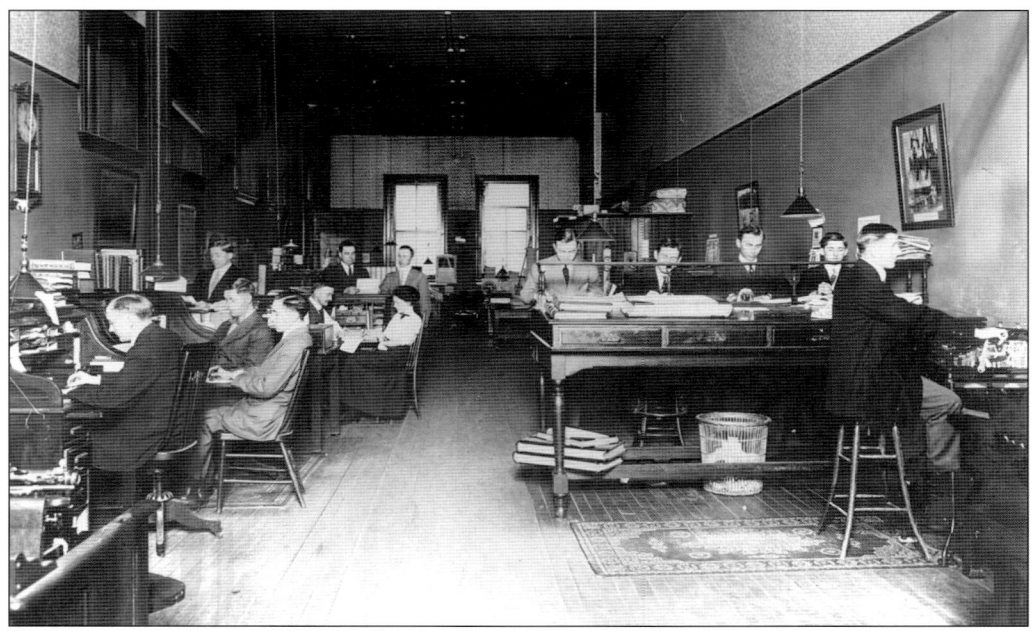

A view of the office of the Lay Brothers Fisheries around 1910 gives an idea of the size of the industry at the time.

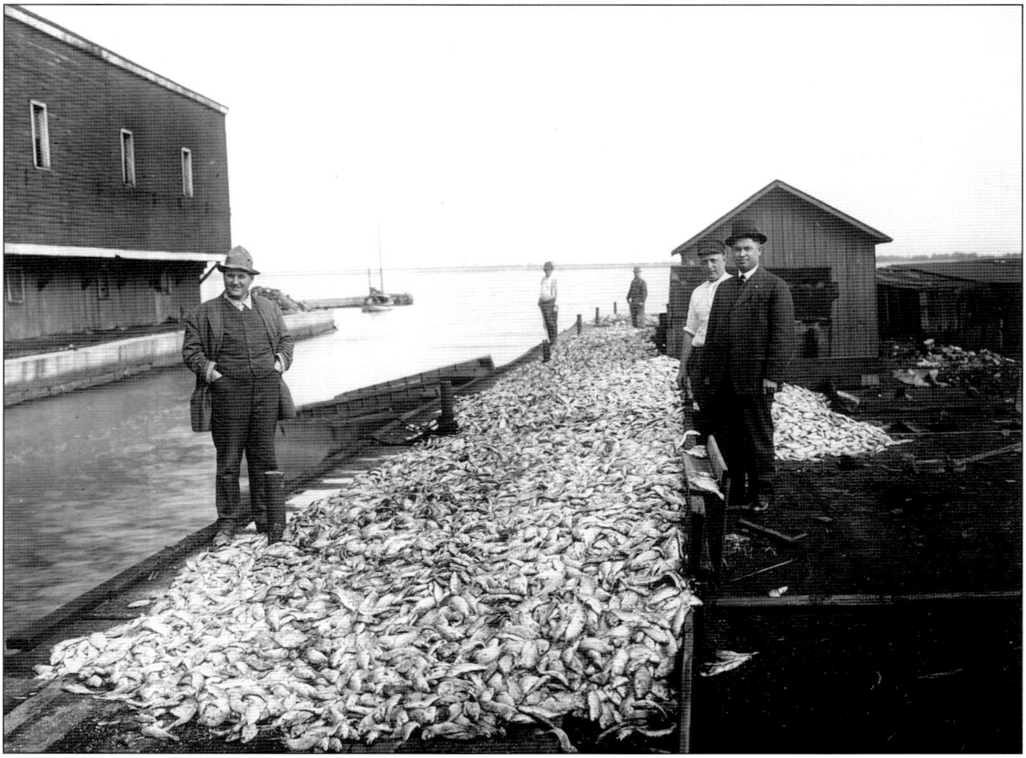

Pictured is another successful catch, c. 1910. Many of the less desirable species of fish were sold to factories to be made into fertilizer.

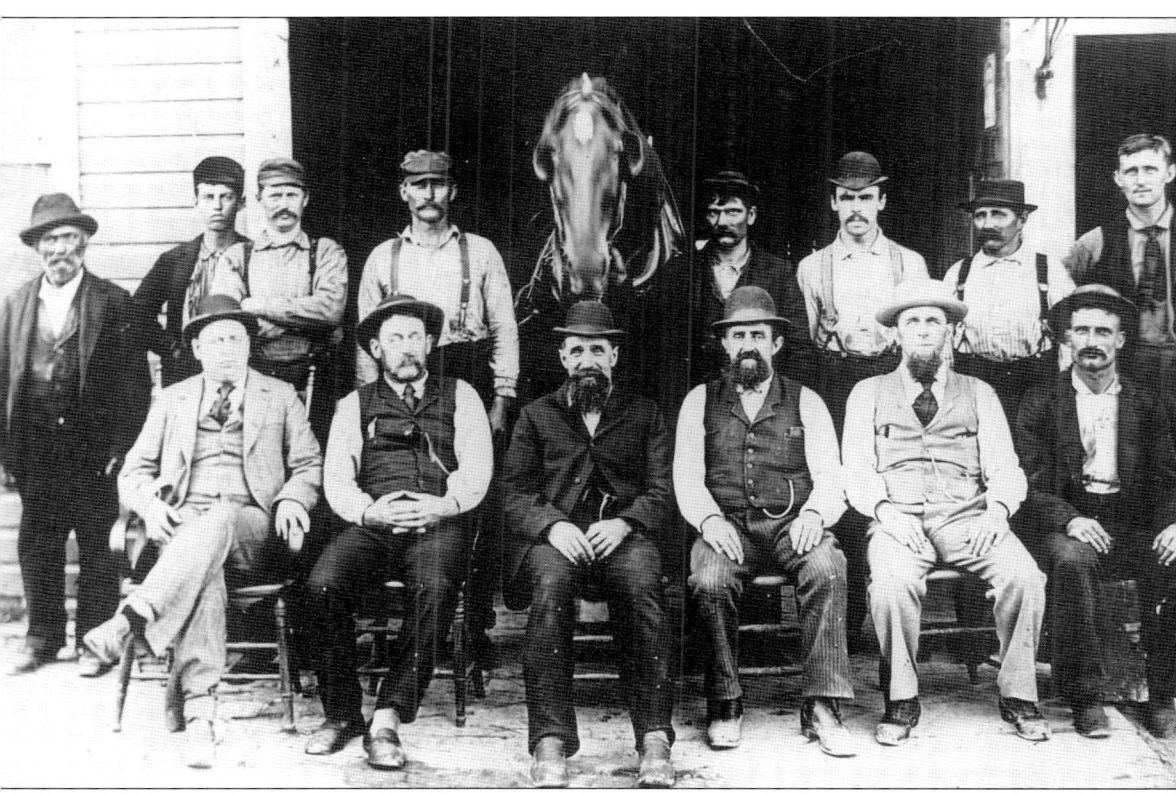

Lay Brothers employees are seen here, c. 1900. These men (and the horse in the back row) were probably in an ice cutting crew. Many of the local fisheries operated their own ice houses, using the ice harvested to preserve their catches. It also kept men employed during the winter months.

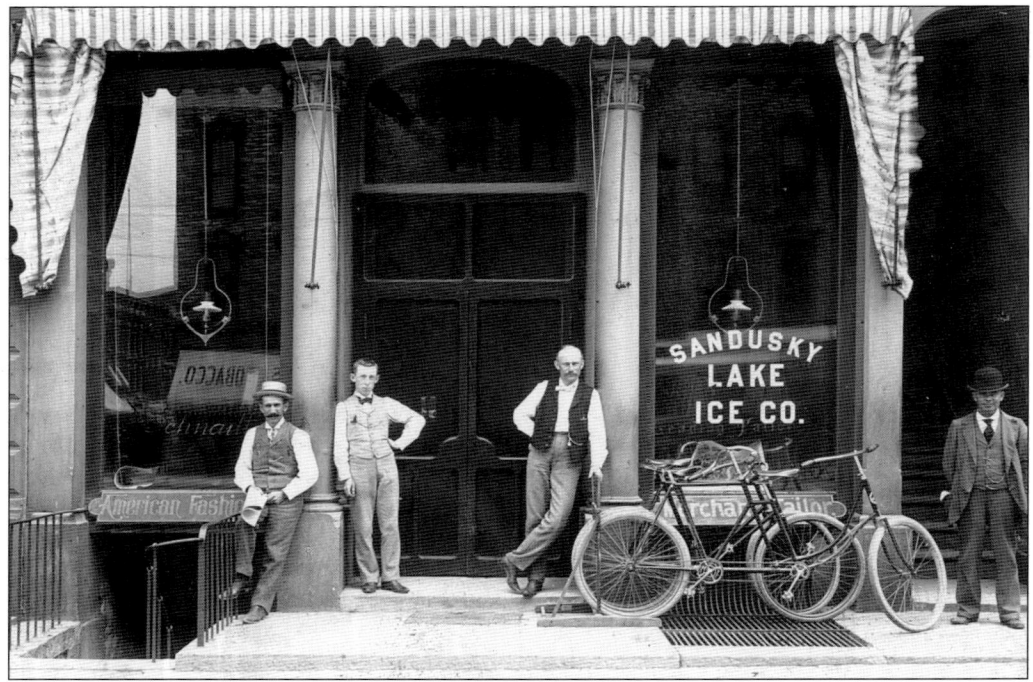

Another now-extinct business that flourished in the 19th century is the ice-harvesting industry. Ice was carved from the bay for use in food preservation before the invention of refrigerators. At the peak of the industry (primarily during the 1880s), Sandusky was home to one of the largest ice industries in the nation—in good years, as many as 2,000 men worked in the ice harvests. More than 50 icehouses lined the shores of Sandusky Bay in these years. In 1881, 22 ice companies were in business. The Sandusky Lake Ice Company had an office at 104 Columbus Avenue in the 1890s.

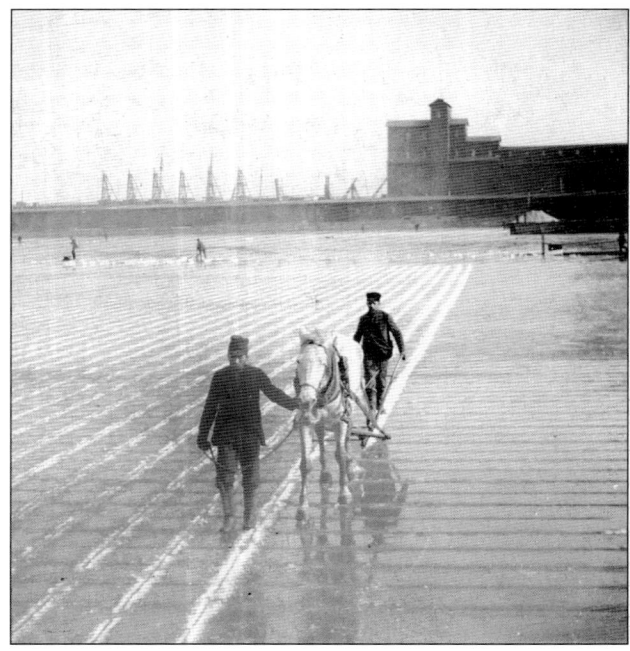

When the ice in the bay became thick enough, crews set out to cut the ice and move it to the icehouses on the shore. Before machines were invented to harvest the ice, heavy saws pulled by horses cut the ice to be harvested.

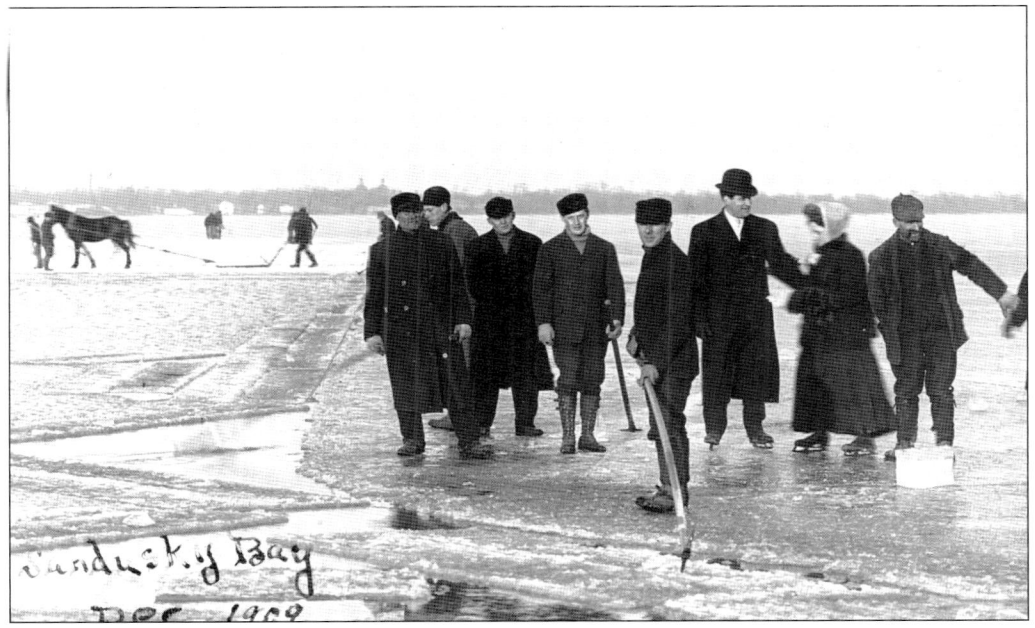

Here a crew is preparing to move blocks of ice cut by the horse-drawn blade seen in the background.

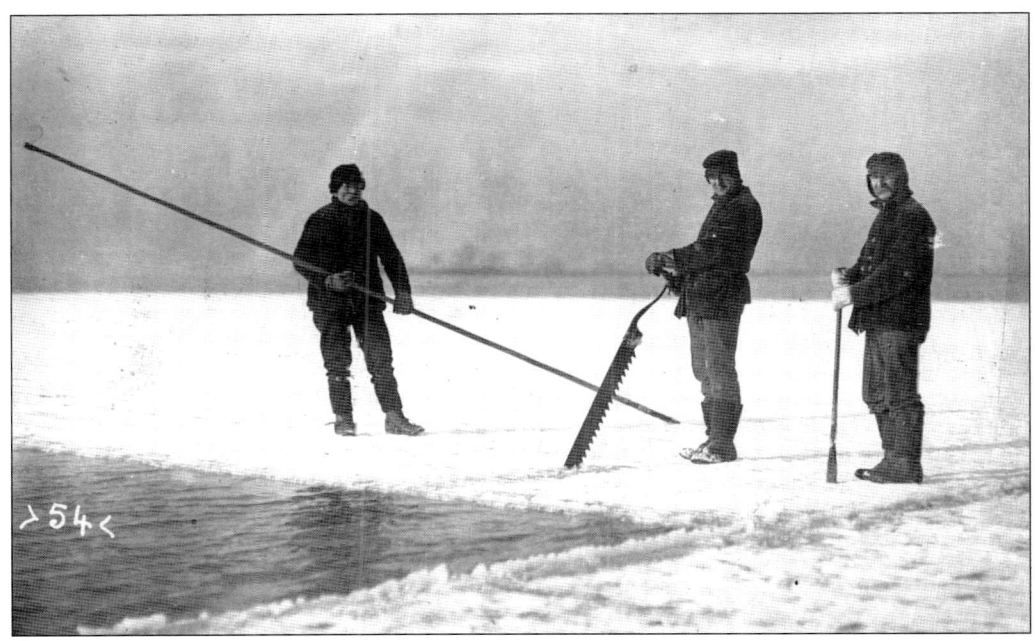

These men are carrying some of the tools of the trade—a large saw to cut the ice and pikes to move the ice along the water to the icehouse.

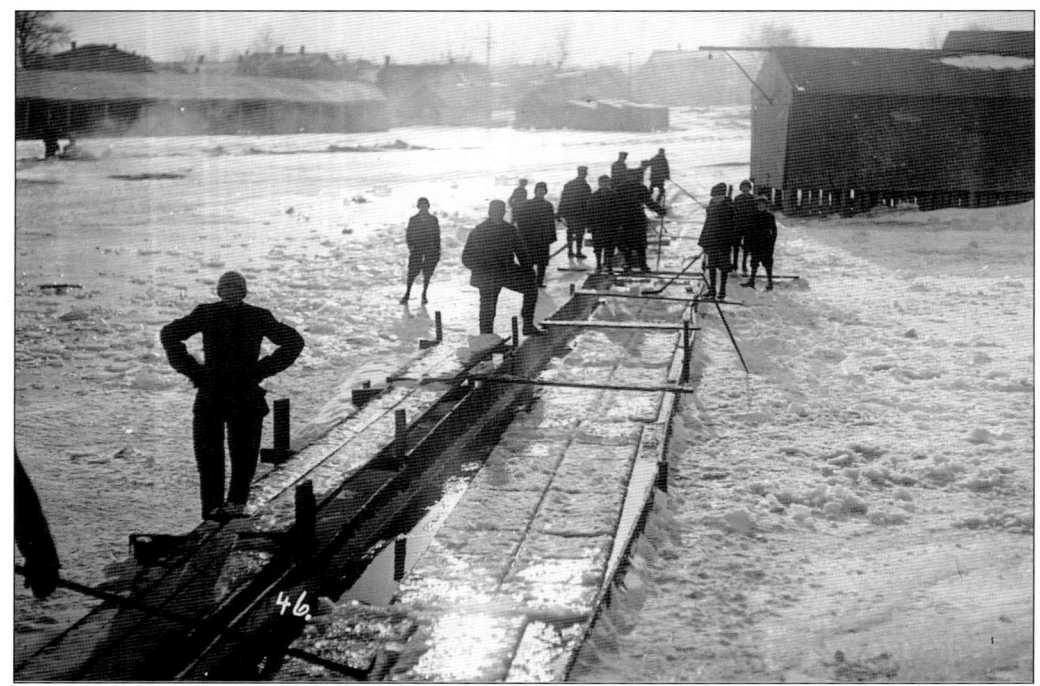

Blocks of ice are being moved along a channel cut to the icehouse.

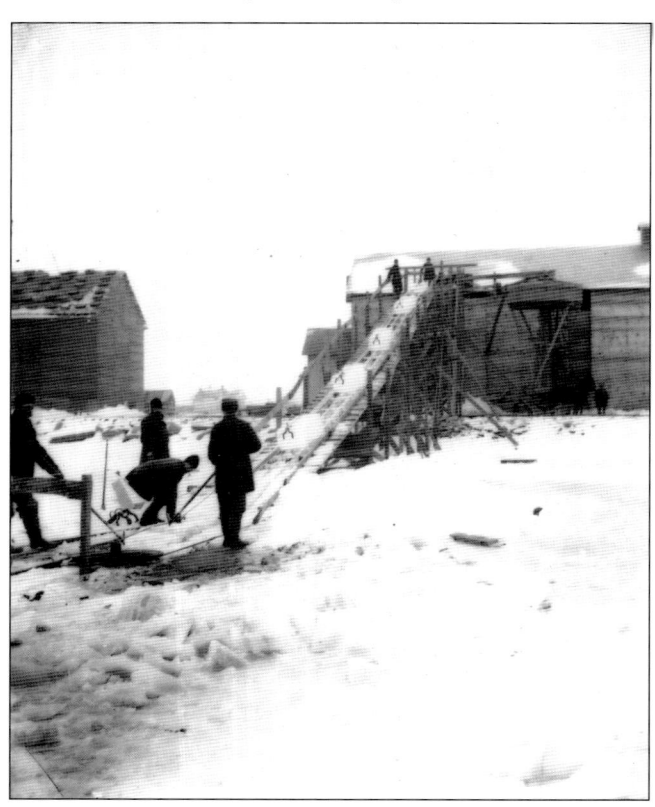

Ice is moved by conveyor into one of the icehouses along the shore of Sandusky Bay.

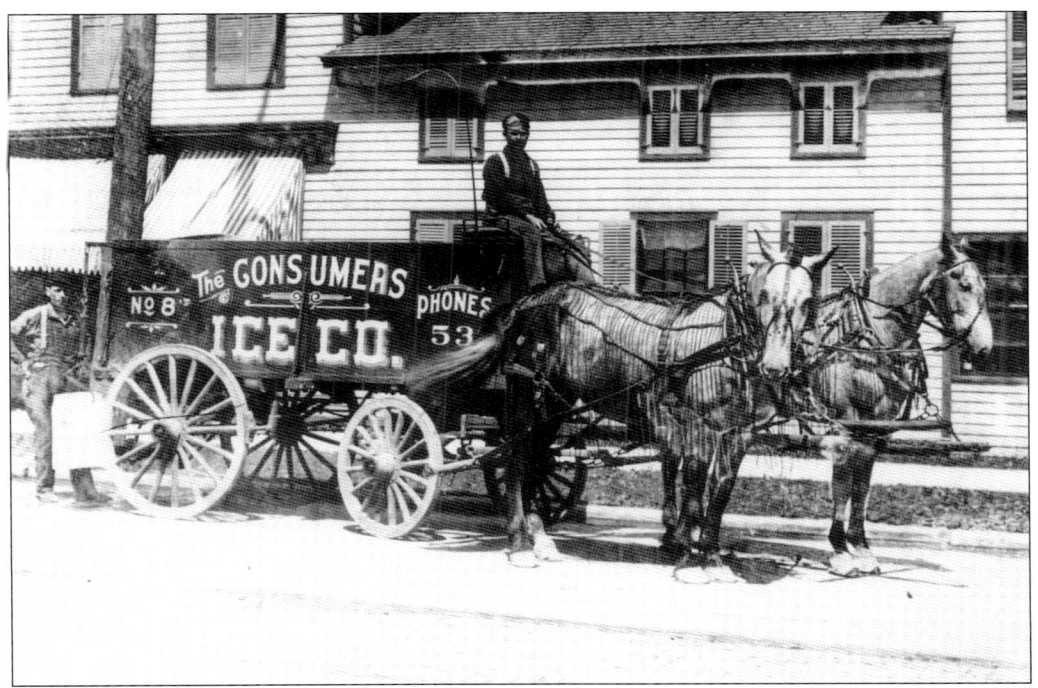

Much of the ice harvested was sold locally to residents and business and delivered by horse-drawn wagons. Some of the ice was shipped as far away as Cincinnati.

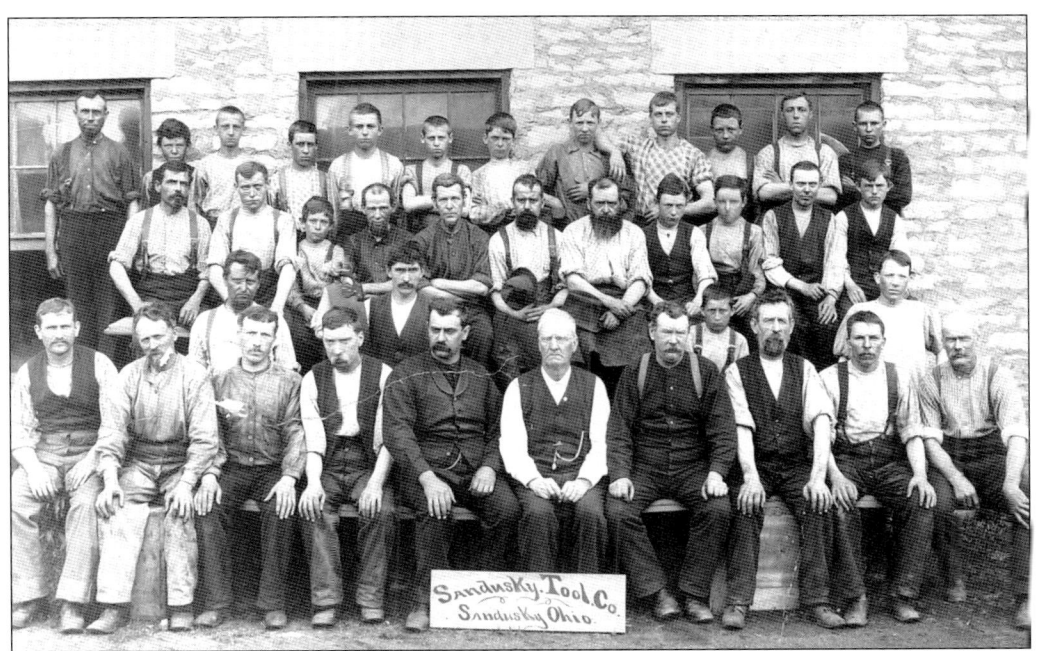

The Sandusky Tool Company made high-quality hand tools for over half a century, beginning in 1869. Many of the handcrafted wood planes made by the company are highly desired by collectors. With the advent of power tools and mass-production, however, the company was unable to survive very long into the 20th century.

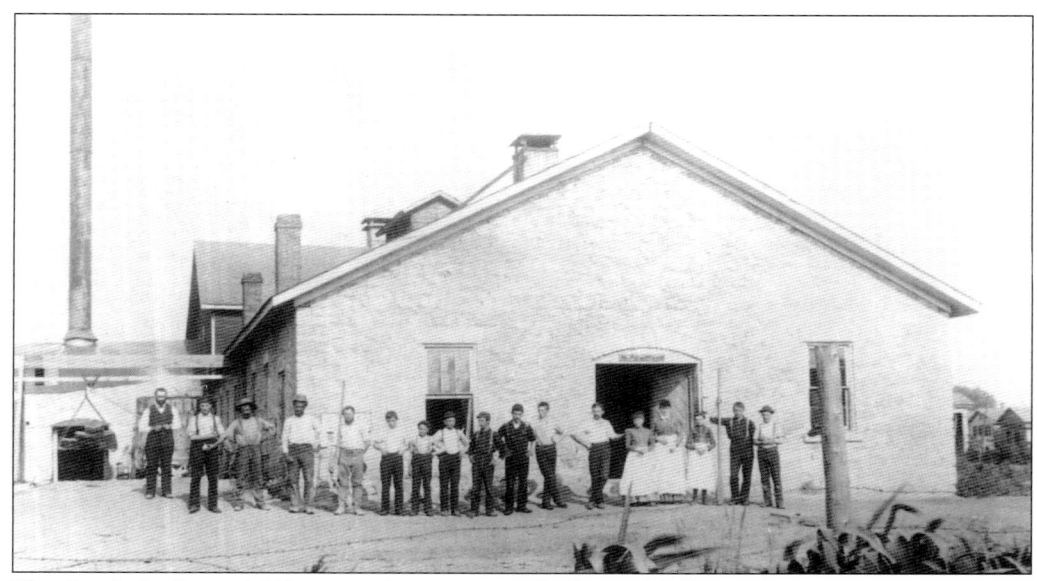

The Sandusky Paper Mill was at the corner of Shelby and Fillmore Streets in 1886. In 1888, businessmen J.J. Hinde and J.J. Dauch leased (and later purchased) the mill. The company eventually became known as the Hinde and Dauch Paper Company.

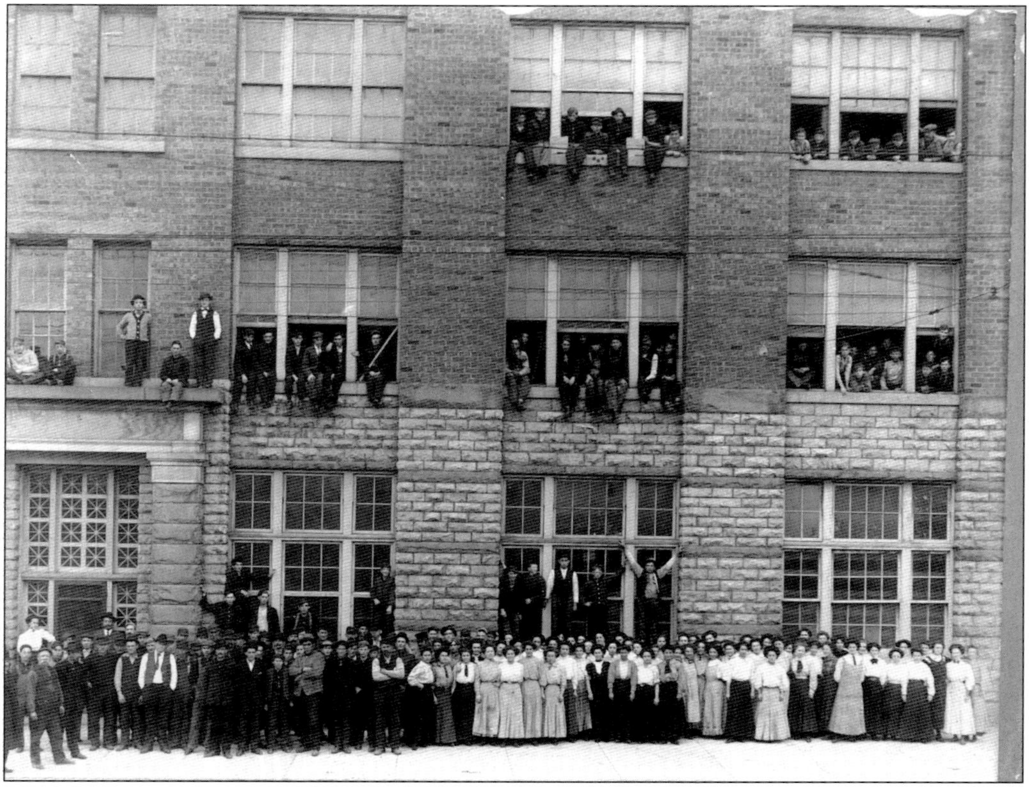

The Hinde and Dauch factory on Water Street began operation around 1896. The company was best known as a maker of corrugated shipping boxes.

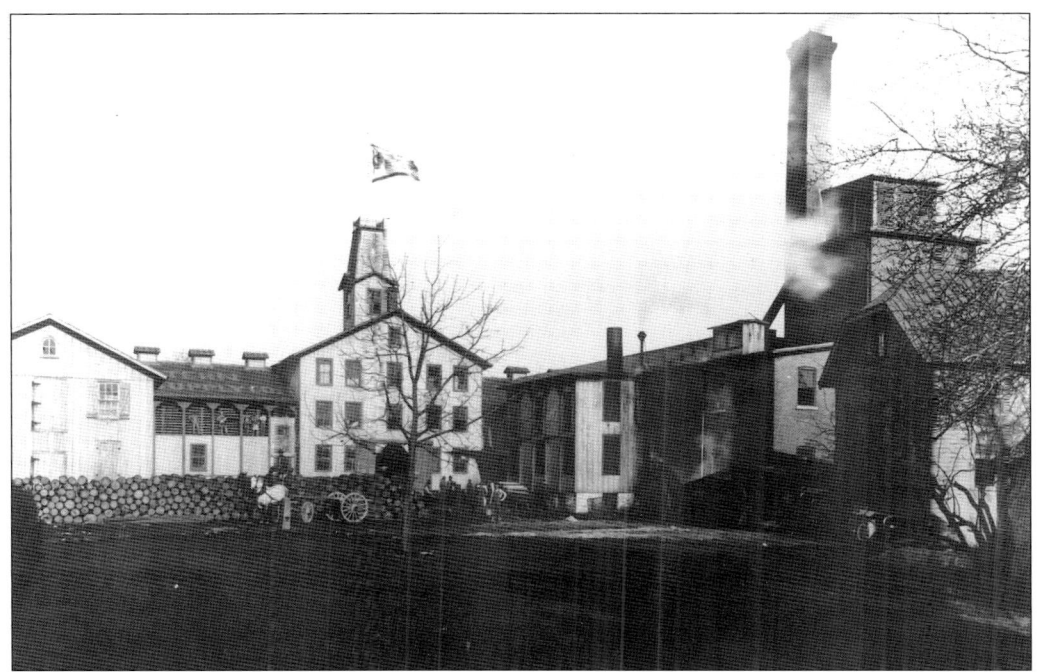

The American Crayon Company traced its origins to 1835, when a school chalk company began business in Sandusky. The Western School Supply Company became American Crayon after merging with two other crayon companies in 1890.

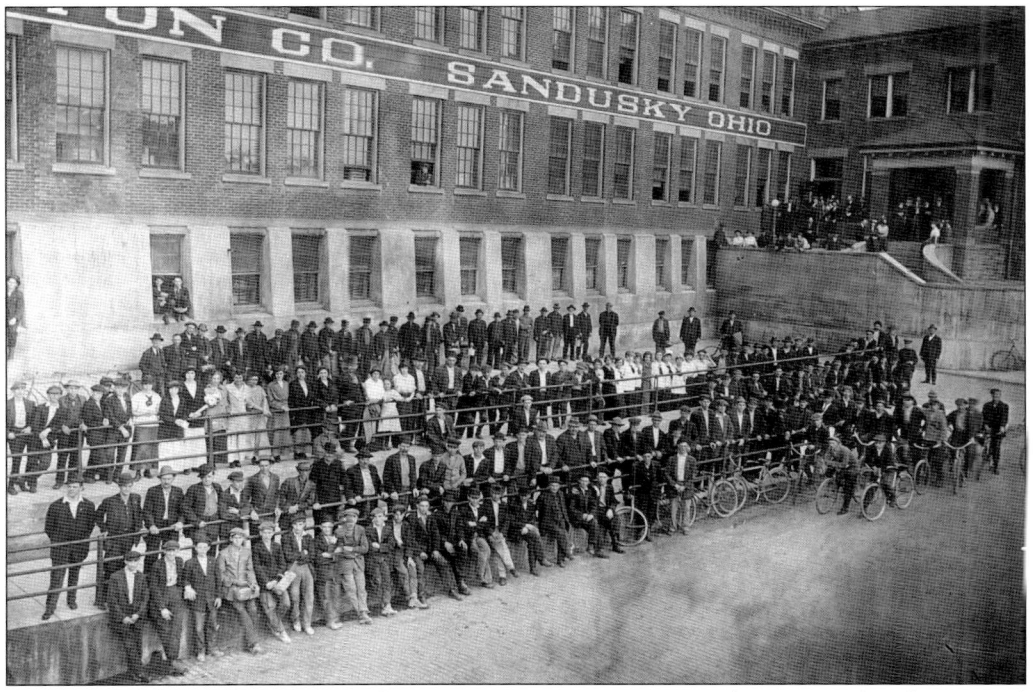

The American Crayon Company factory on Hayes Avenue opened in 1901, after the original building was destroyed by fire.

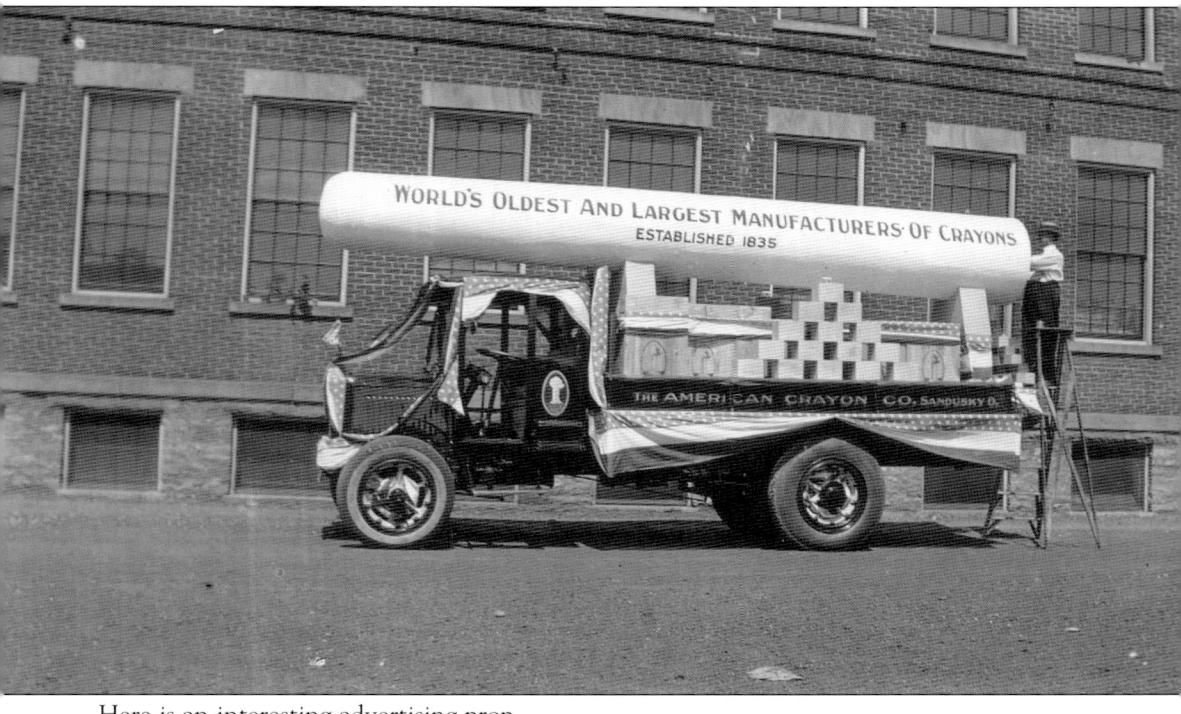

Here is an interesting advertising prop.

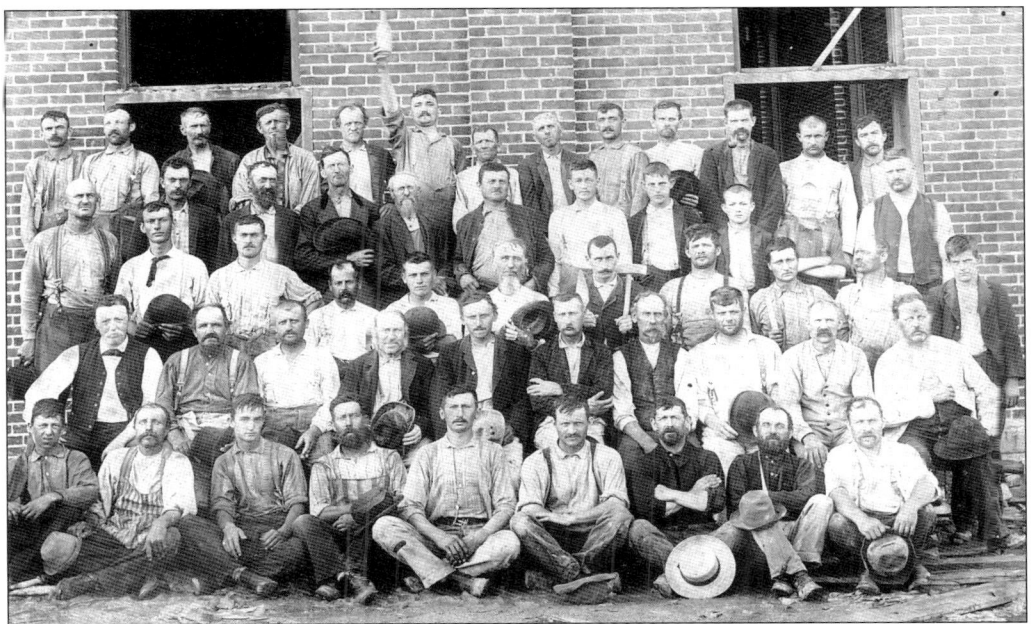

The construction crew that built the Jackson Underwear factory at North Depot and McDonough Streets in 1899 poses for a formal picture. Although the identity of these men is not known, it is reasonable to believe that some of these men were immigrants from Europe. There was a substantial German population in Sandusky in the 19th and early 20th centuries.

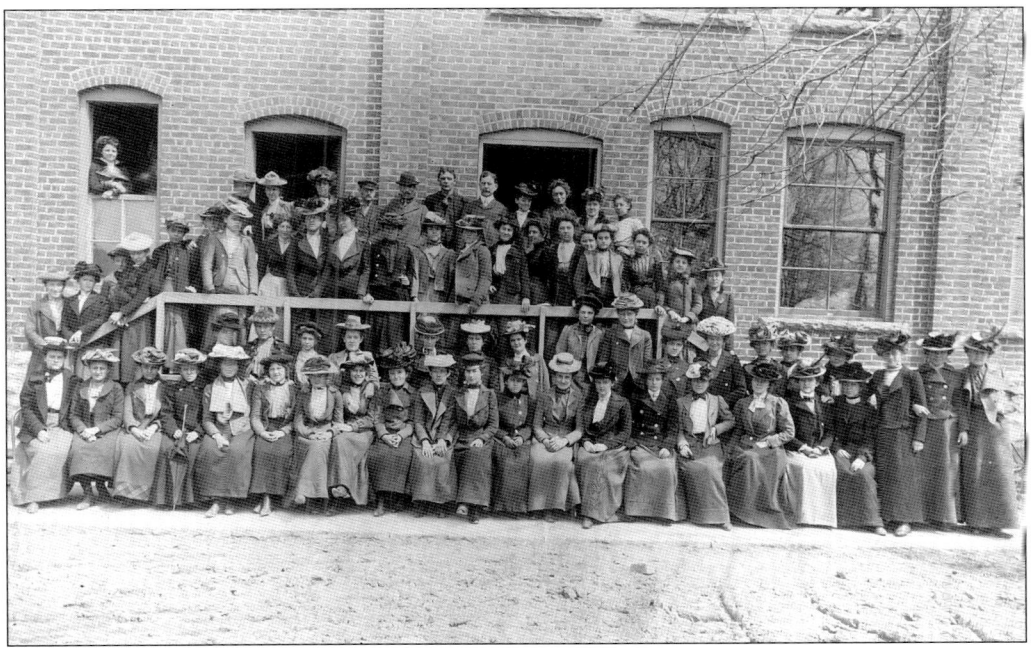

Pictured are employees of the Jackson Underwear Factory, c. 1906. This factory operated in Sandusky from 1899 to 1933, making nightgowns and pajamas for women and children. The company employed mostly women to operate the sewing machines at a time when it was rare for a woman to work outside the home.

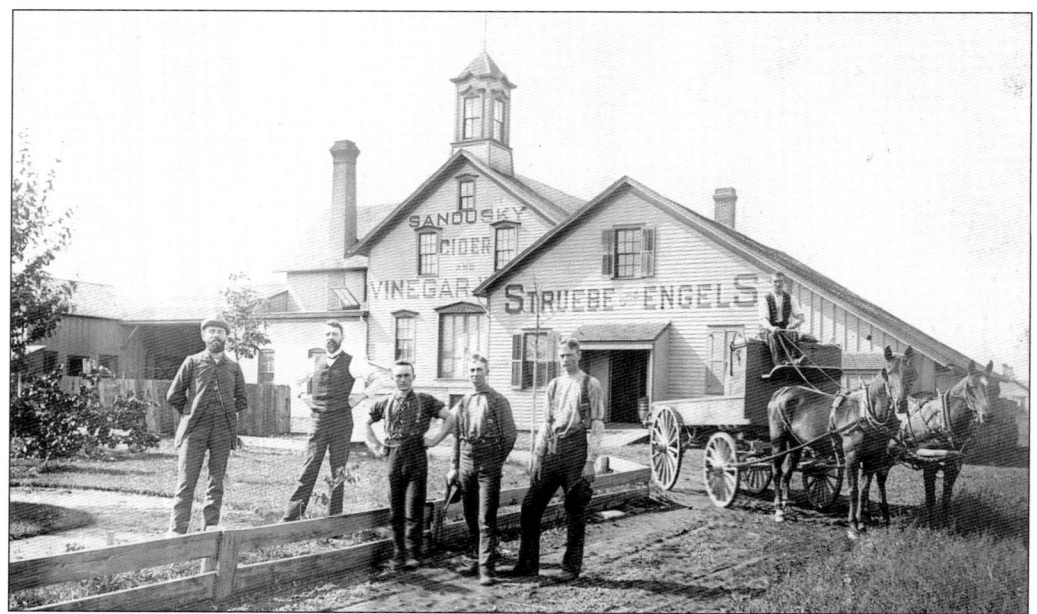

The Struebe and Engels plant produced cider and vinegar in Sandusky into the early 20th century. Cider was a popular drink in early America. C.H. Struebe was also involved in the wine business—not surprising, since the manufacturing process for wine, cider, and vinegar are similar.

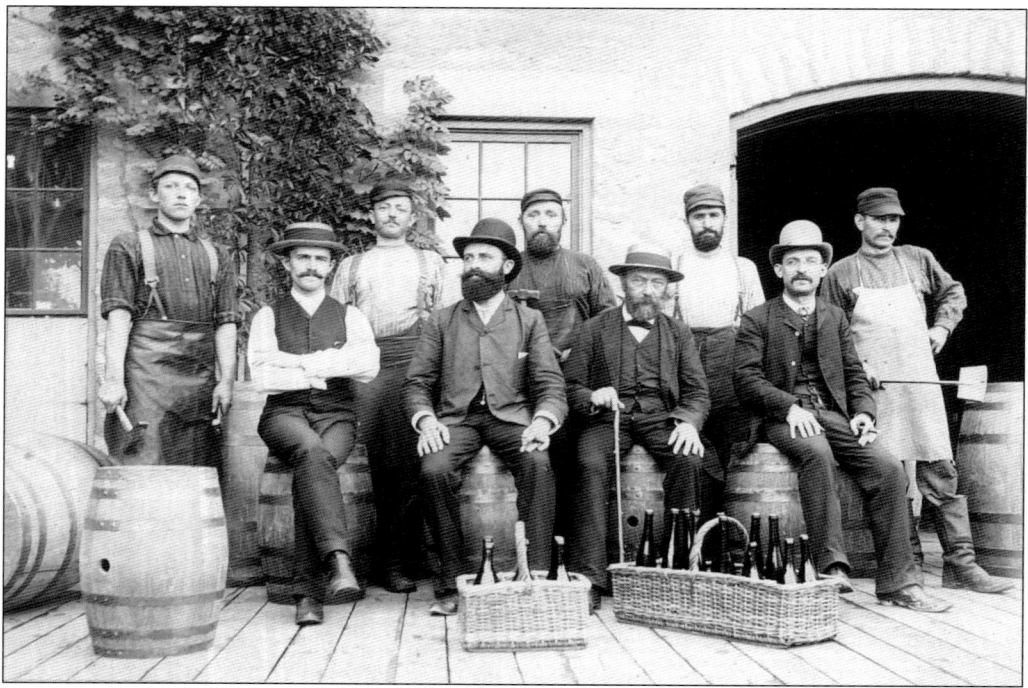

The Engels and Krudwig Wine Company, founded in 1878, was one of nearly two dozen wineries operating in and around Sandusky in the late 19th and early 20th centuries. Their wines sold throughout the eastern United States. Some wineries are still in business in nearby communities.

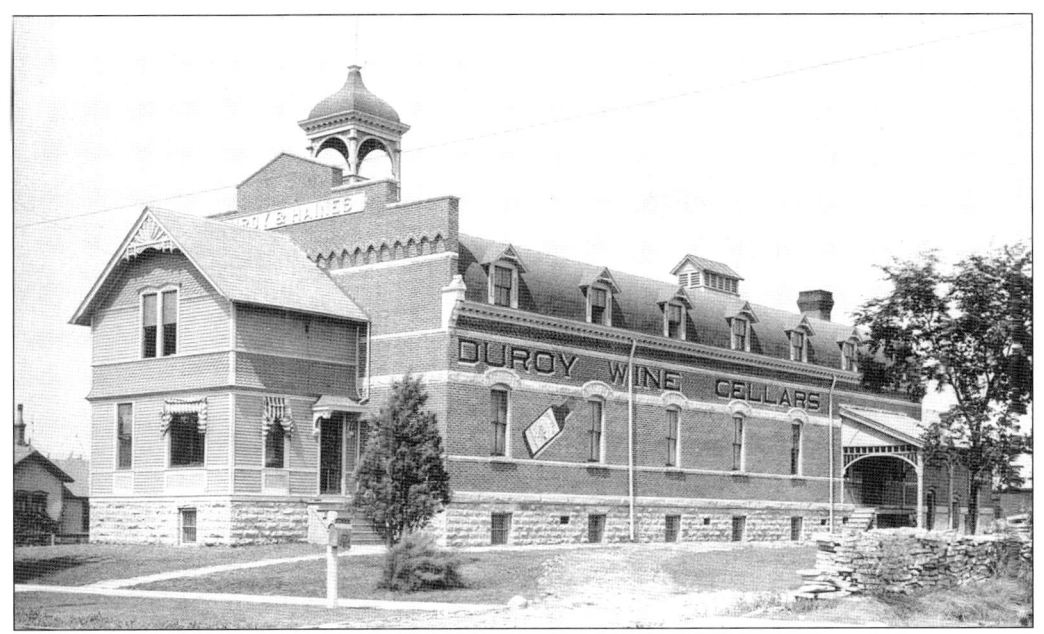

Founded in 1888 by Martial Duroy and E.J. Haines, the Duroy and Haines Wine Cellars operated on Columbus Avenue for nearly 30 years. The company also made champagne and grape juice.

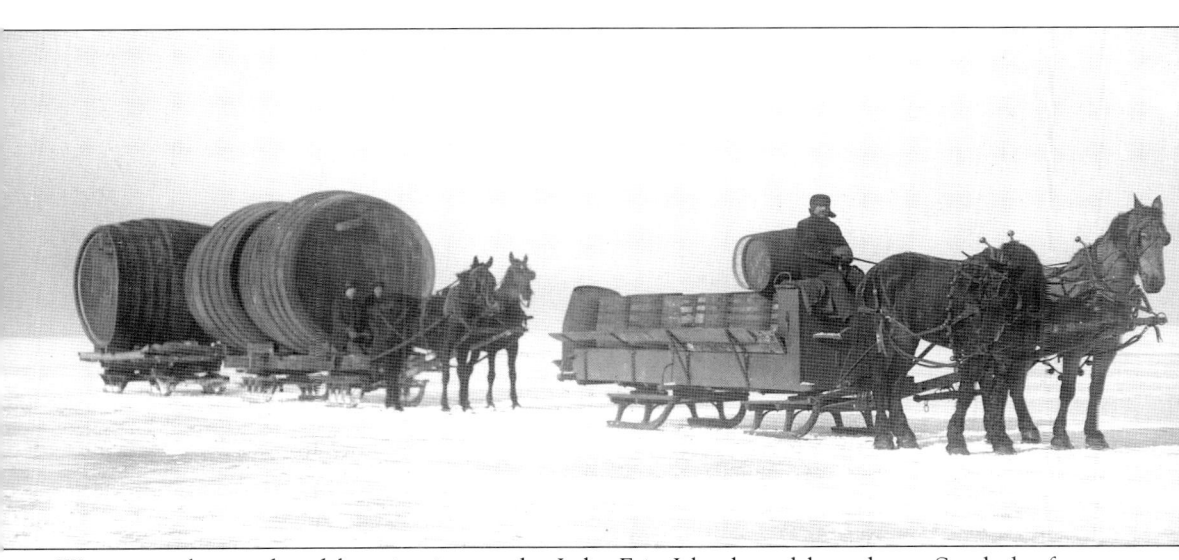

Wine was also produced by wineries on the Lake Erie Islands and brought to Sandusky for distribution. When the lake was frozen in the winter, horse-drawn sleds often brought wine casks across the Lake Erie ice, as in this scene, c. 1900. Sandusky and the Lake Erie Islands region was one of the largest grape and wine centers east of California, with nearly 6,000 acres in Erie and Ottawa Counties used for growing grapes.

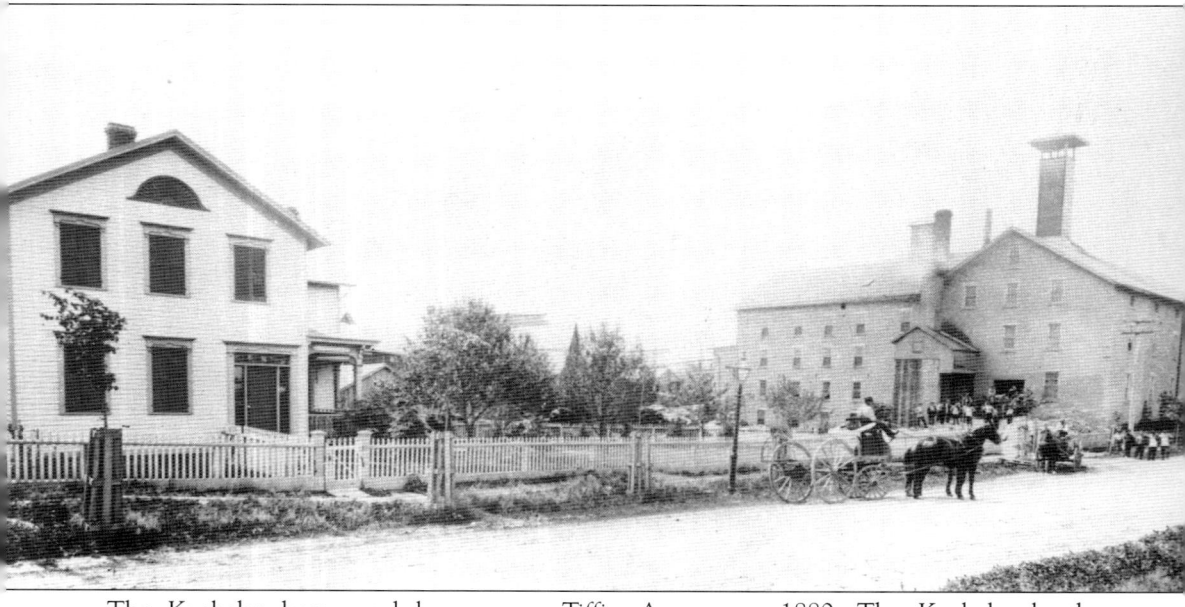

The Kuebeler home and brewery on Tiffin Avenue, c. 1880. The Kuebeler brothers, Jacob and August, founded the Kuebeler Brewing Company in 1867. They imported over 50,000 pounds of hops from Germany to produce over 100 barrels of lager beer daily. The beer garden at Cedar Point sold their beer. In 1885, Jacob built a mansion on the site of the house in the photo; August built an identical house across the street, which is still standing at 1319 Tiffin Avenue.

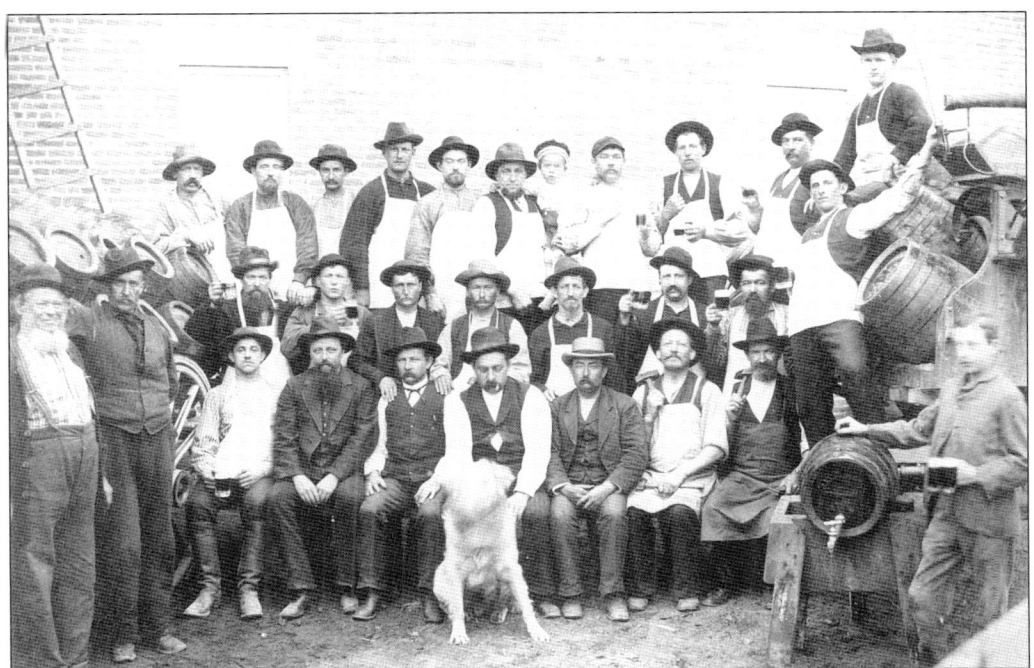

In 1892, the Jacob Kuebeler Brewing Company became incorporated as the Jacob Kuebeler Brewing and Malting Company. The company's employees from that time are posed for a picture.

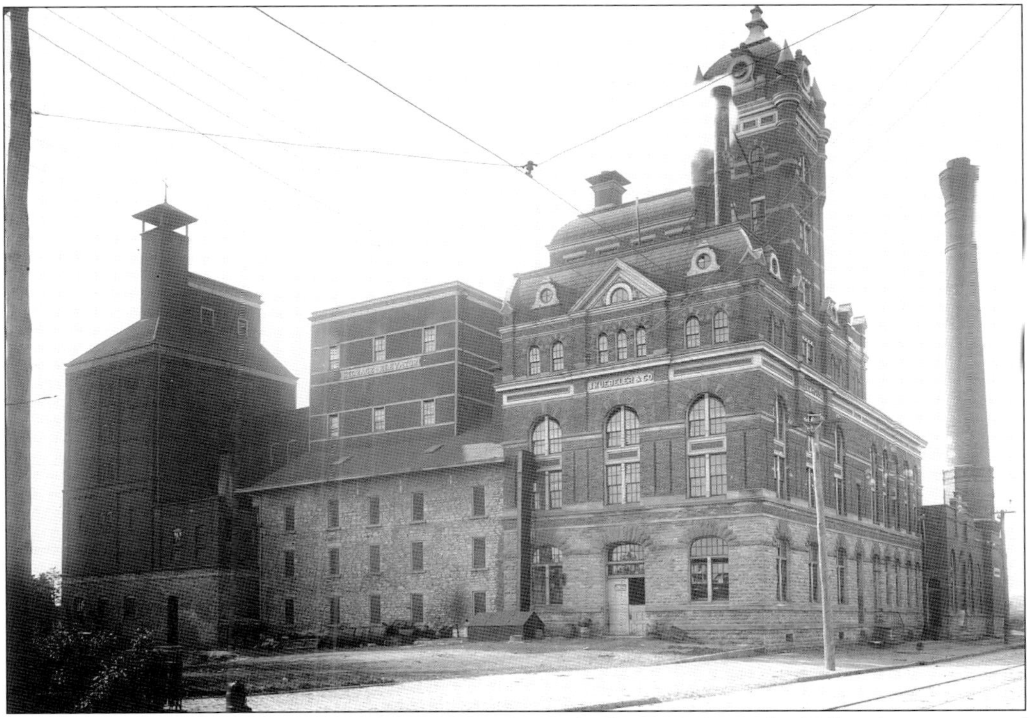

The Kuebeler brewing plant seen here, c. 1895, was built in 1893 on the Tiffin Avenue site of the previous plant, which burned down in 1892.

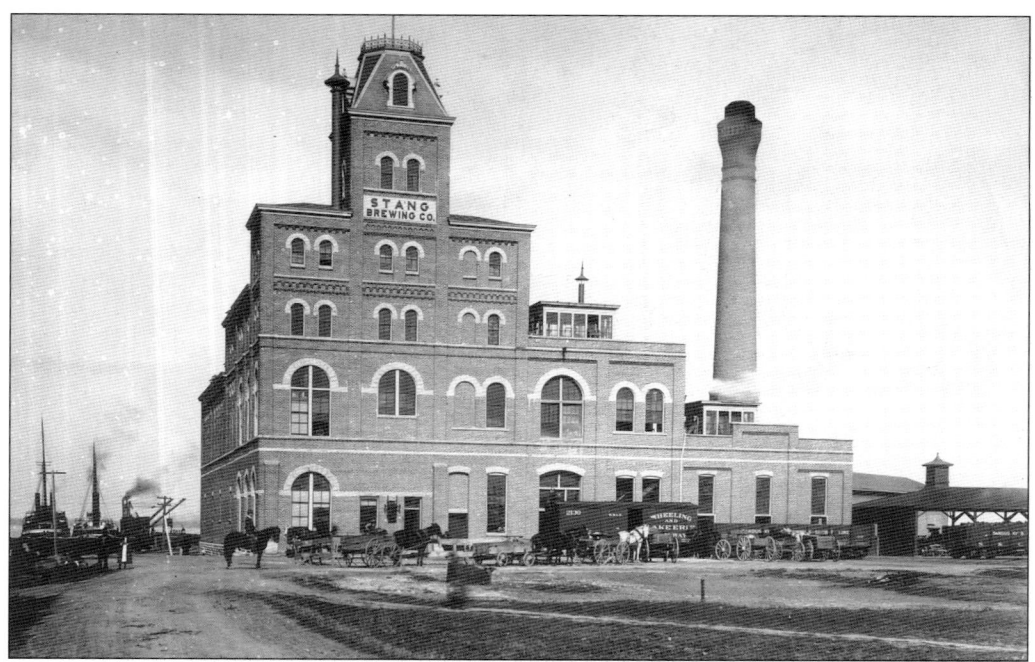

Around 1880, Frank Stang purchased the "Old Dauch" Brewery (founded in 1857) and created the Stang Brewing Company. This building on King Street was built in 1893. Frank's brother John became president of the company in 1890.

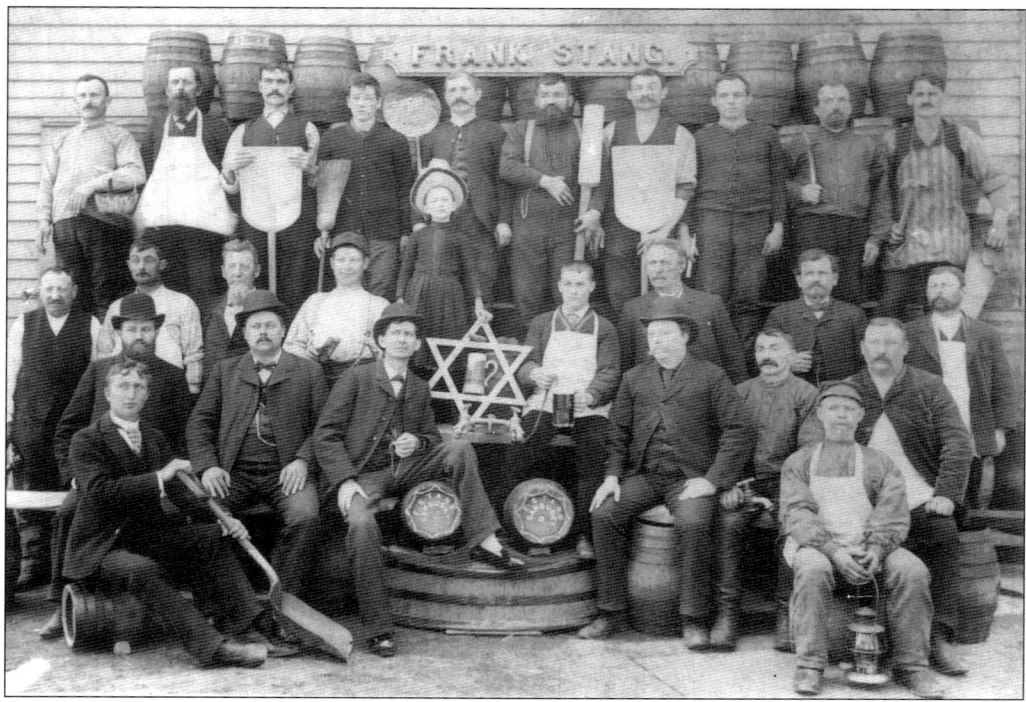

Frank Stang's daughter Ida is near the center of this photograph of brewery employees in 1887. Frank and John Stang may be among the men in the front row.

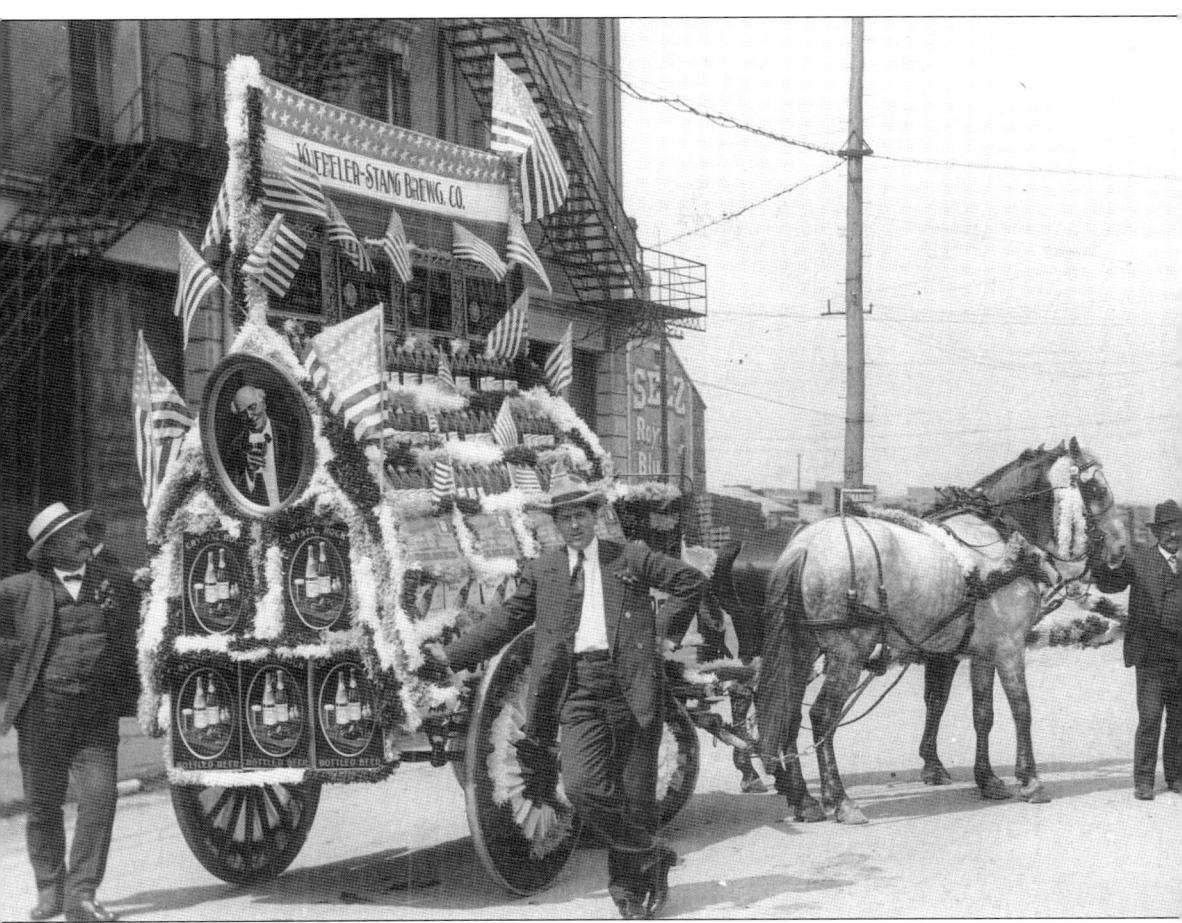

This decorated wagon advertising Crystal Rock Beer could have been in a parade. The Kuebeler Brewery and the Stang Brewery merged in 1896, forming the Kuebeler-Stang Brewing Company. Two years later, the company merged with seven breweries in Cleveland to form the Cleveland and Sandusky Brewing Company. These breweries produced the Crystal Rock brand locally. Not surprisingly, Prohibition drove these plants out of business. The Stang plant briefly reopened after Prohibition, but closed for good in 1935.

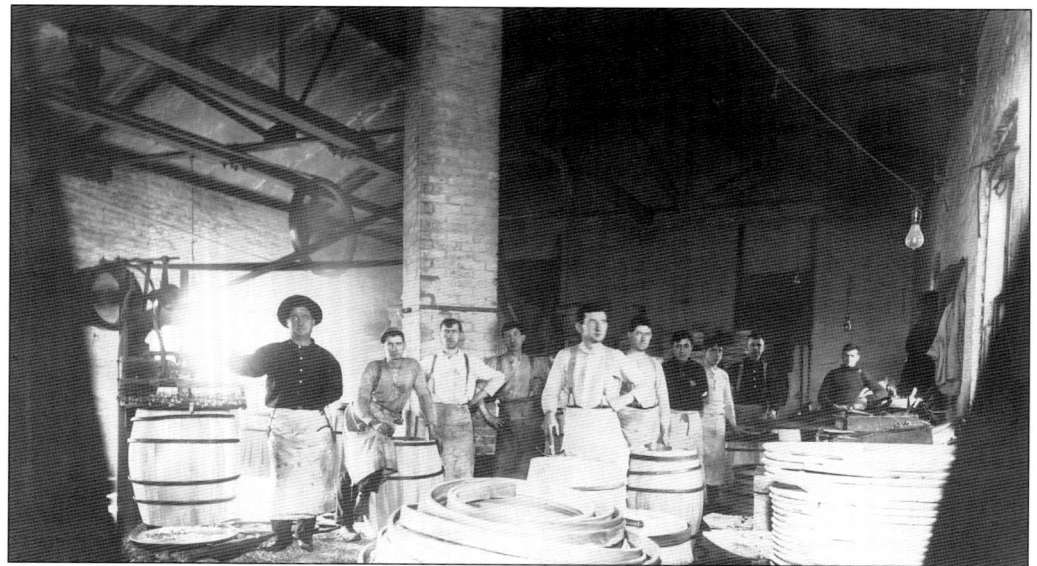

Both breweries and wineries used barrels to store their products, so it is not surprising that cooperages did significant business making barrels in Sandusky.

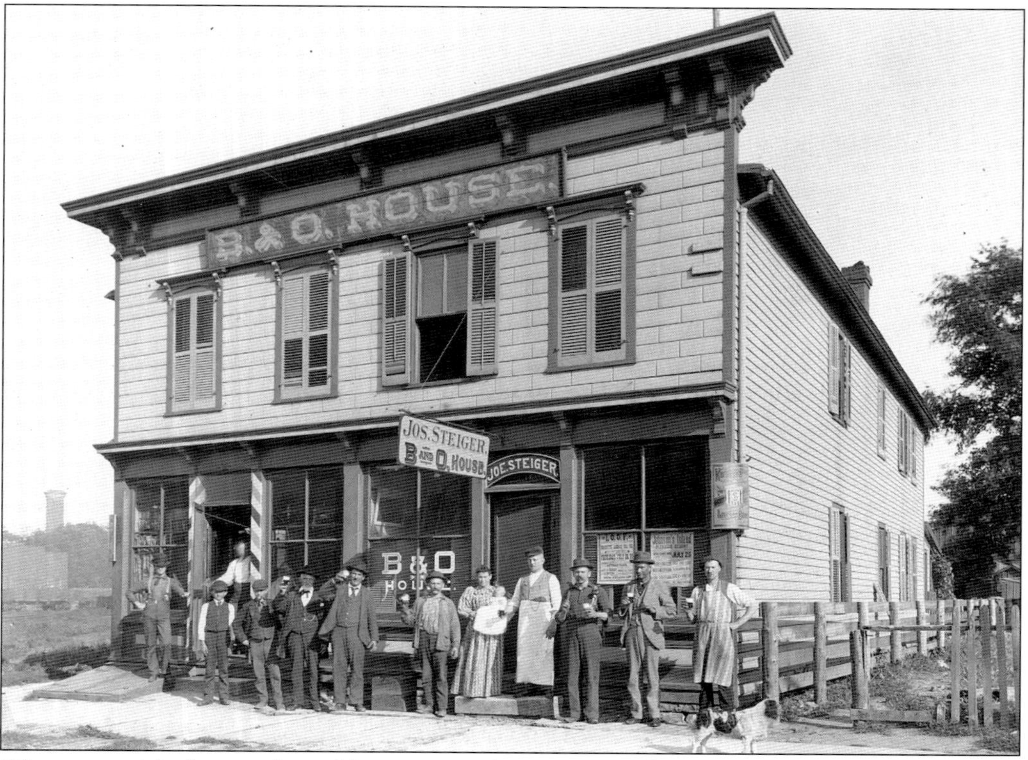

Of course, with the number of breweries and wineries in the area, saloons were common in Sandusky, particularly in the 19th century. The 1896–1897 city directory listed over 150 saloons in Sandusky. Joseph Steiger operated a saloon in the first floor of the B&O House Hotel on Water Street. An advertisement for the Johnson's Island Pleasure Resort is in the window.

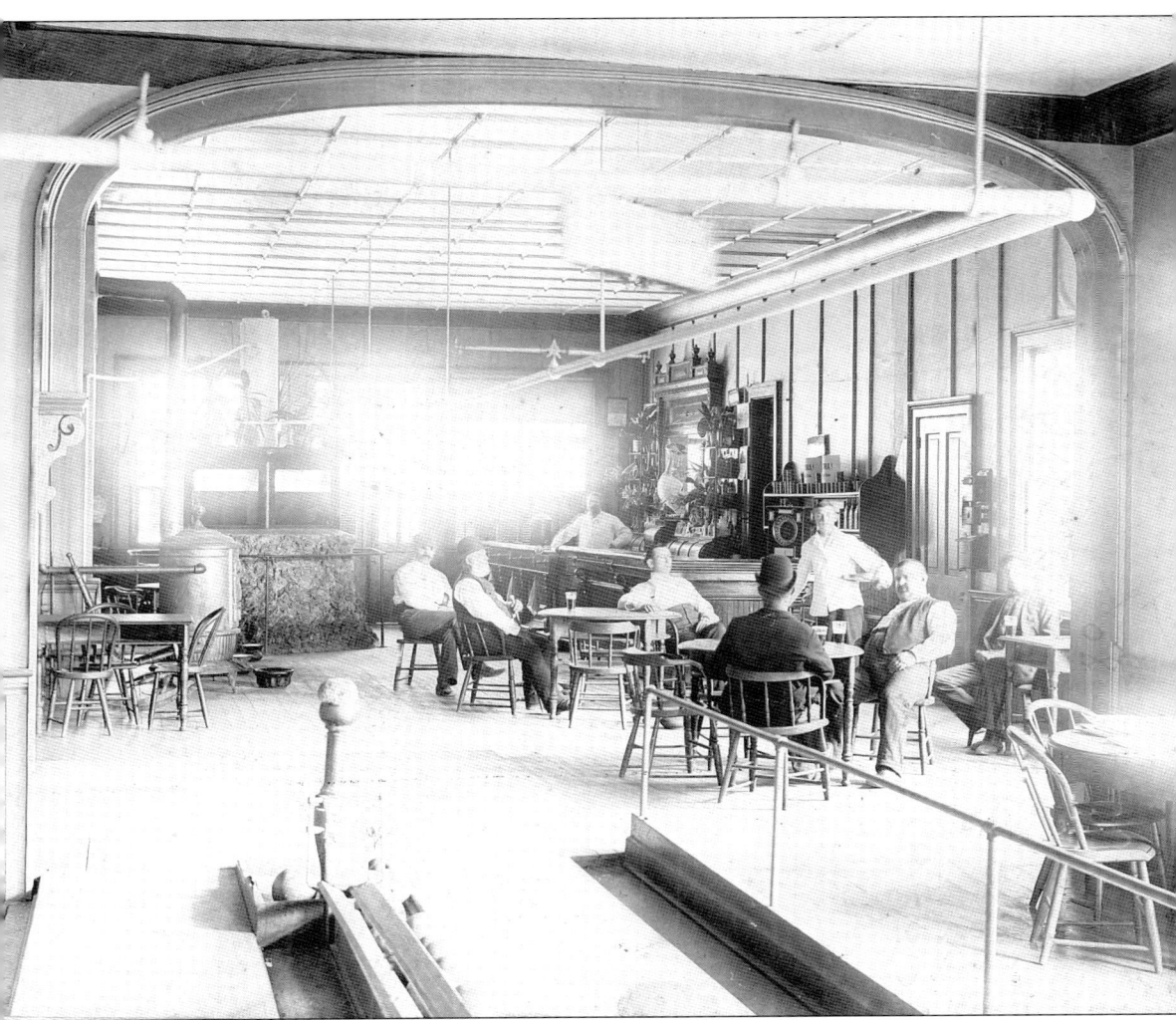

Interior of the Atlantic Pleasure Gardens located on Meigs Street in the 1890s. Louis Zistel operated Atlantic Pleasure Garden, which opened in 1873. The complex included a boat yard, bathing establishment, and a "Mammoth Aquarium." In addition to these attractions there was a bar (saloon) and bowling alley (seen in the foreground). In the late 19th century, recreation activities were growing as people had more time for leisure. While local bars had always been popular among men, some places were beginning to try to attract families.

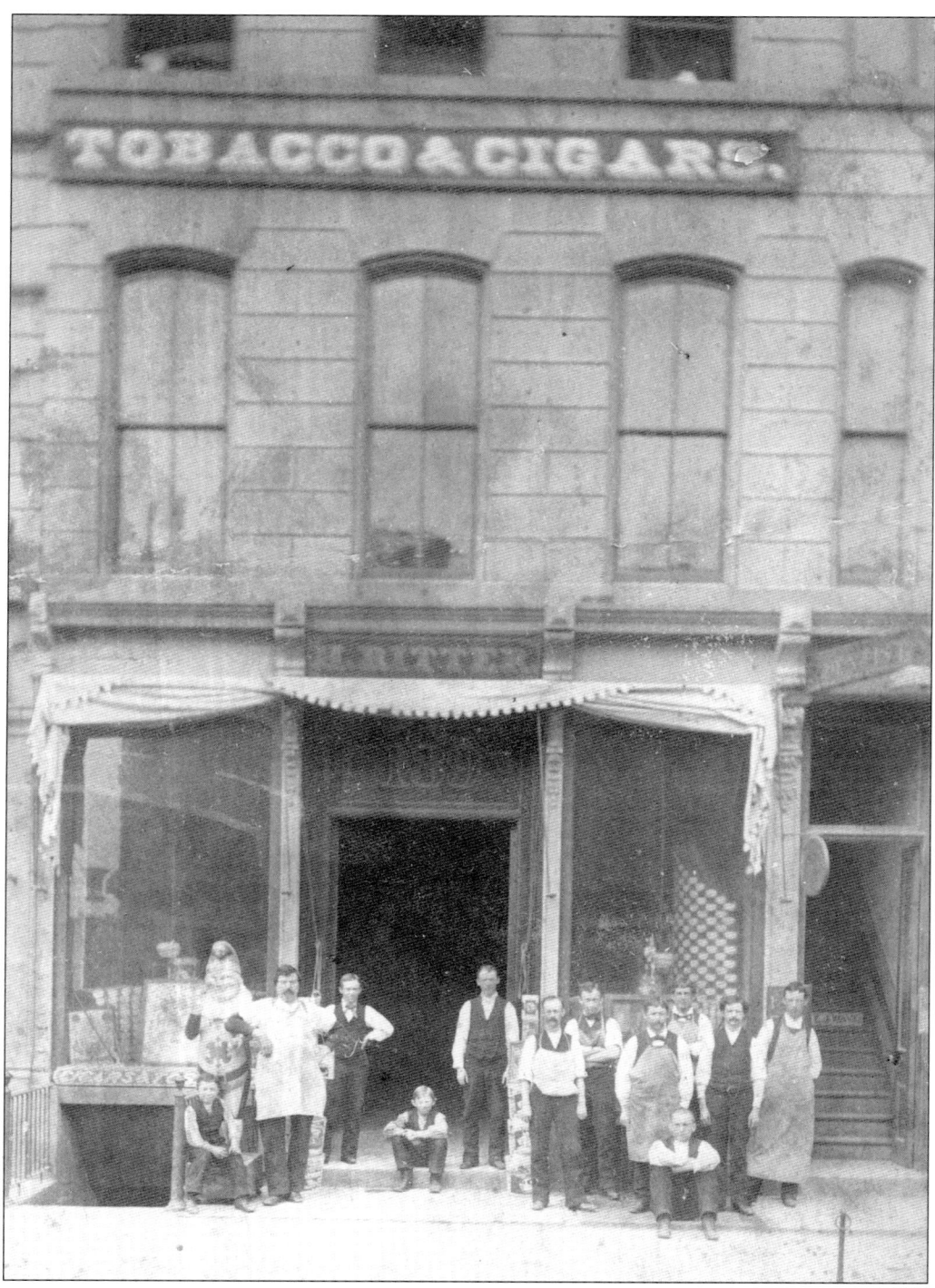

Exterior of Henry Ritter's Columbus Avenue cigar store in the 1890s. Ritter and his family operated the cigar store for over 70 years, beginning in the 1860s. His storefront contained a wooden statue of "Punch" carved from the spar of an old sailing vessel (seen at the left of the picture). Punch is now exhibited in the Follett House Museum.

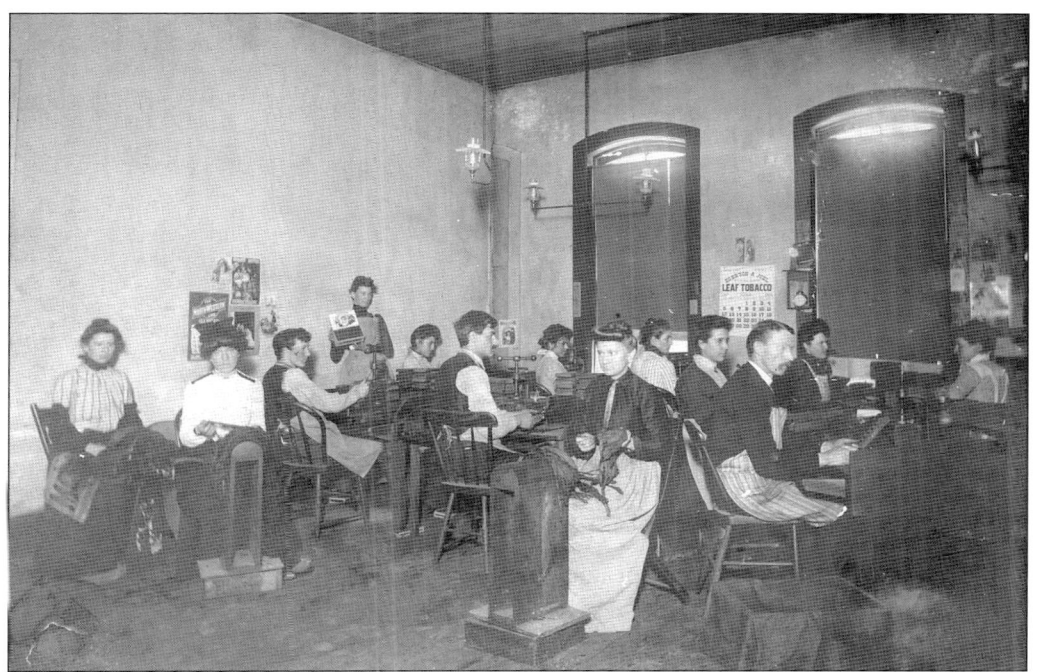

Here is an interior view of Henry Ritter's Sons' cigar factory, 1903. Ritter was also a cigar manufacturer. Henry Ritter's cigar company became a family affair when he passed it on to his sons. They continued the family business into the 1930s.

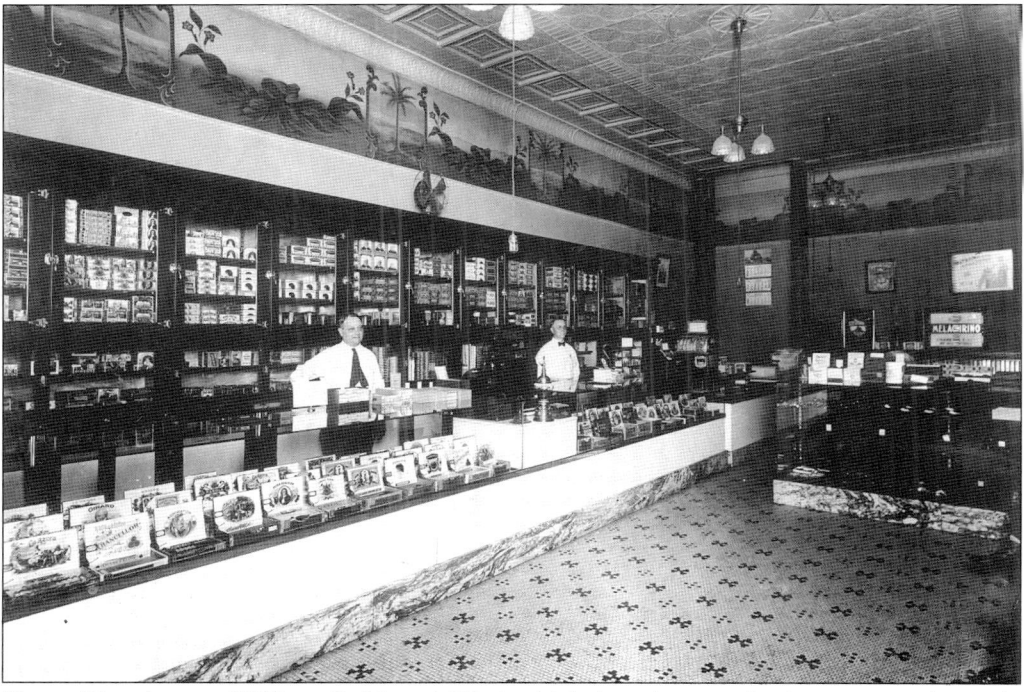

Henry Ritter's sons William (left) and Edwin (right) took over the business in the early 20th century.

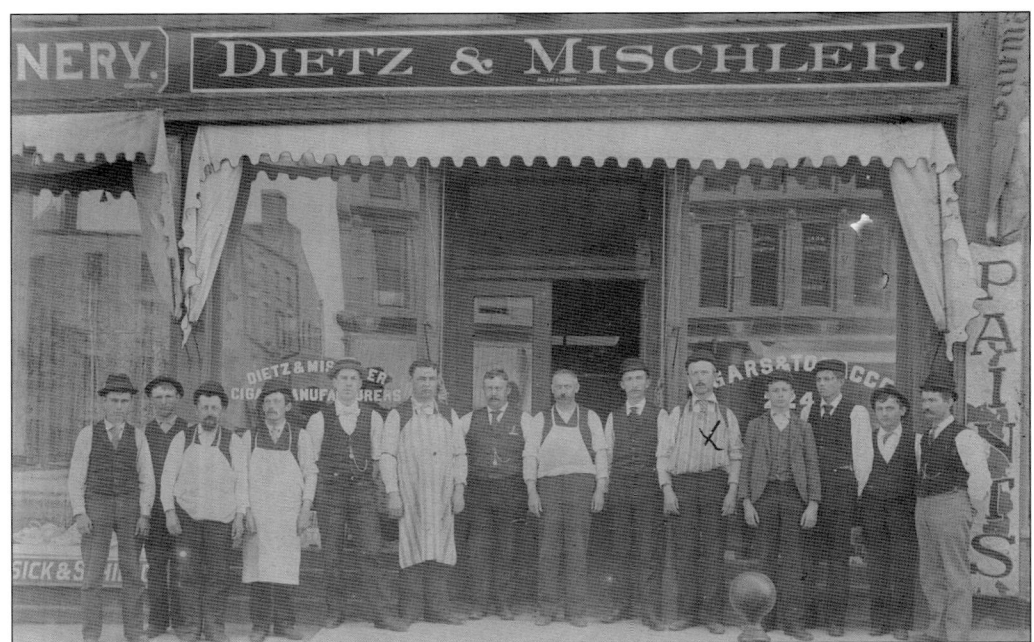

Seen here is the exterior of the Dietz and Mischler cigar store on Columbus Avenue in the 1890s. Dietz and Mischler was just one of the over one dozen cigar manufacturers in Sandusky in the late 19th century. This cigar store was also home to a local landmark, a zinc statue of Shakespeare's *Midsummer Night's Dream* character, Puck.

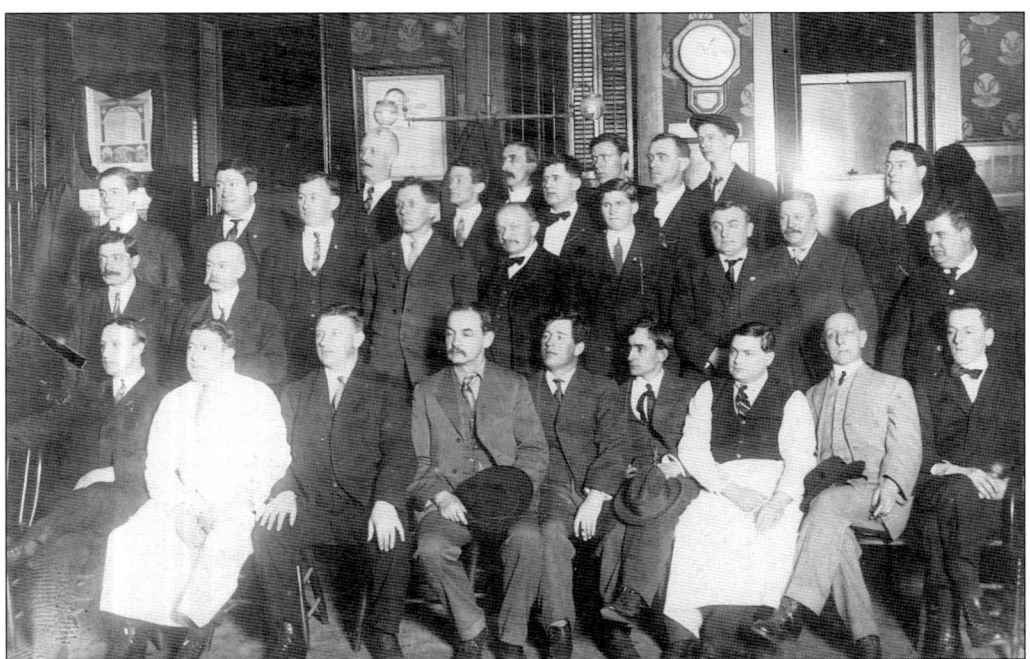

A cigar makers' union meeting for the Sandusky chapter was held in 1905. As cigar making had become a very prominent business in Sandusky and the surrounding area, many company employees unionized. Some, such as Ritter's, did not join the union.

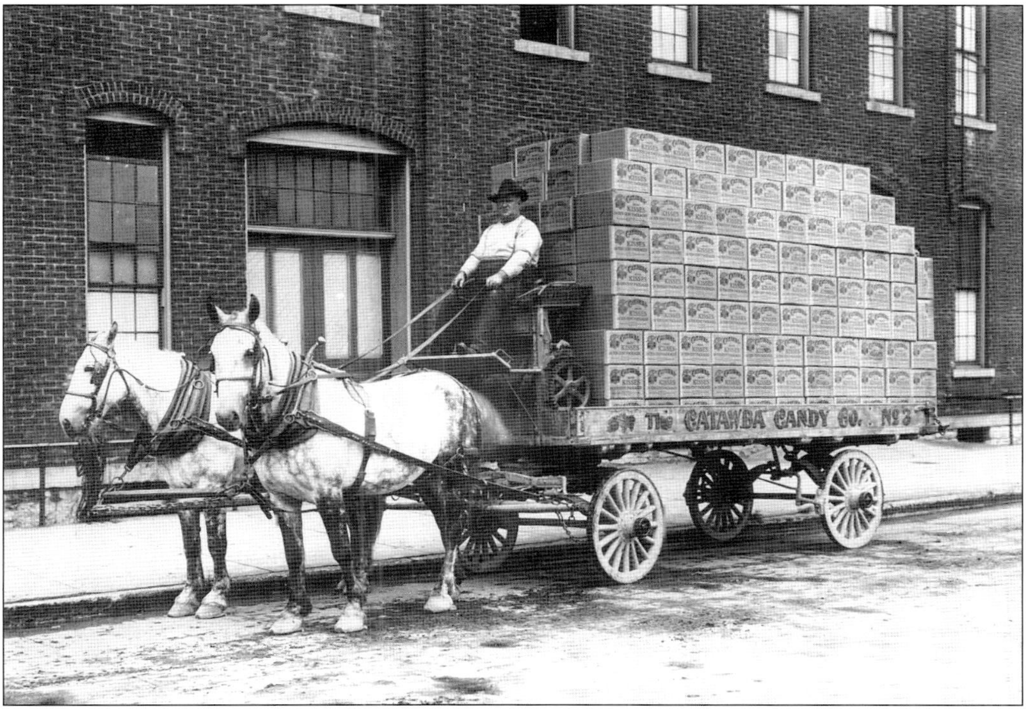

Here is a delivery wagon for the Catawba Candy Company, 1905. The candy company was established in 1905. The workers melted chocolate in large copper kettles and then hand-dipped the candies. At one point, the Catawba Candy Company was considered the largest candy company in the United States, but by 1938 the company had gone out of business.

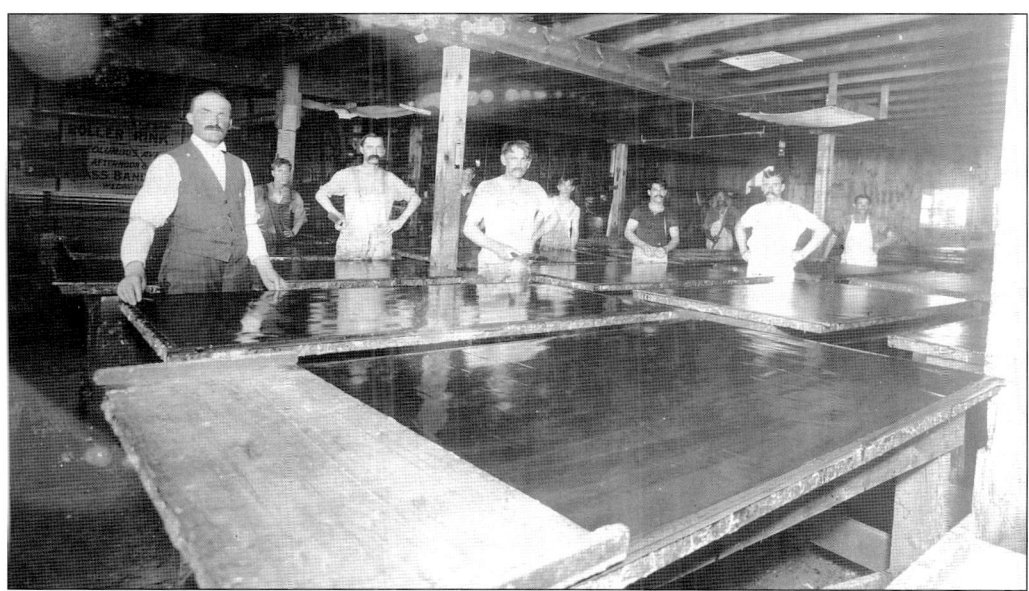

Pictured is the interior of the Catawba Candy Company. These were the fudge tables where fudge was spread out in order to set. Fudge was just one of the many types of candy that the company made.

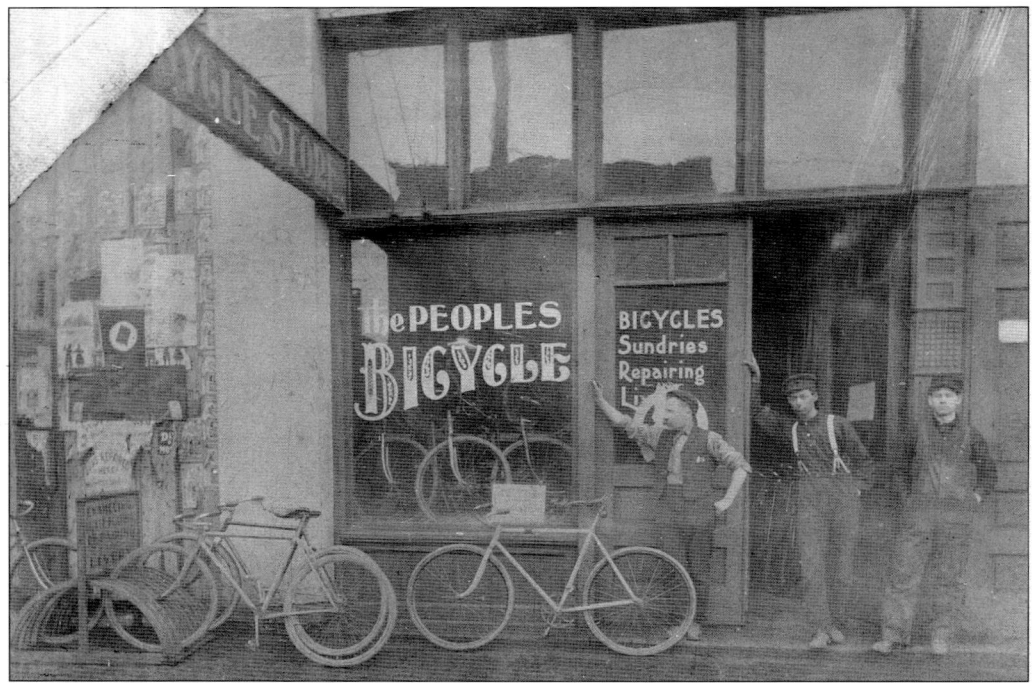

Seen here is the exterior of the People's Bicycle Shop. The modern bicycle was developed by 1880 and became very popular by the turn of the century. It provided local transportation throughout Sandusky, just as it did in many cities around the United States. By 1900, seven shops in Sandusky sold and repaired bicycles.

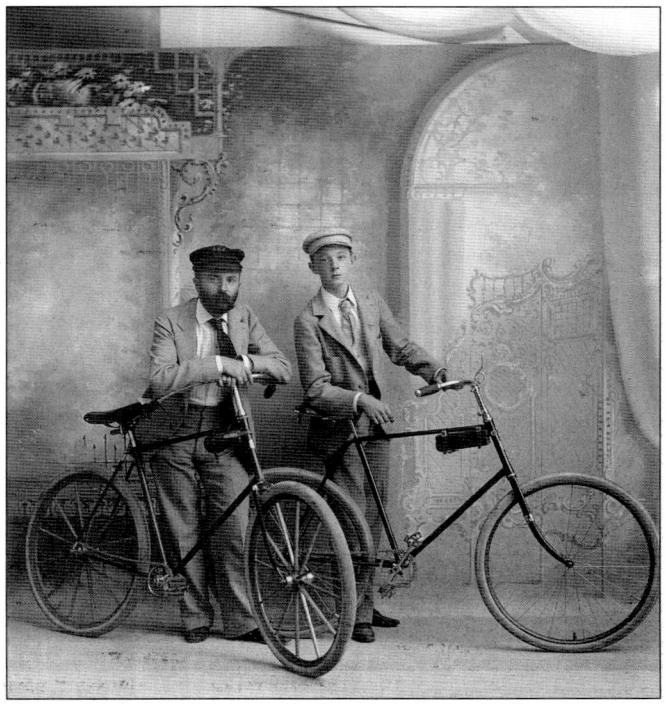

It is interesting to note that bicycles were so important to some people that they chose to pose for professional portraits with their bicycles in front of a backdrop, as in this portrait from 1894.

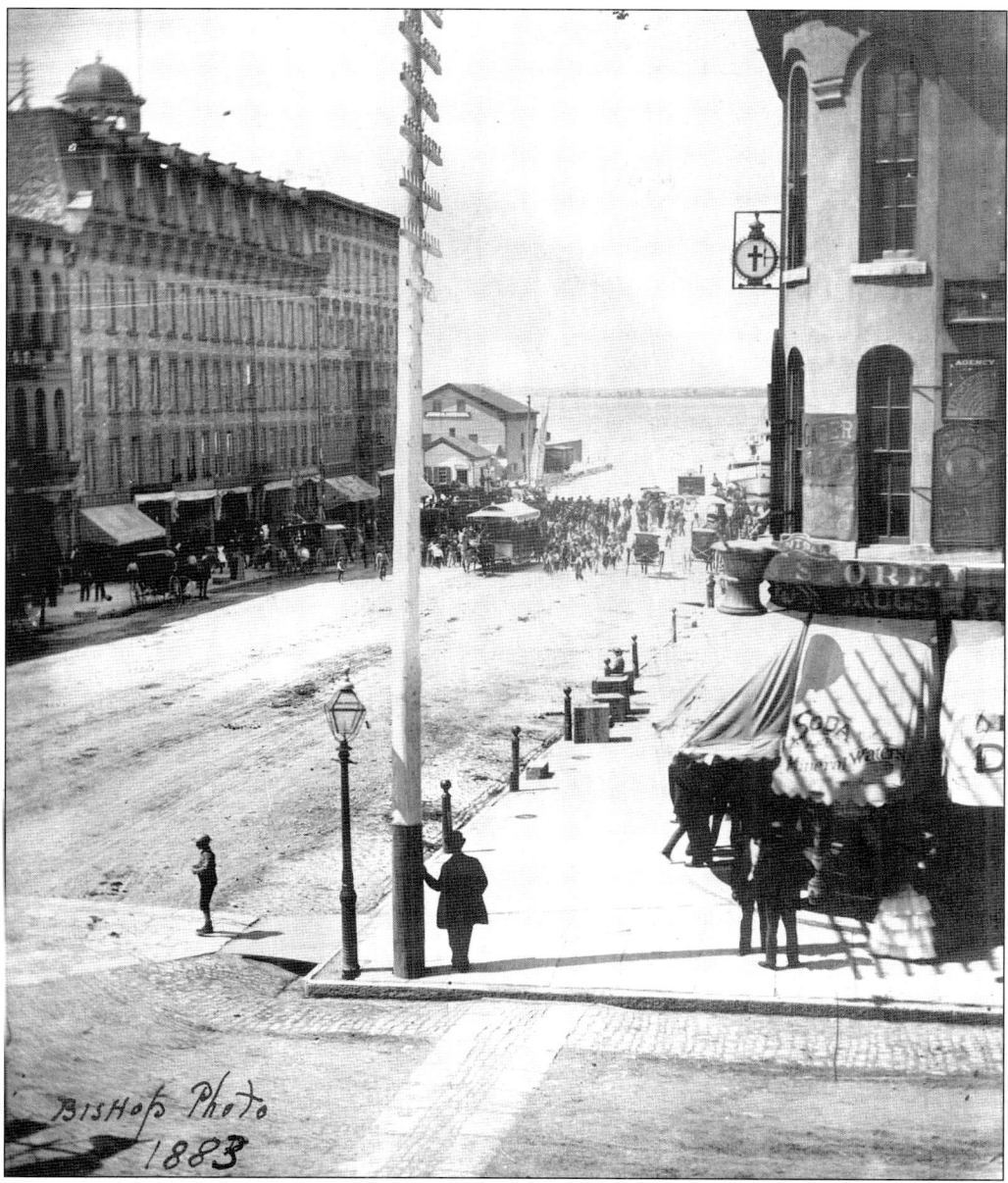

Sandusky's first streetcar is pictured here on its maiden run up Columbus Avenue, with a crowd of onlookers following. The Sandusky Streetcar Company was organized in 1881. The first horse-drawn streetcars were put into service in 1883. The cars were drawn on single tracks with a two-horse team.

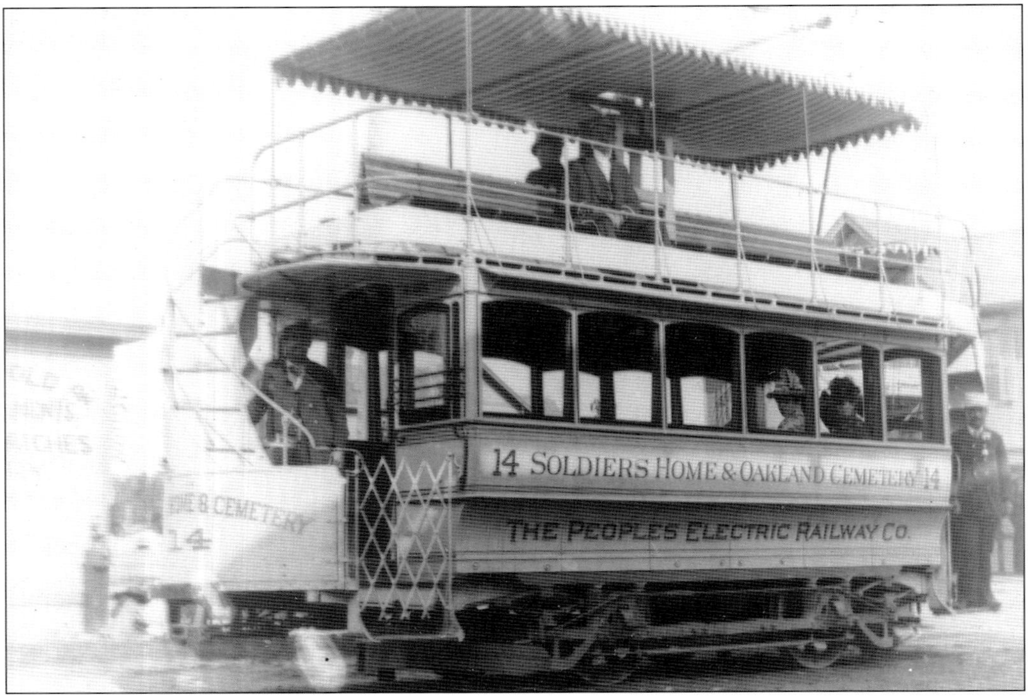

Seen here is a People's Electric Railway Company car c. 1890s. The first electric streetcar in Sandusky began service in 1889, running from Scott Street and Columbus Avenue to the Soldiers' Home. This line was purchased in 1890 by the People's Electric Railway Company (commonly called the White Line because of the color of its cars). The company operated double-decker cars on some of its routes.

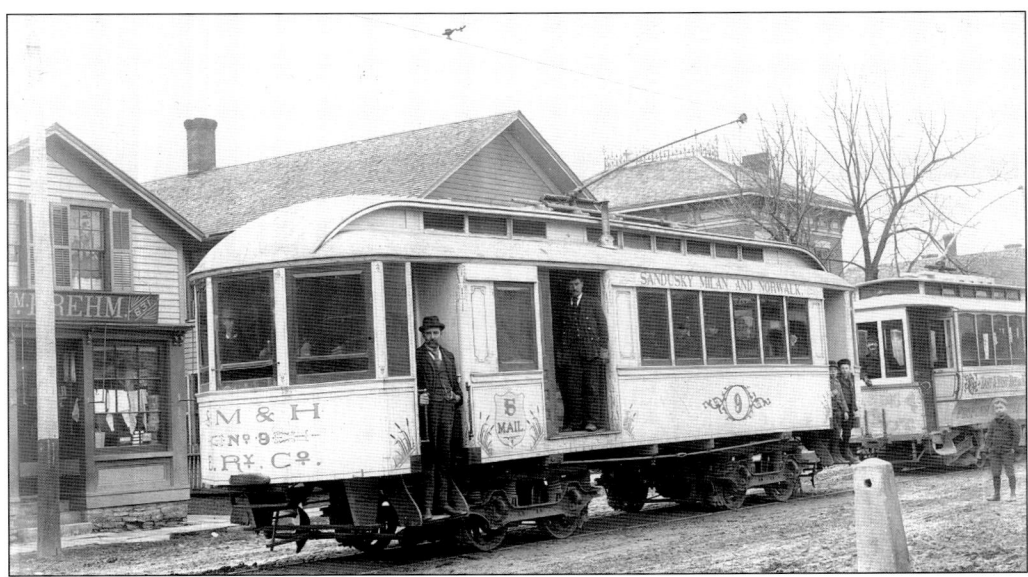

Pictured is a car of the Sandusky, Milan, and Norwalk Railway, 1893. This interurban railway was built between these cities in 1892. Service began in May of 1893. The car is followed in the picture by a People's Electric Railway car.

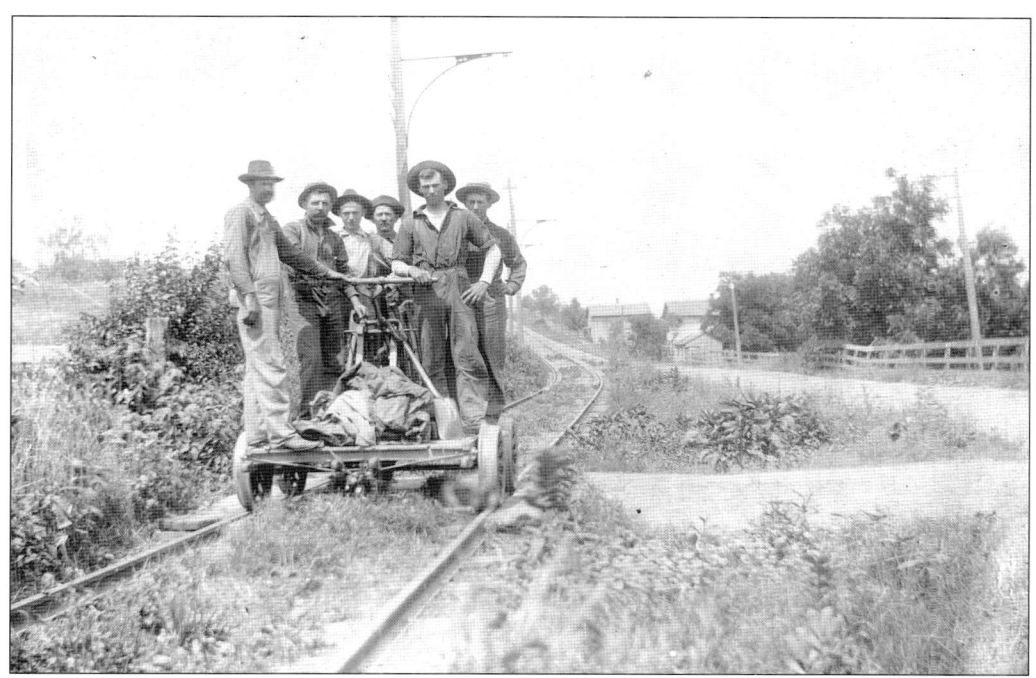

A maintenance crew riding a handcar on the railway lines, *c.* 1895.

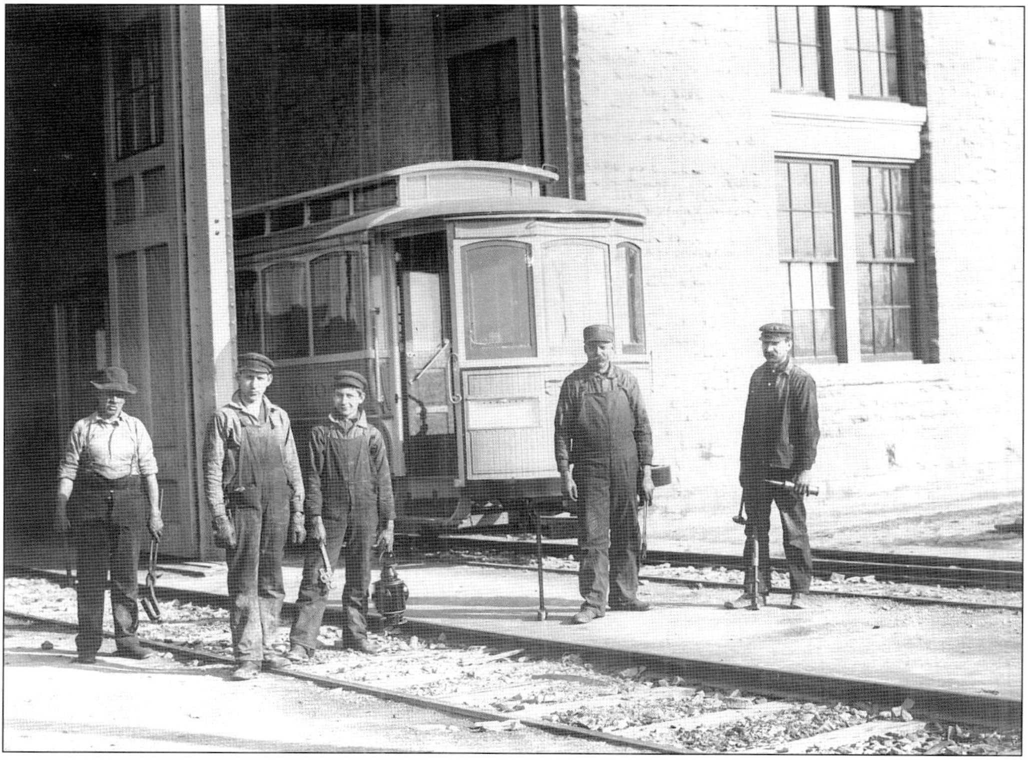

Maintenance employees pose in front of the Sandusky car barns, *c.* 1902.

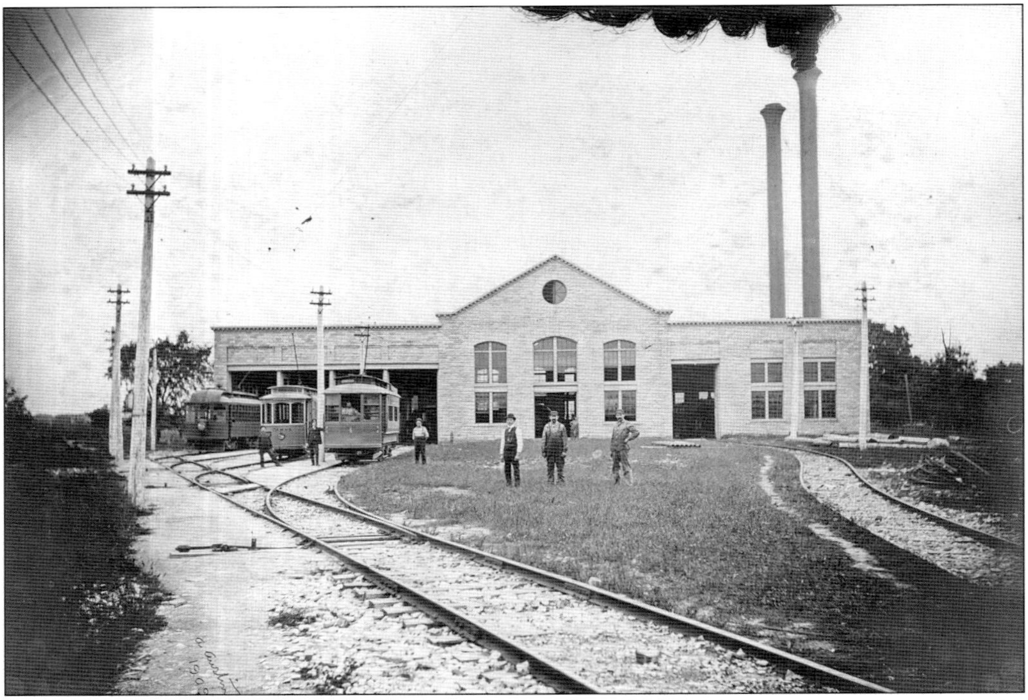

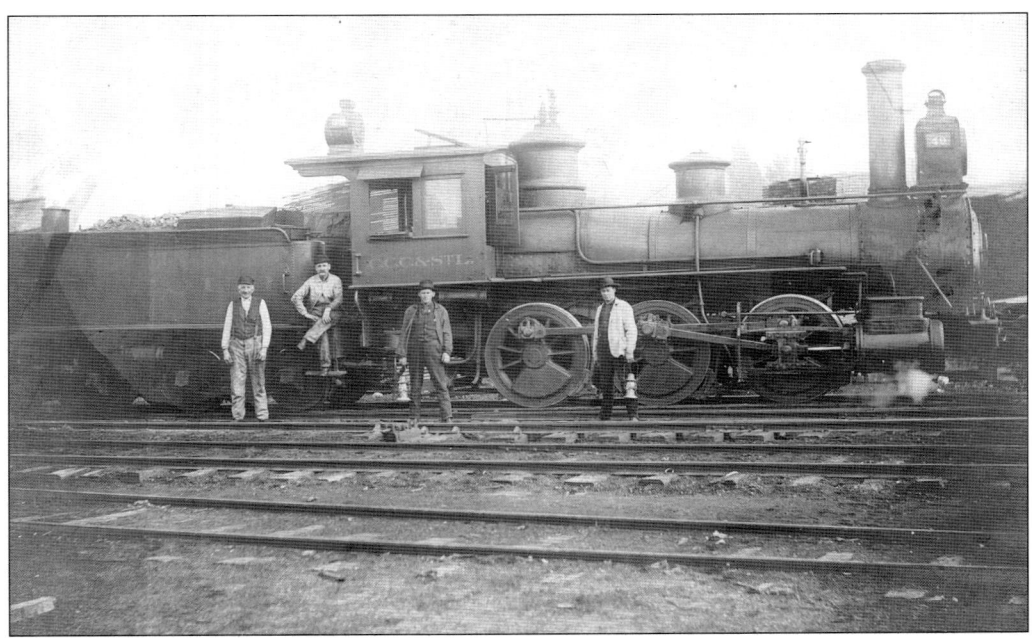

The Sandusky car barns housed the streetcars as well as a repair shop and powerhouse for the electric railways in Sandusky.

Railroads, of course, were still the primary means of long-distance transportation at the turn of the 20th century. Sandusky was a transit point for several lines. The Cleveland, Cincinnati, Chicago, and St. Louis Line, also known as the "Big Four," formed in 1889 with the merger of three railroads. It operated well into the 20th century.

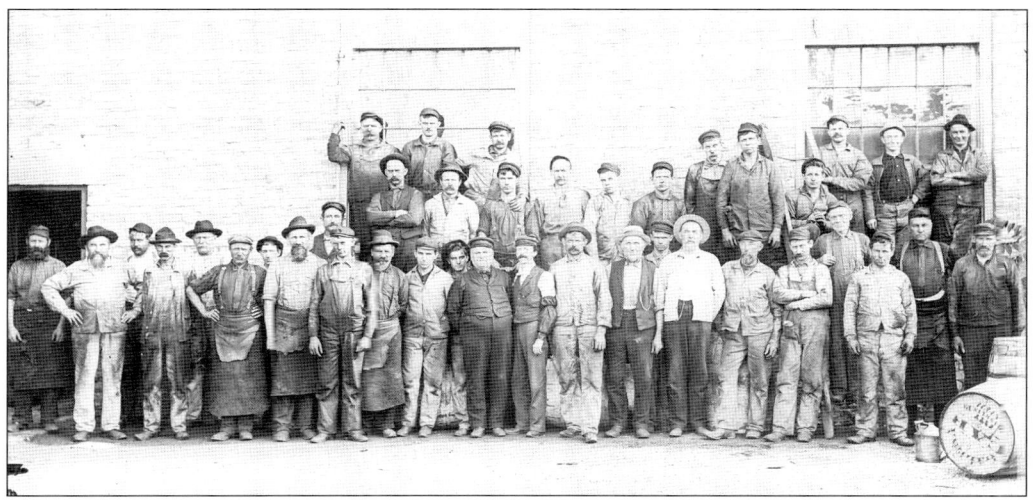

The Big Four had a maintenance shop on the west end of Market Street. Here the crew poses for a photo in 1901.

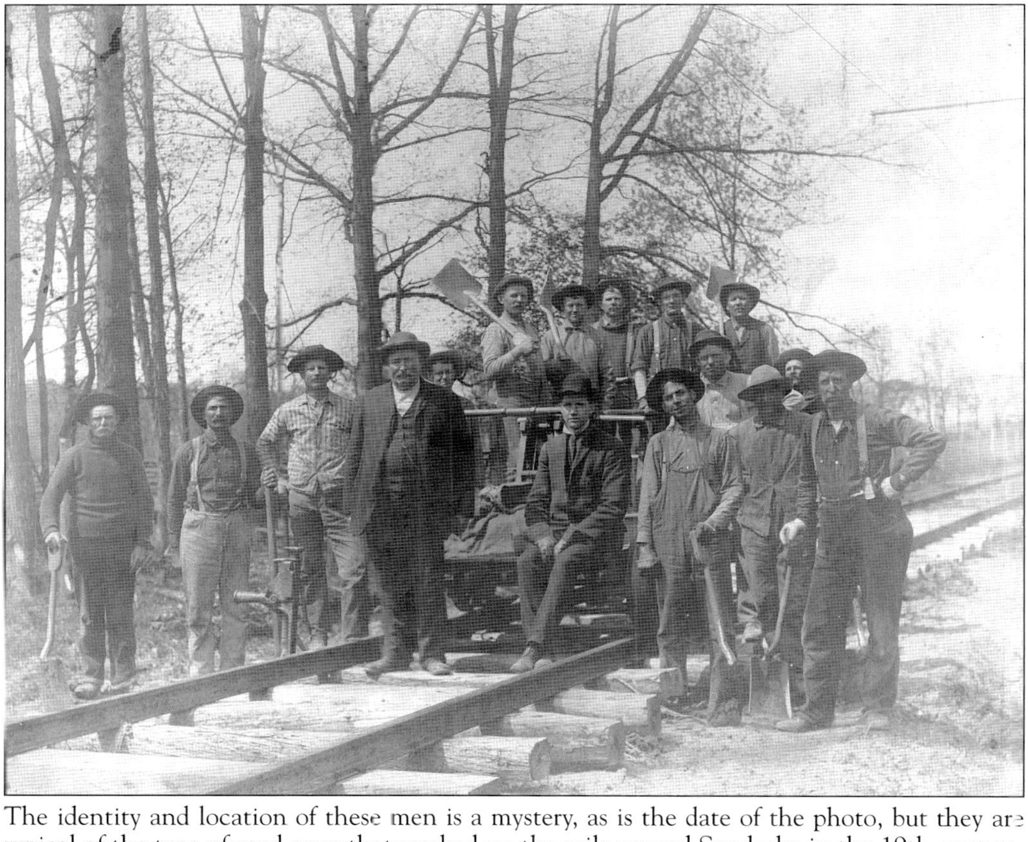

The identity and location of these men is a mystery, as is the date of the photo, but they are typical of the type of road crew that worked on the rails around Sandusky in the 19th century.

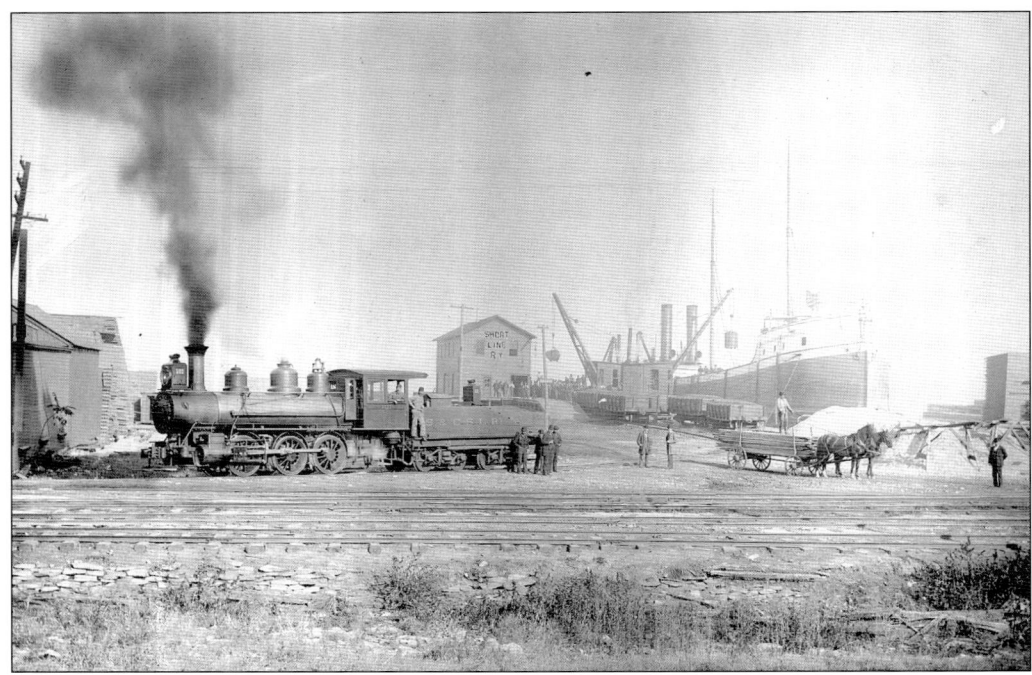

The lower lakes dock was at the foot of Decatur Street.

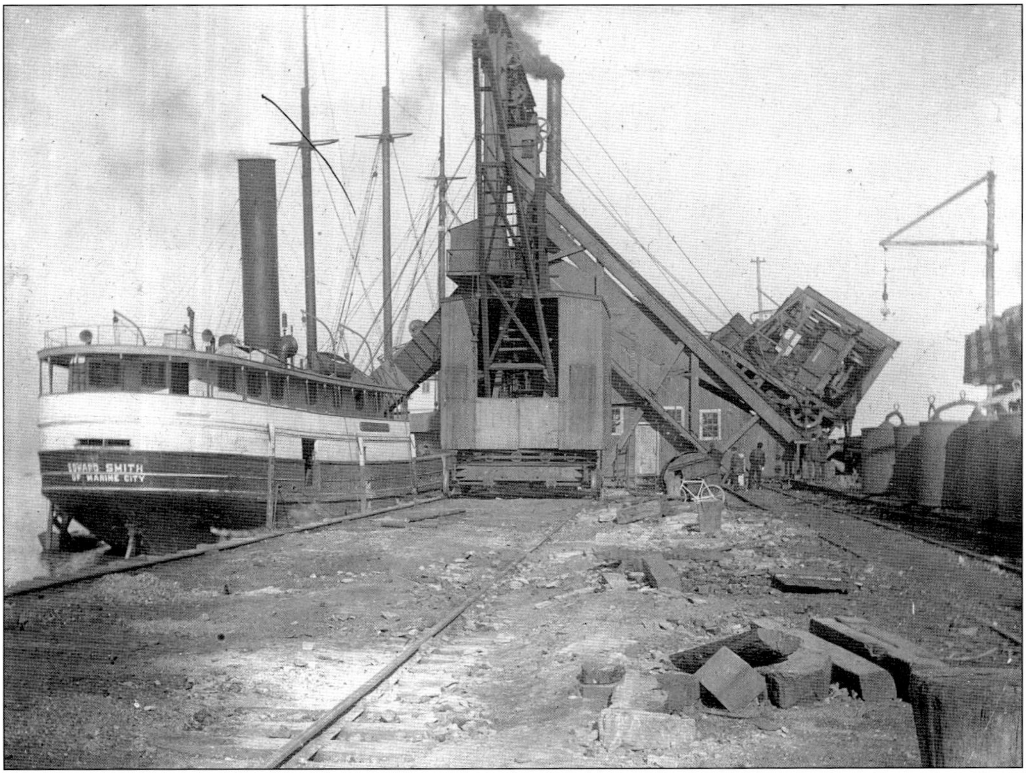

Coal is loaded at the docks.

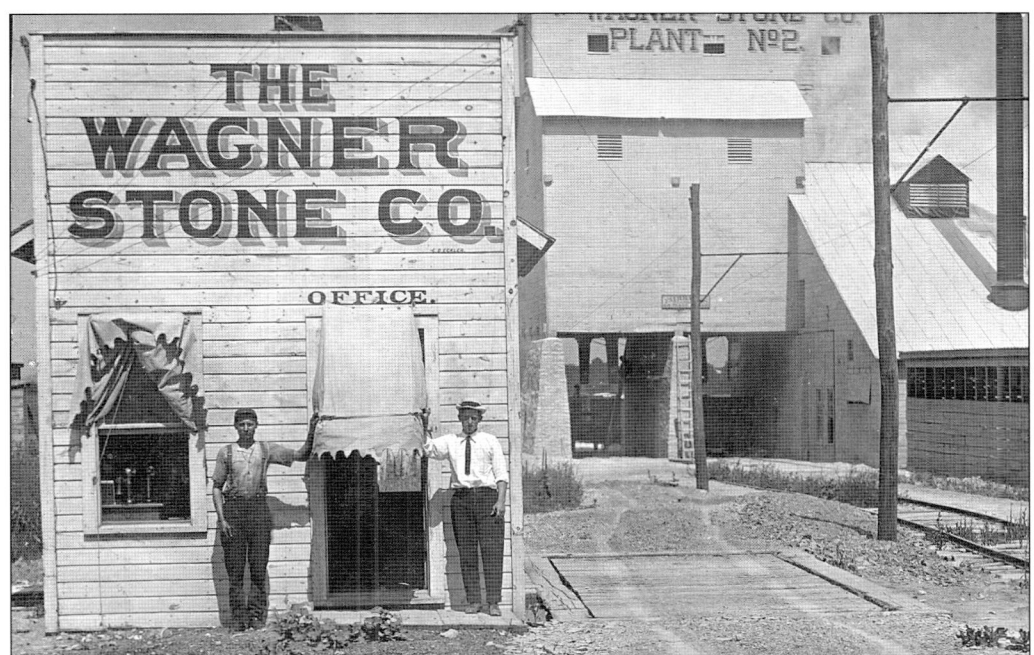

The Wagner Stone Company was incorporated in 1903, although it had begun its quarrying business on Milan Road ten years earlier. The quarry is still in operation today. The total capitalization of the company in 1903 was $50,000.

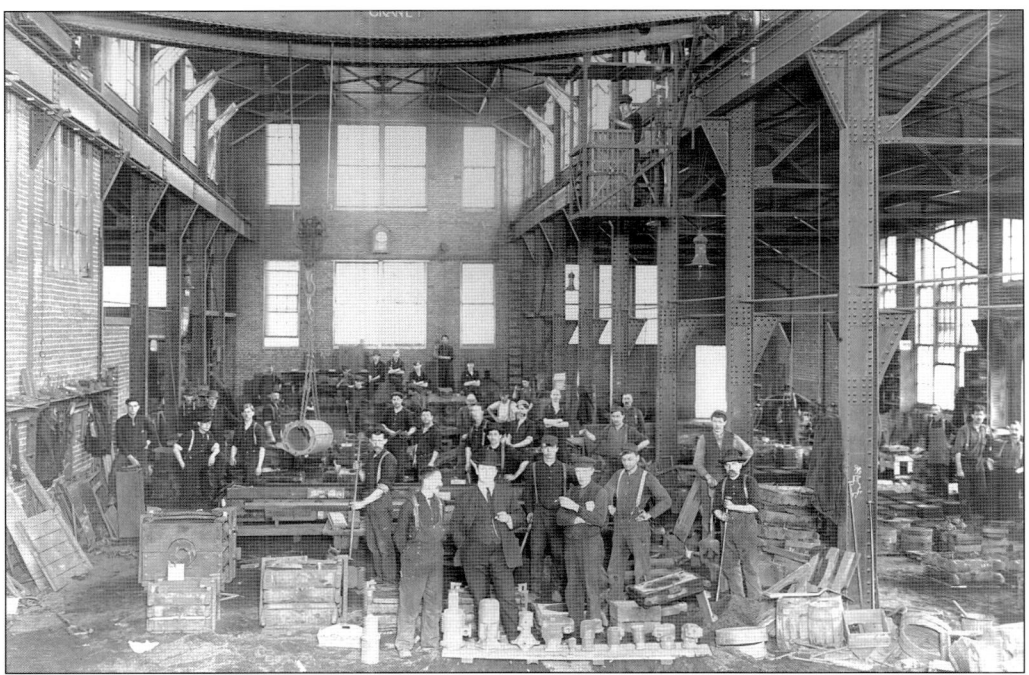

The Bay View Foundry, on McDonough Street, between Market and Water Streets, was incorporated in 1908, as heavier industries began to overtake the smaller crafts businesses for dominance in the marketplace.

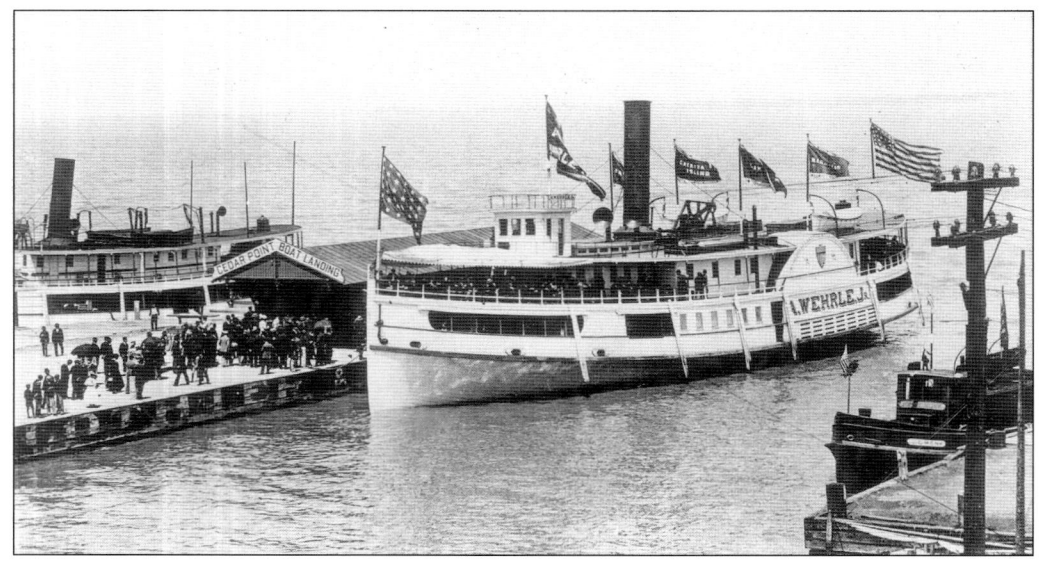

A Cedar Point ferry is at the dock in downtown Sandusky, 1900. As the peninsula developed as a recreation area, ferries began to provide service to Cedar Point. During peak times boats ran every half hour between downtown Sandusky and Cedar Point.

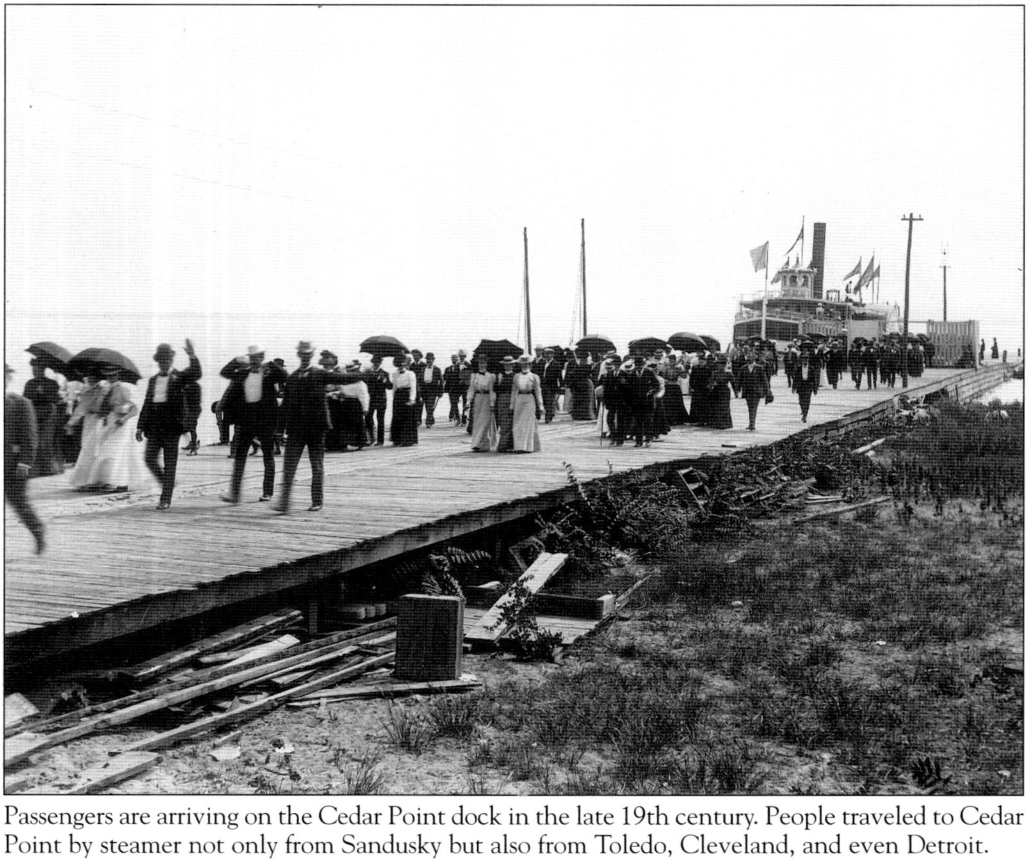

Passengers are arriving on the Cedar Point dock in the late 19th century. People traveled to Cedar Point by steamer not only from Sandusky but also from Toledo, Cleveland, and even Detroit.

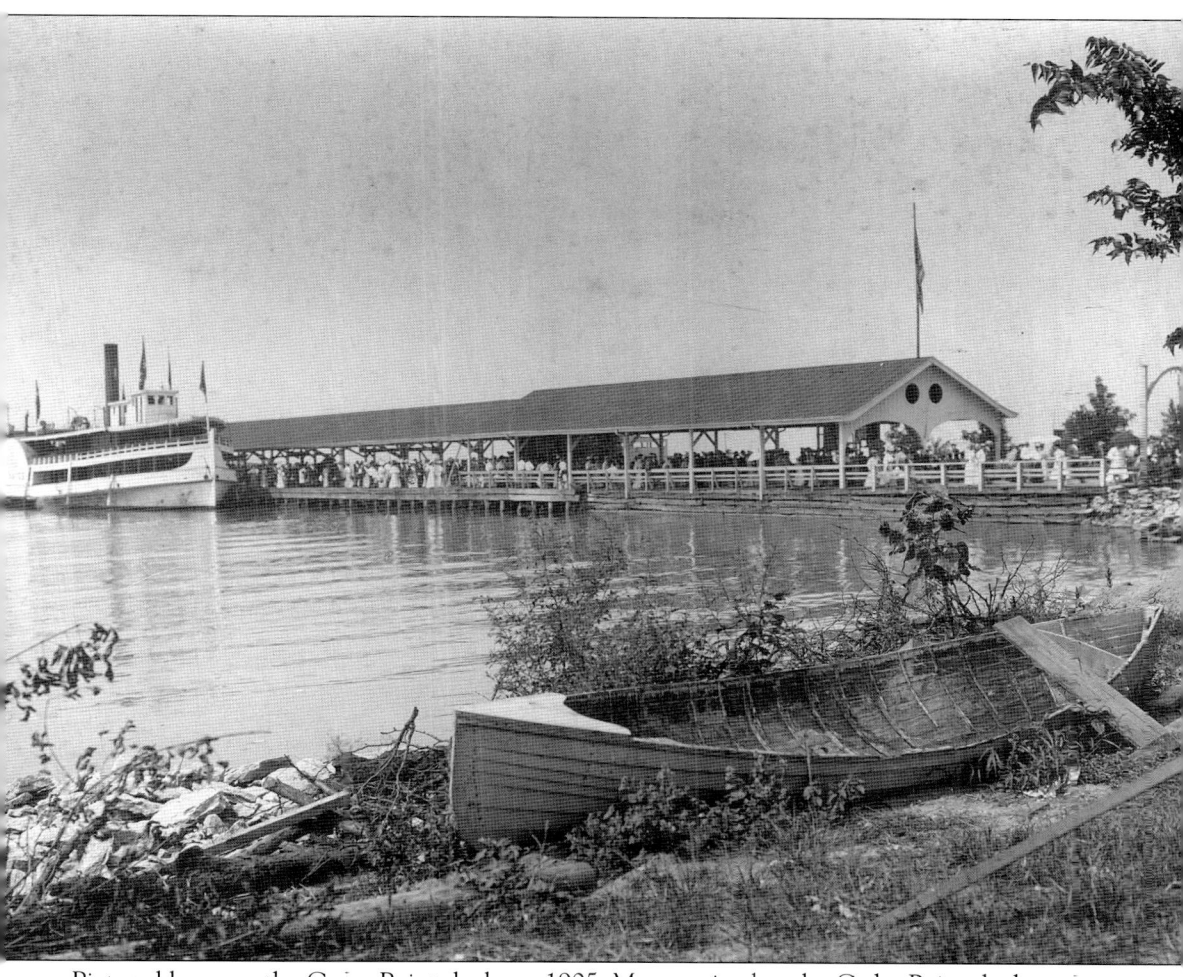
Pictured here are the Cedar Point docks, c. 1905. Many arrived at the Cedar Point dock ready to leave the hectic life of the city for the vast sandy beaches and warm water of Cedar Point. Cedar Point also offered wooded picnic grounds.

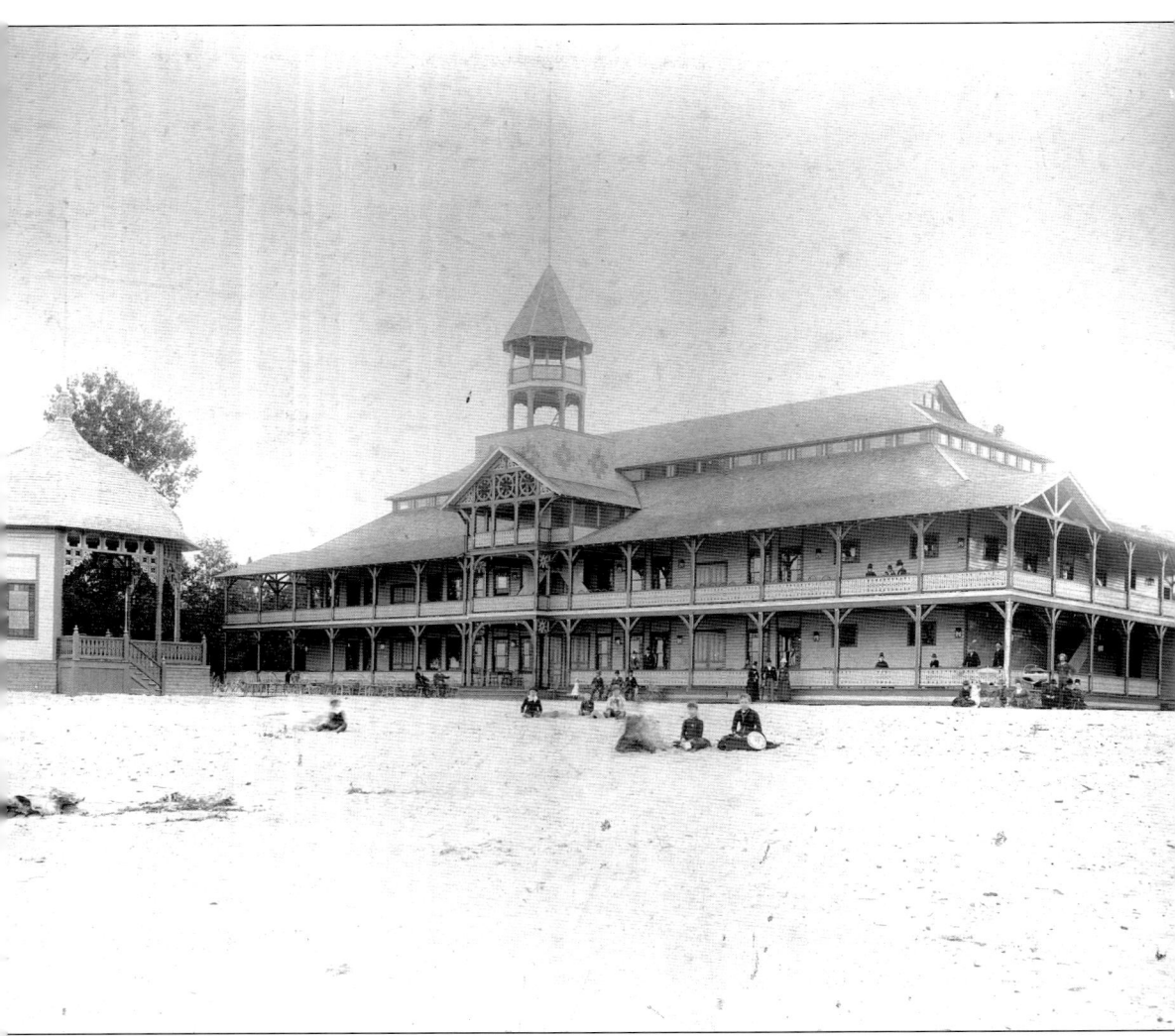

The first summer resort on Cedar Point began in 1870, when Louis Zistel opened a small beer garden and dance hall, along with a nearby bathhouse on the Point, bringing visitors from Sandusky via steamboat. It was in the 1880s, however, that Cedar Point's popularity began to explode. The picnic areas were expanded, and the bathing beach further developed. The Grand Pavilion, shown here with the bandstand alongside it, opened in 1888.

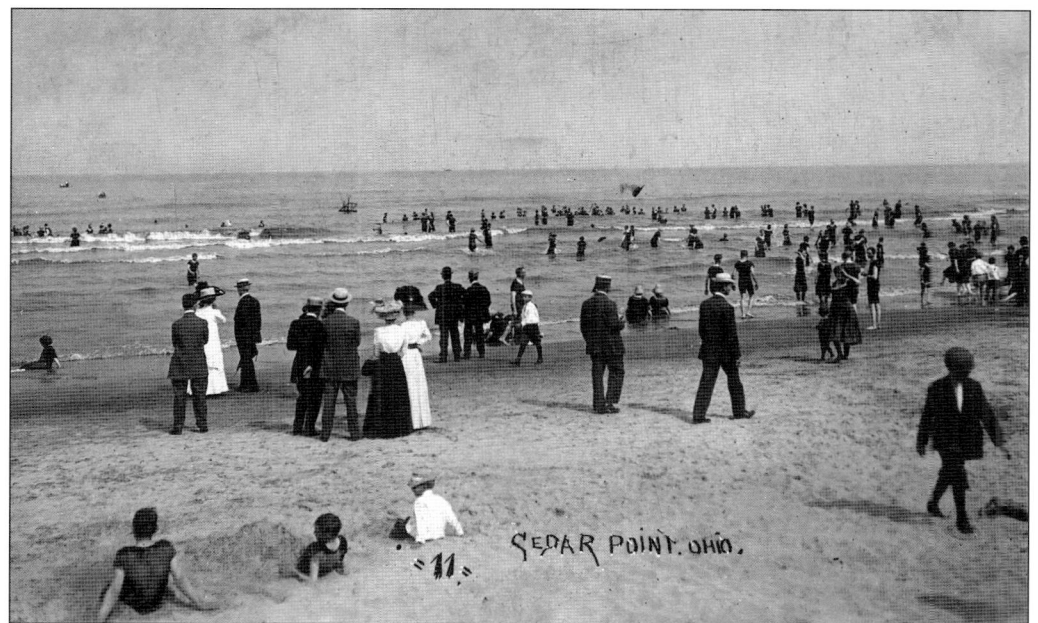

These people are enjoying the Cedar Point beach at the turn of the century. In bath houses on the Cedar Point beach, people were able to rent bathing suits or change into their own. At one point, a screen ran from these bath houses to the water in order to allow privacy for the more modest ladies of that day.

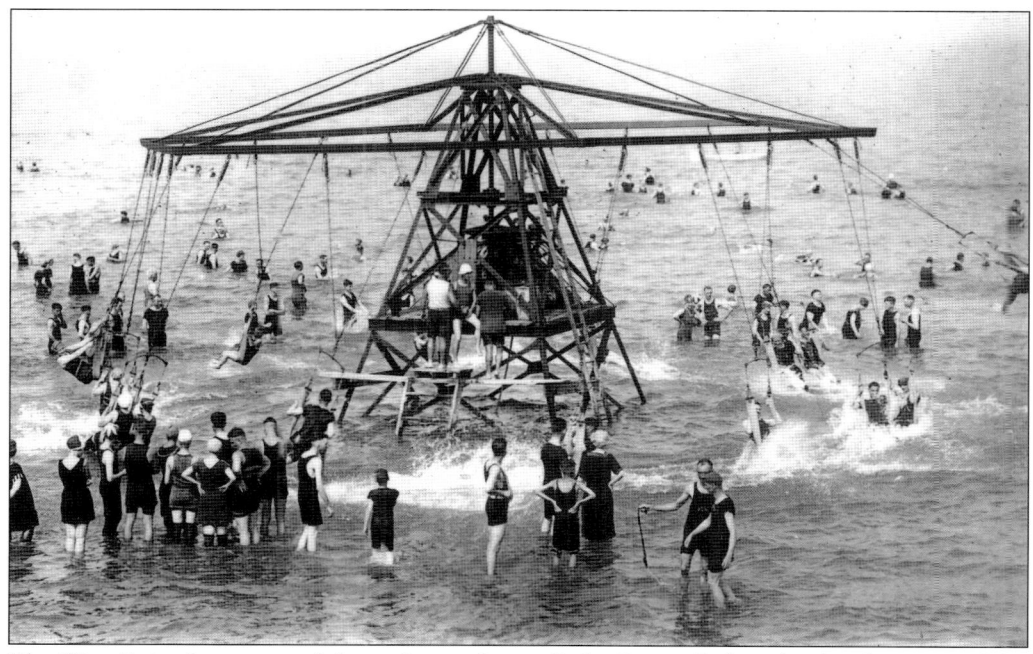

The "Sea Swing" was one of the earliest rides at Cedar Point. Before the development of the amusement park, the beaches were the largest attraction for Cedar Point. Now, rides (especially the many roller coasters) have become the primary attraction.

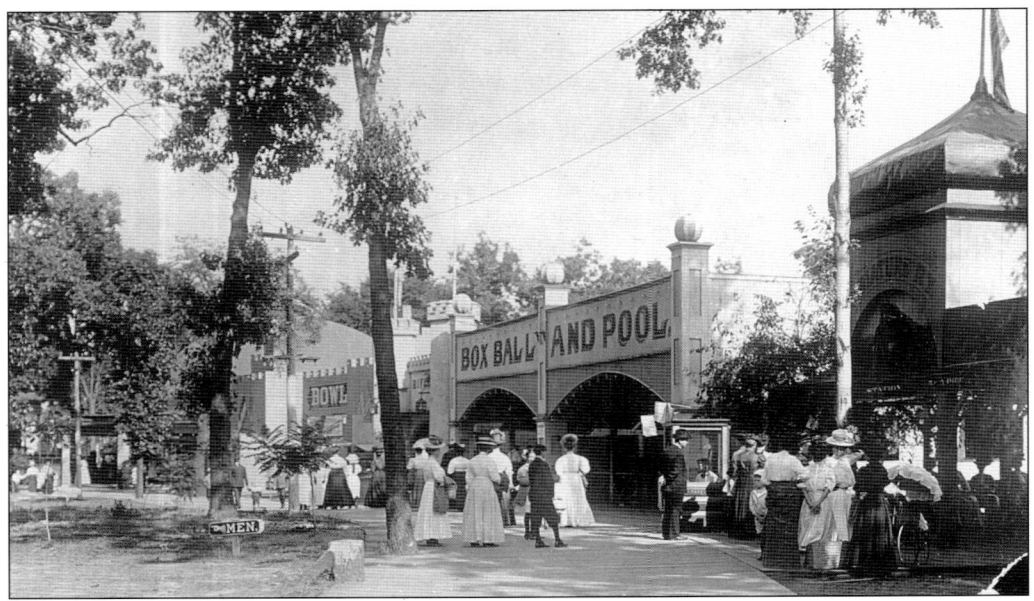

Here is a post card view of the Midway at Cedar Point, 1910. The Midway, also known as the Amusement Circle, developed in 1906 when some electric rides, funhouses, and other gaming activities came to the peninsula.

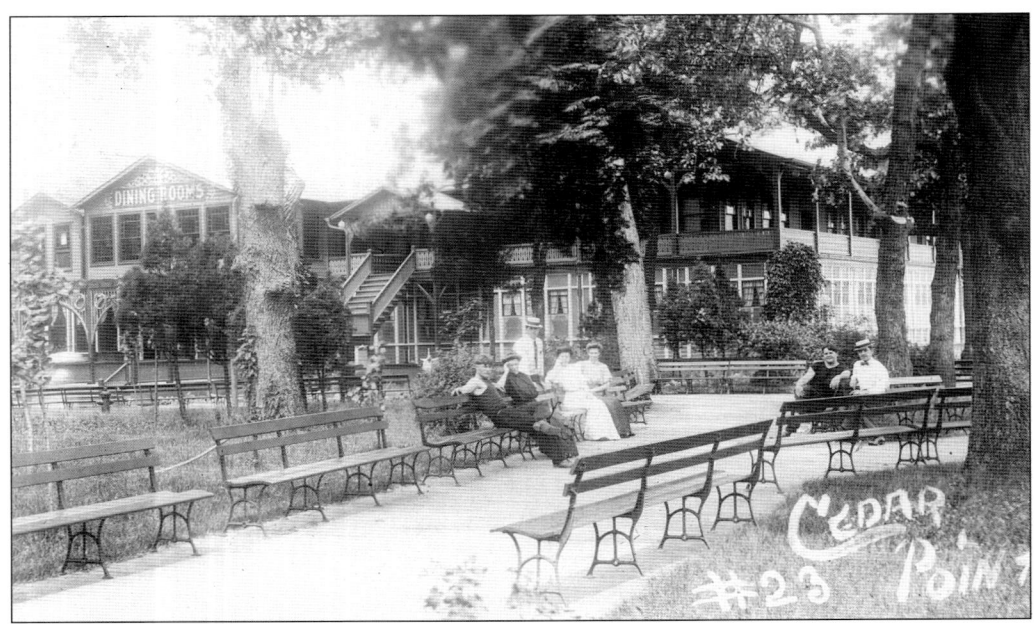

The dining rooms at Cedar Point are seen here around the turn of the century. Many people spent entire days at Cedar Point enjoying its features and attractions. The dining rooms were one alternative for lunches and dinners.

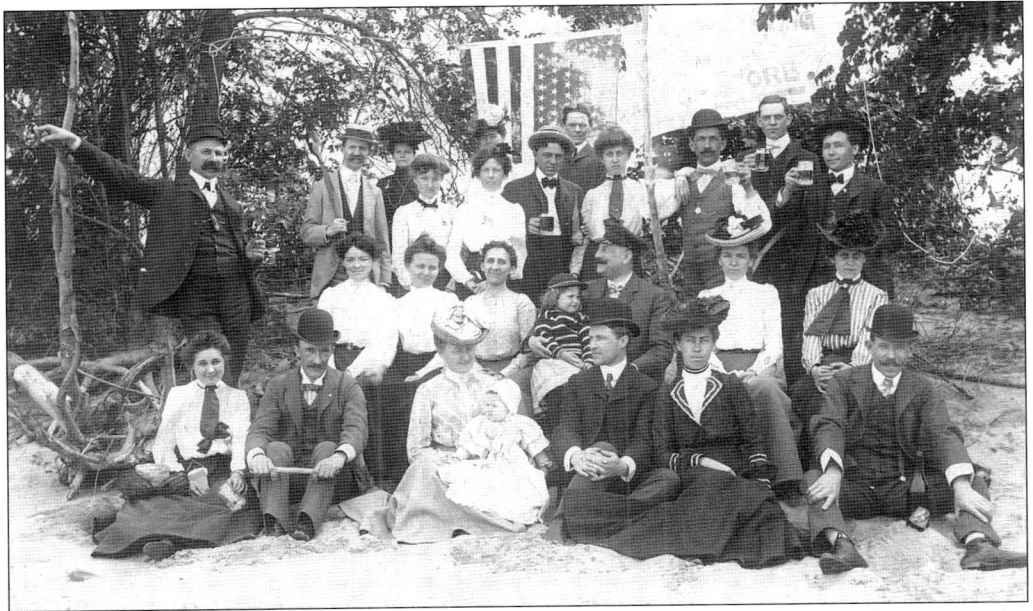

Here is a C.C. Engels Picnic at Cedar Point in 1902. Picnicking was a popular activity for visitors to Cedar Point, particularly in its early years.

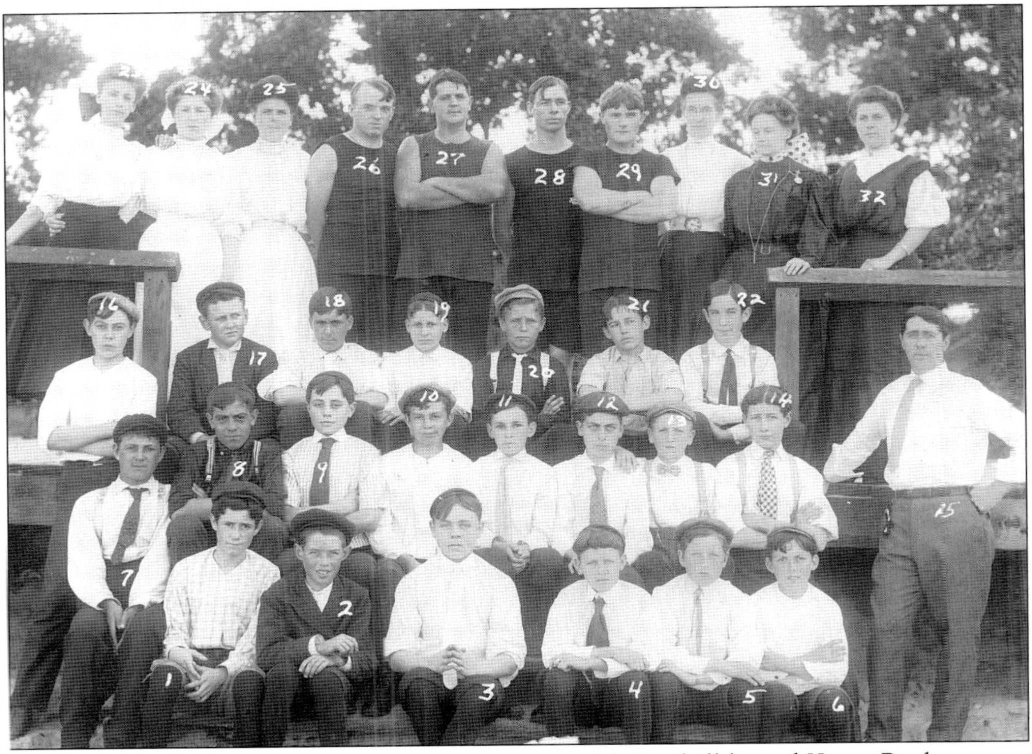

The crew of the Cedar Point bath house posing in 1906. Football legend Knute Rockne was a lifeguard at Cedar Point in 1913 while a student at Notre Dame. Legend says that he perfected the forward pass while playing on the beaches of Cedar Point.

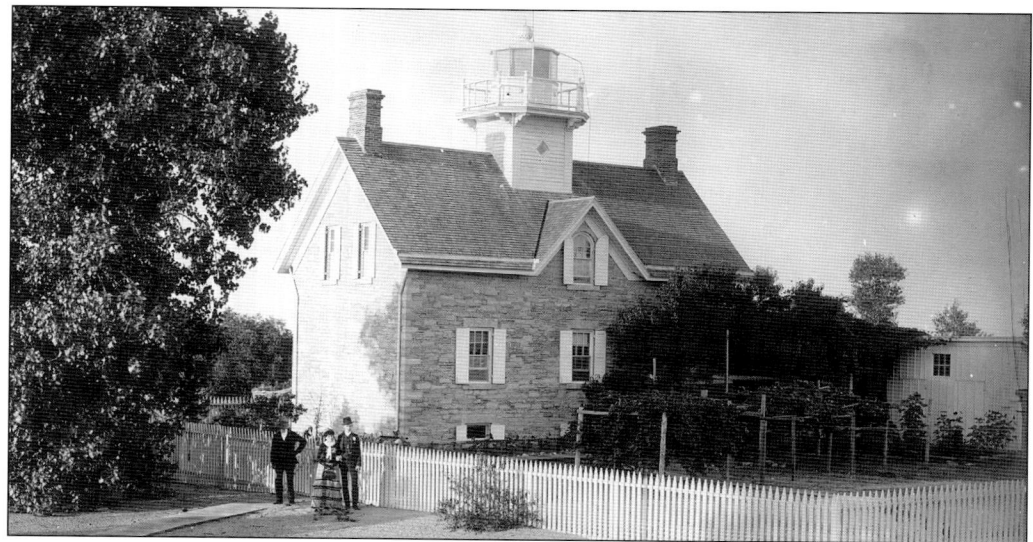

The Cedar Point Lighthouse is seen here in the 1890s. Because Cedar Point is such a prominent feature of the Lake Erie coast, lighthouses were built on the point from the earliest years in order to aid navigation of the Sandusky Bay and the lake. A new lighthouse was built in 1862 to replace an earlier lighthouse.

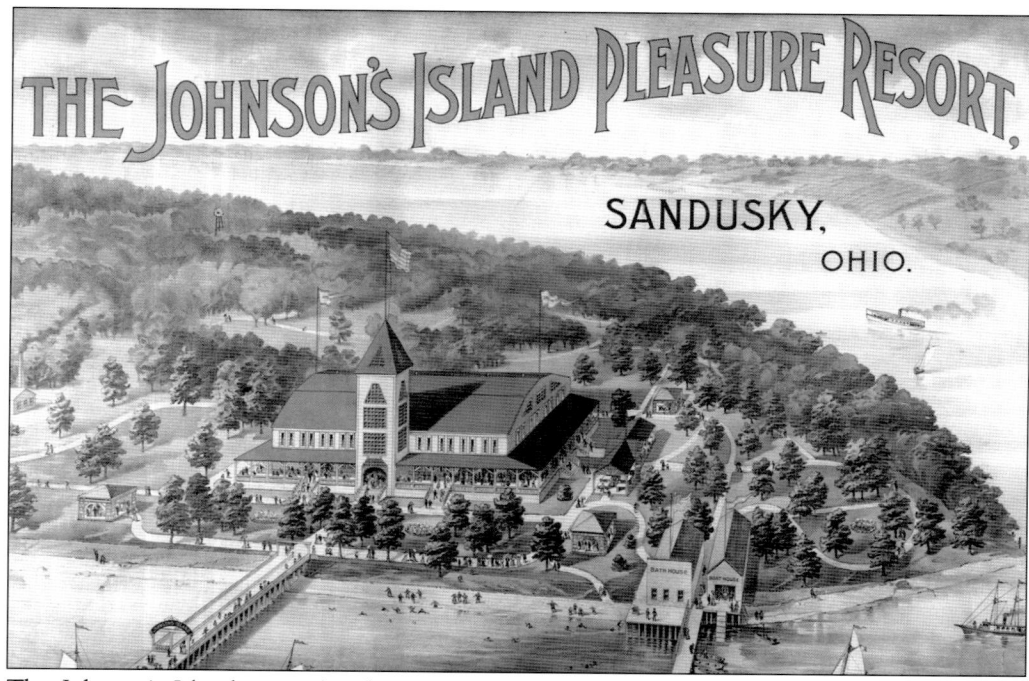

The Johnson's Island resort briefly attempted to compete with Cedar Point for the summer recreation business. An advertising print of the Johnson's Island Pleasure Resort at the end of the 19th century shows the features the resort offered. However, business difficulties, compounded by a fire that destroyed the main pavilion in 1897, doomed the resort, and it closed after only a few years of operation. An attempt to reopen the Johnson's Island resort in 1904 was short-lived, and ultimately the property was bought by Cedar Point in order to eliminate any future competition.

Three
MODERN TIMES

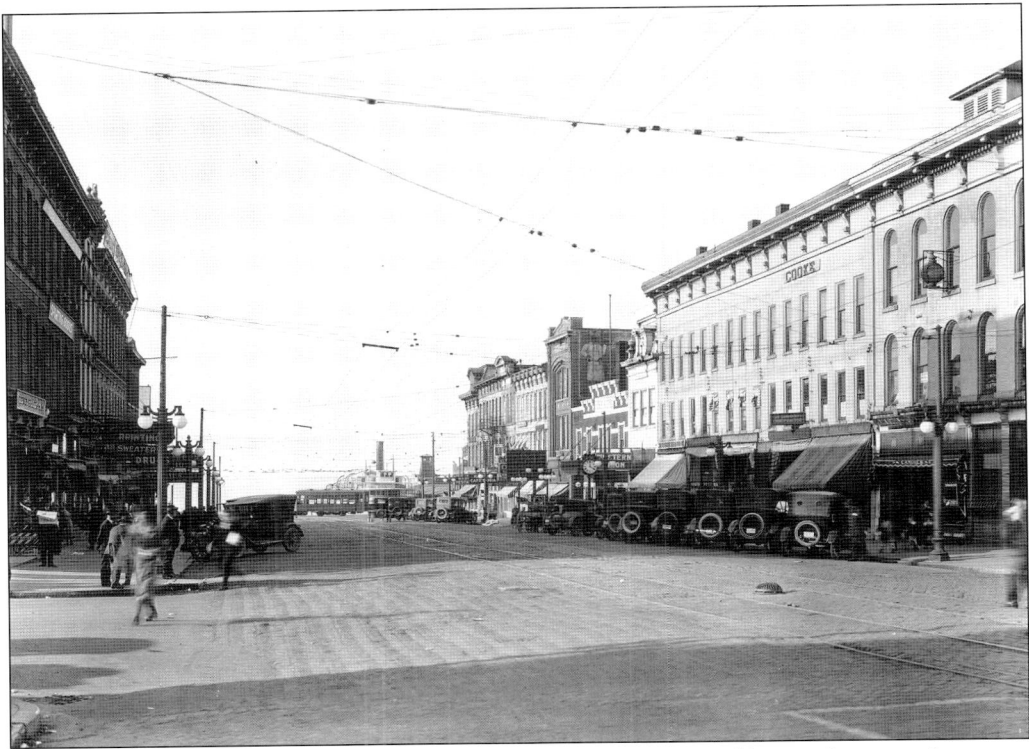

By the early 20th century, Sandusky was a complete city, with a stable population and a secure economic base. Although life in Sandusky in the last 100 years has developed quite differently than in the first 100 years, it is still the same strong community. In 1922, the center of commercial activity was along Columbus Avenue. Note the overhead line for the electric trolleys.

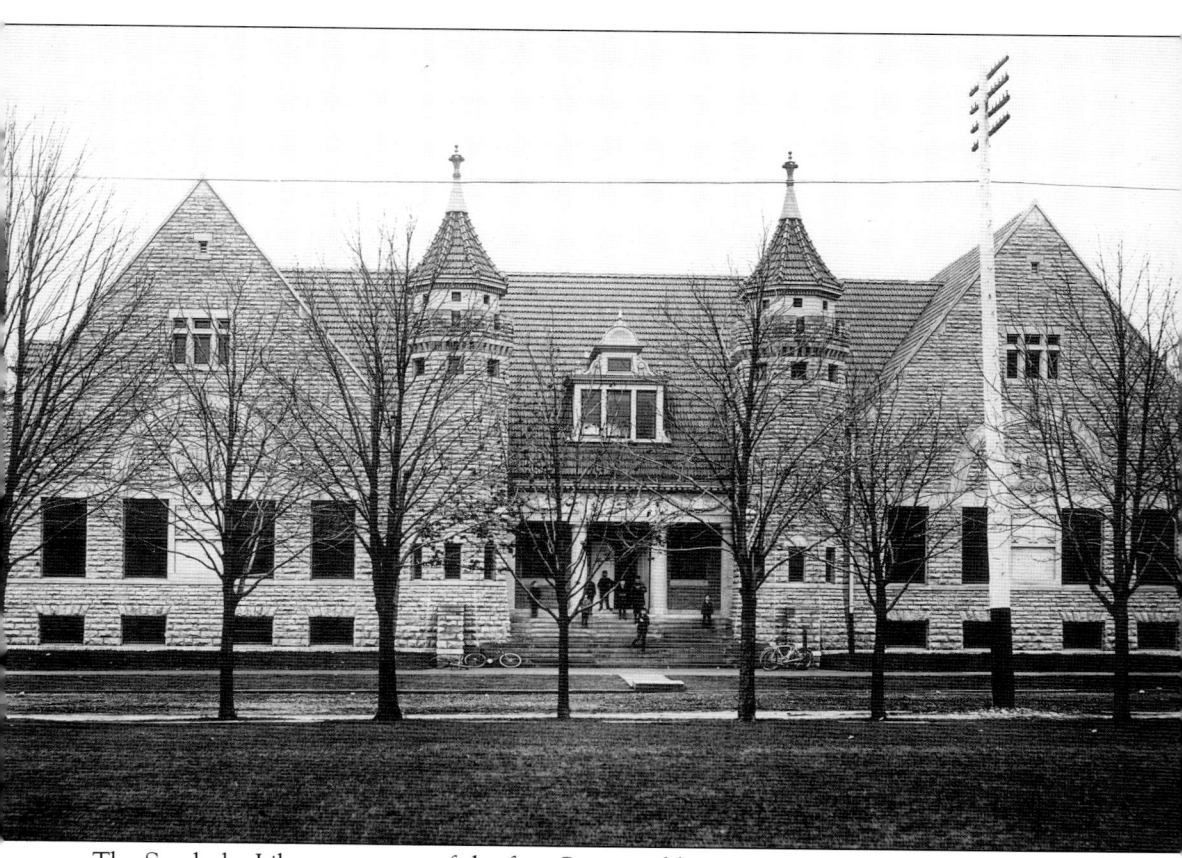
The Sandusky Library was one of the first Carnegie libraries in Ohio. Opened in 1901, it was built with the aid of a $50,000 grant from the industrialist Andrew Carnegie.

Mrs. Jay O. Moss, a member of the Library Association, was instrumental in securing the grant from Andrew Carnegie. She was a personal acquaintance of Carnegie and was able to persuade him to select Sandusky from among the many applicants for funding throughout the country.

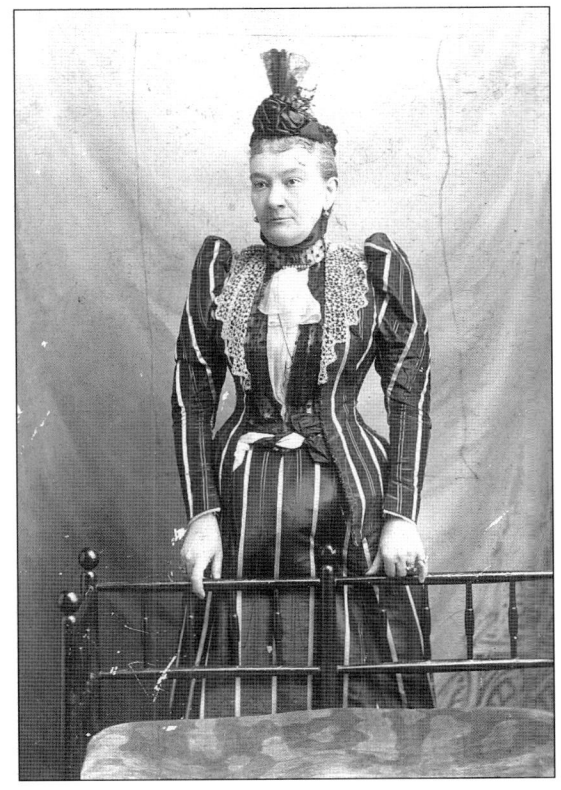

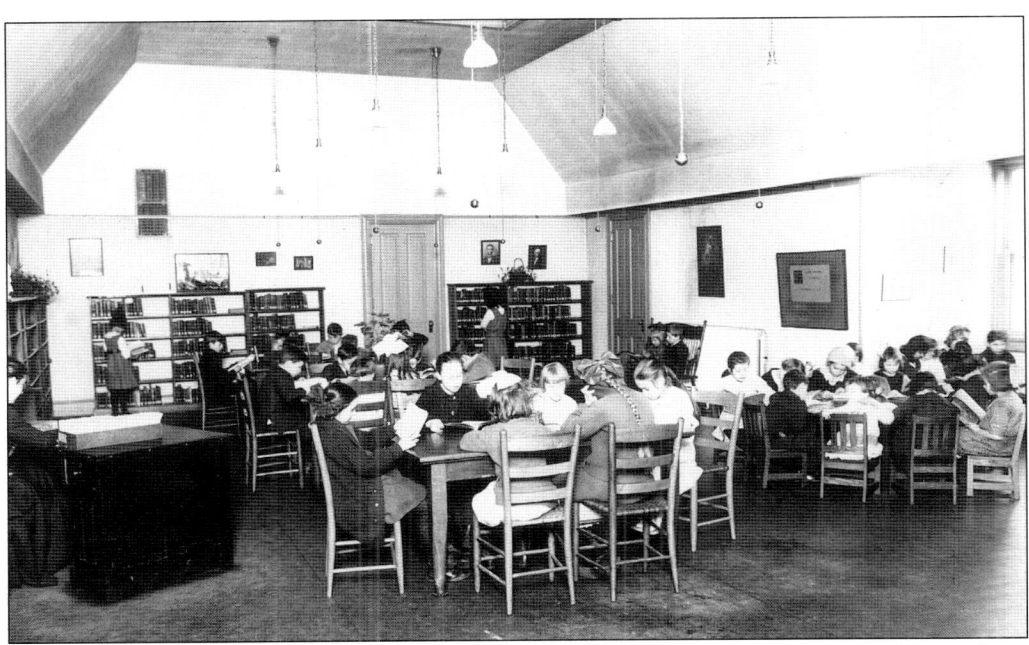

The children's room of the Sandusky Library in 1917 looks quite different than it does today.

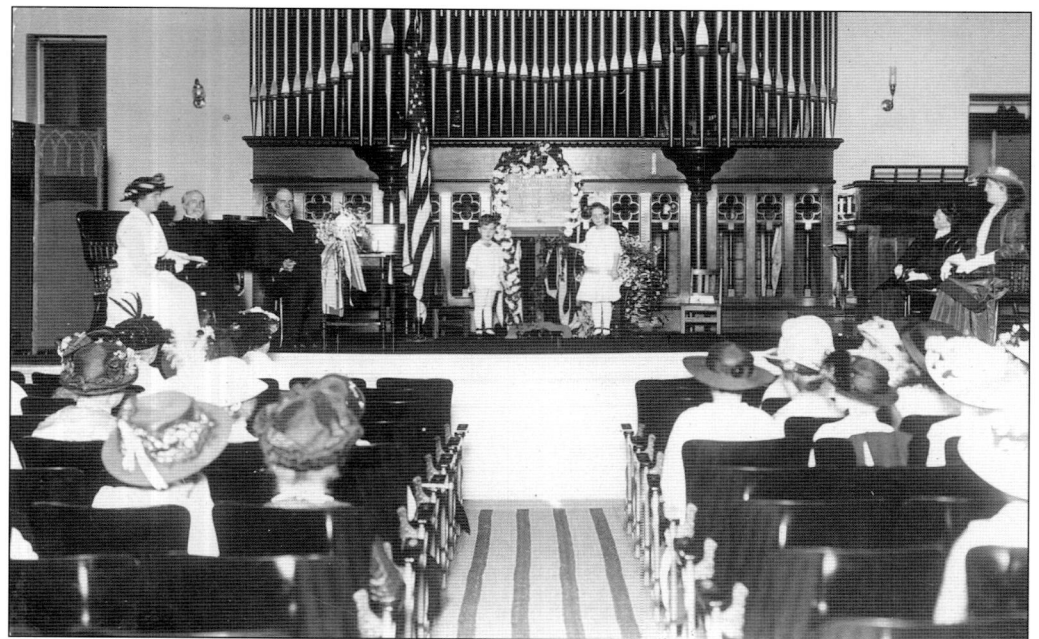

As with many early Carnegie libraries, the Sandusky Library building included an auditorium for public events. This view shows the massive pipe organ at the rear of the stage. The auditorium was eliminated around 1920 to provide more room for books and reading.

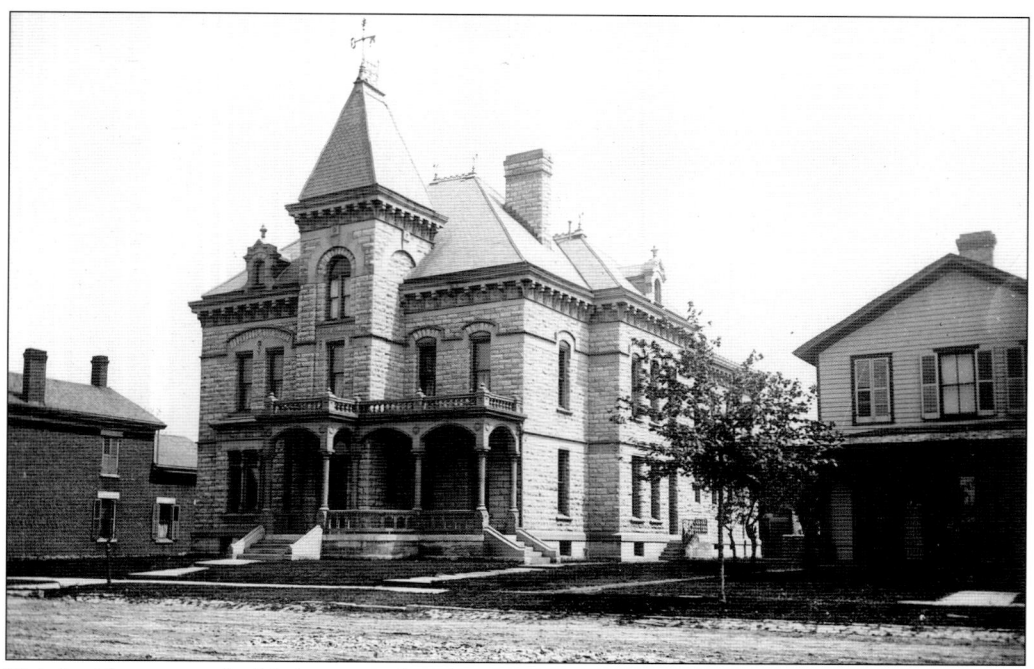

This building, near the library, served as the Erie County Jail from 1883 until 1990, when a new facility opened in Perkins Township. The sheriff and his family often lived in the front of the building (perhaps explaining its "homey" design). Today this building has been incorporated as part of the recently expanded Sandusky Library.

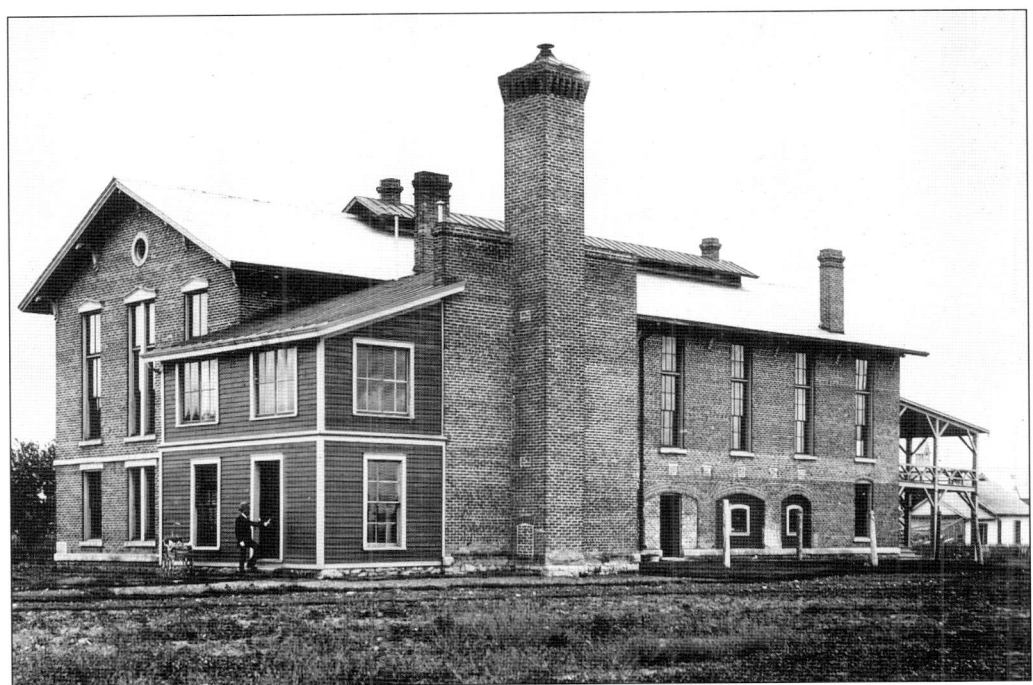

The cornerstone of the Good Samaritan Hospital (the predecessor to the Firelands Hospital) was laid in June 1876, on land donated by C.C. Keech, one of Sandusky's greatest philanthropists. However, because of financial difficulties, the hospital did not accept patients until October 13, 1886.

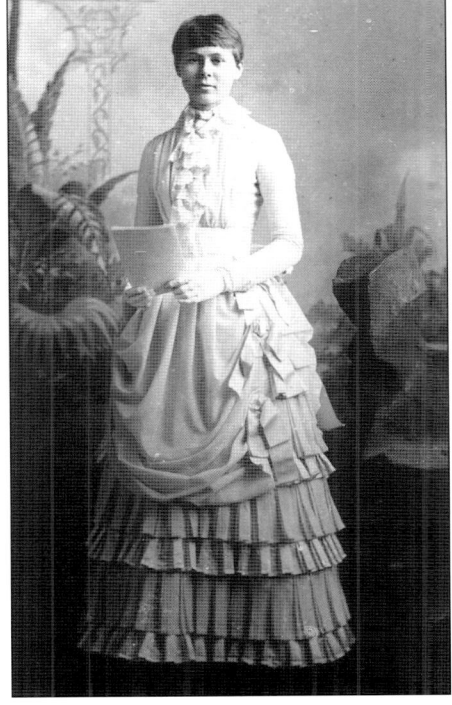

After some difficulties in attracting patients to the new concept called the hospital, the first Good Samaritan Hospital closed in 1898. But in 1909, a movement led by Dr. Carrie Chase Davis succeeded in getting the hospital reopened to the public. The Women's Advisory Board of the hospital helped to solicit financial support from the public to maintain the hospital, which was reopened on June 27, 1910.

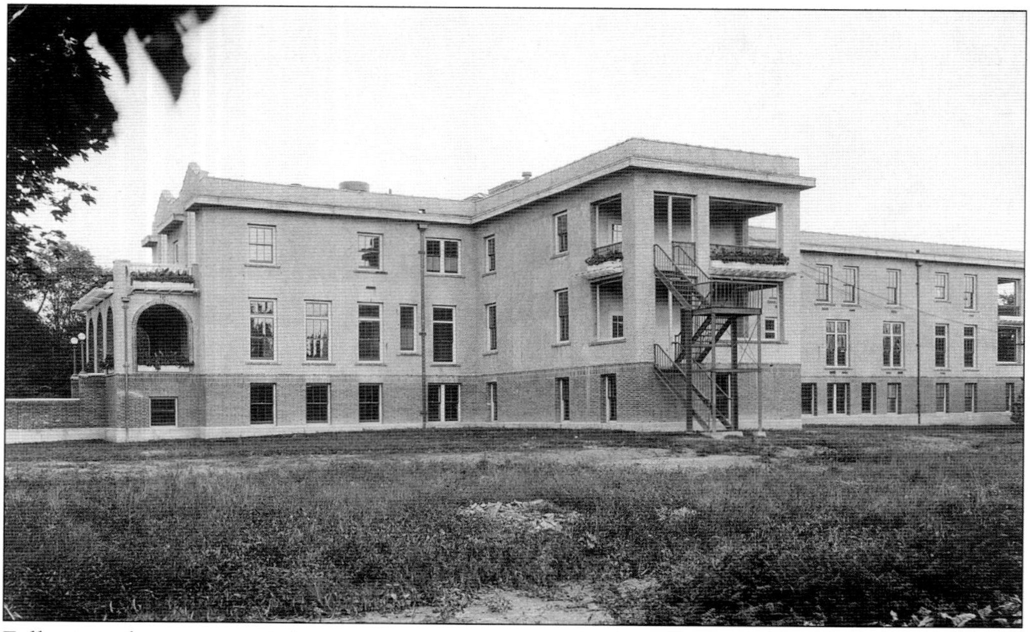

Following the success of the movement to reopen the hospital and the accompanying fund drive, Good Samaritan hospital was rebuilt in 1918 on Van Buren Street.

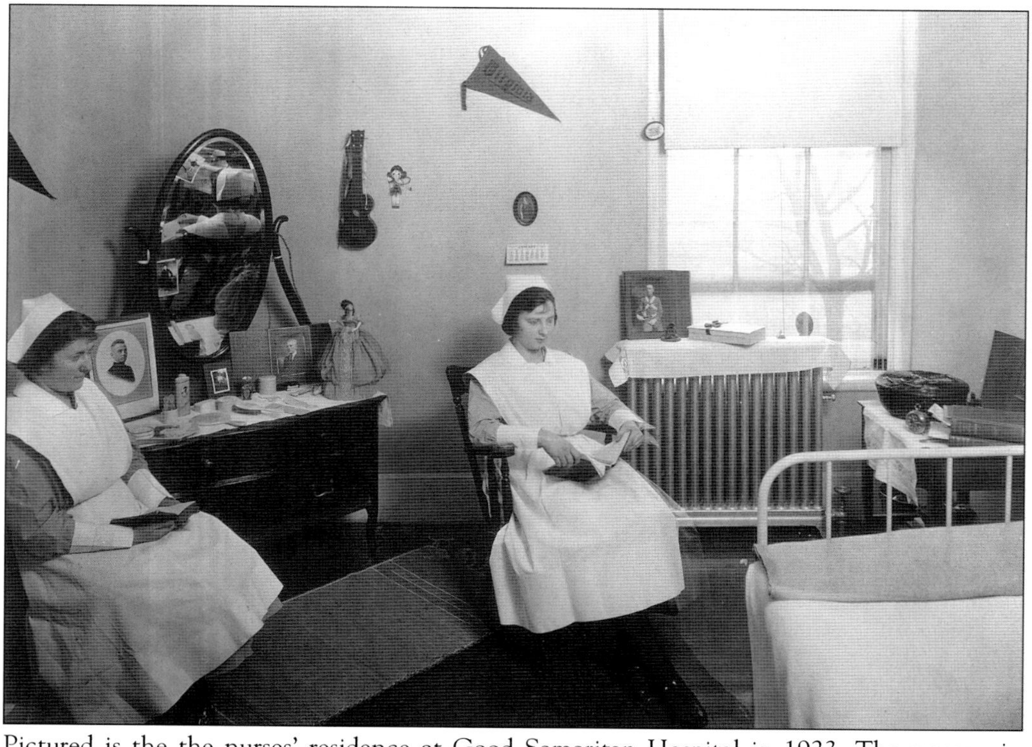

Pictured is the the nurses' residence at Good Samaritan Hospital in 1923. The women in the photograph could have been students at the hospital's school of nursing, which trained students from 1910 to 1937.

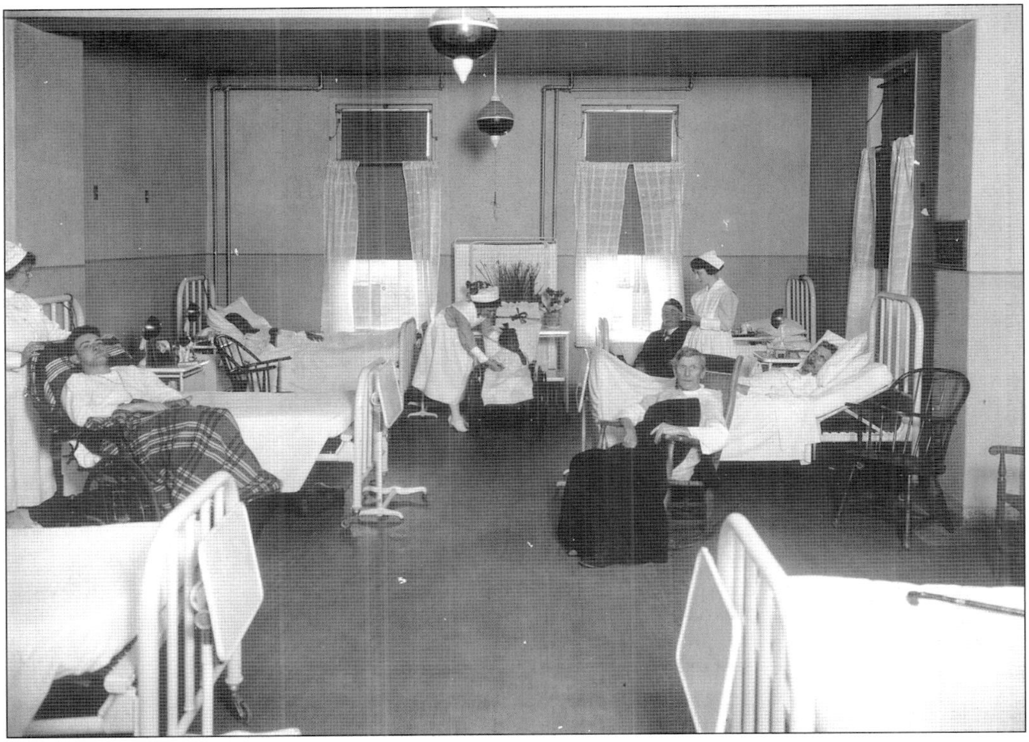

Seen here is a ward at Good Samaritan Hospital, 1923.

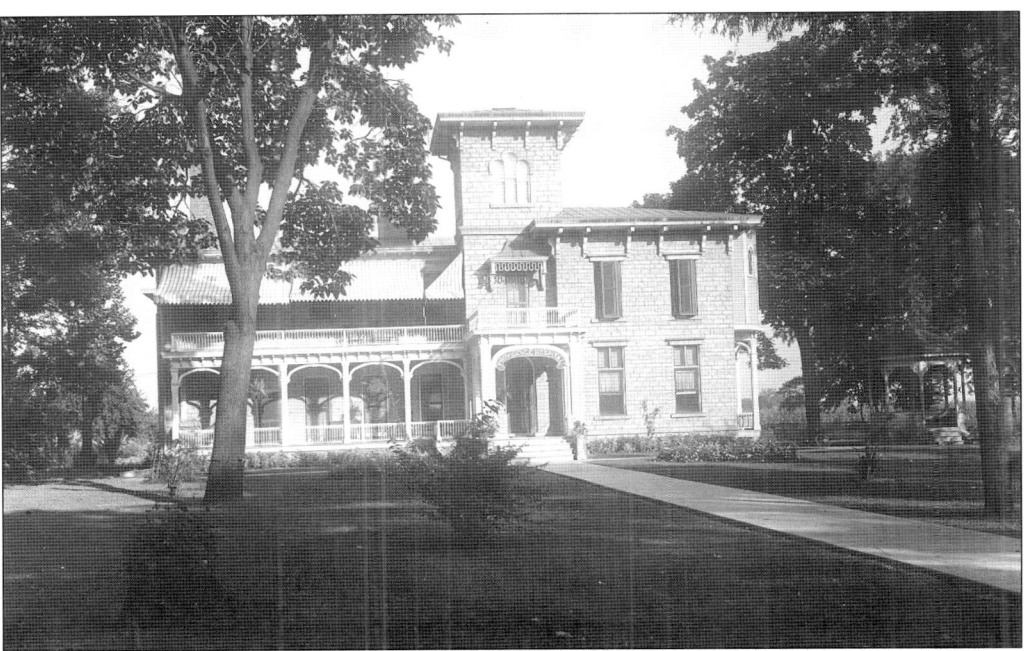

Providence Hospital opened in 1902 in the former home of C C. Keech (who died in 1891) on Hayes Avenue. The Sisters of Charity of St. Augustine founded the hospital. The home was later used as nurses' quarters when the new hospital building was constructed.

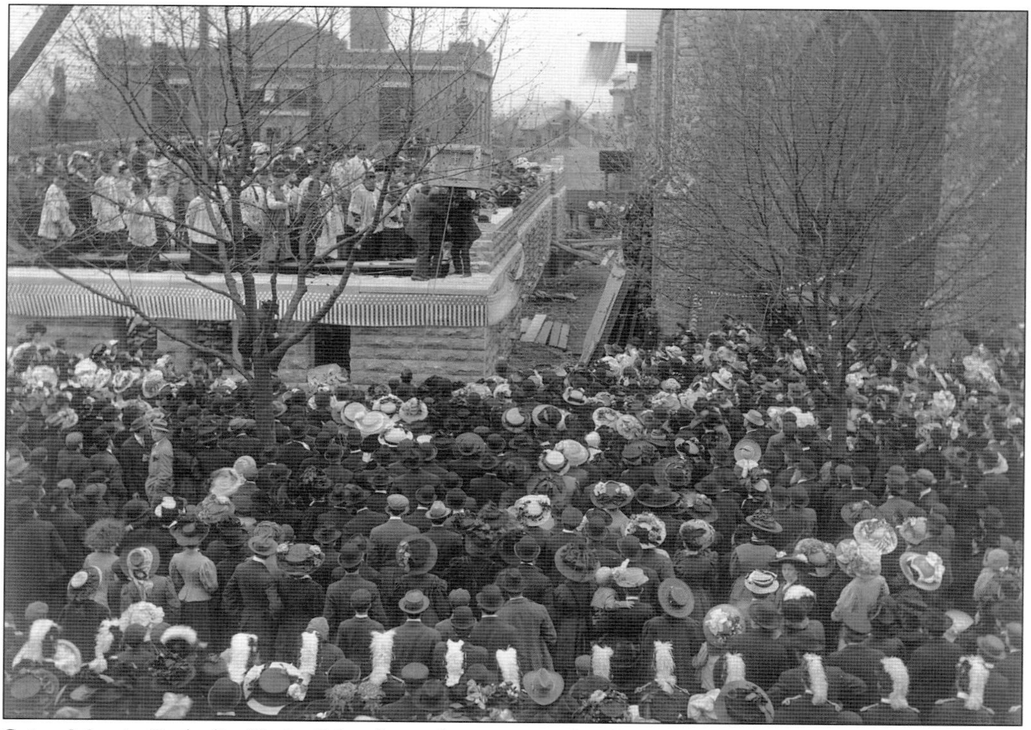

Saint Mary's Catholic High School, at the corner of Jefferson and Decatur Streets, opened to students in 1910. Here we see the cornerstone laying ceremony for the building on April 25, 1909.

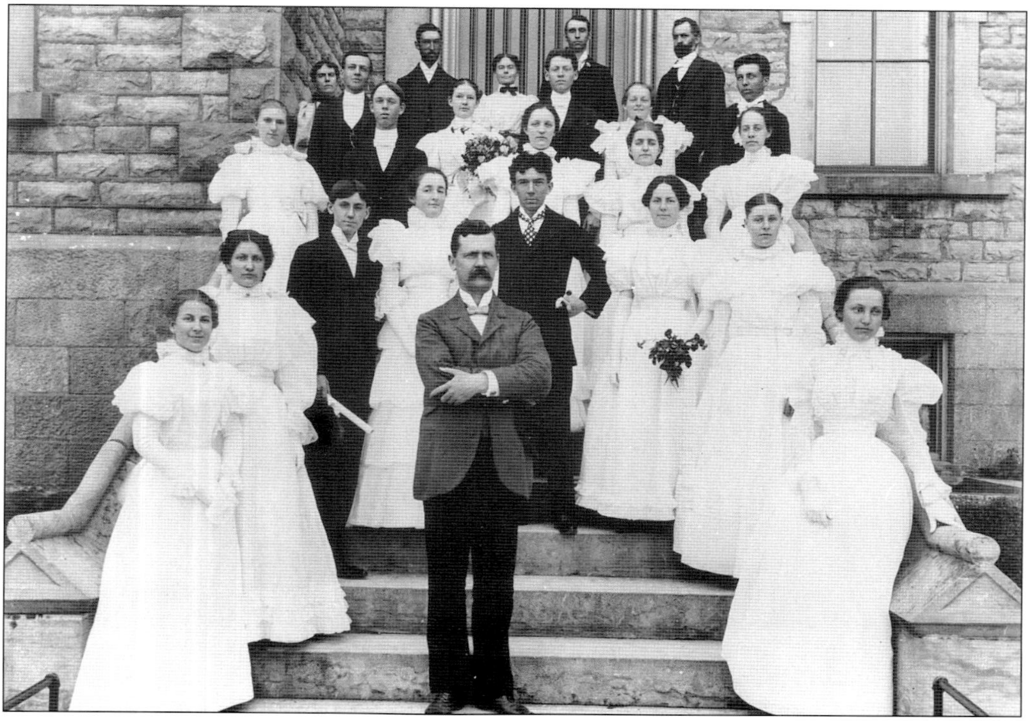

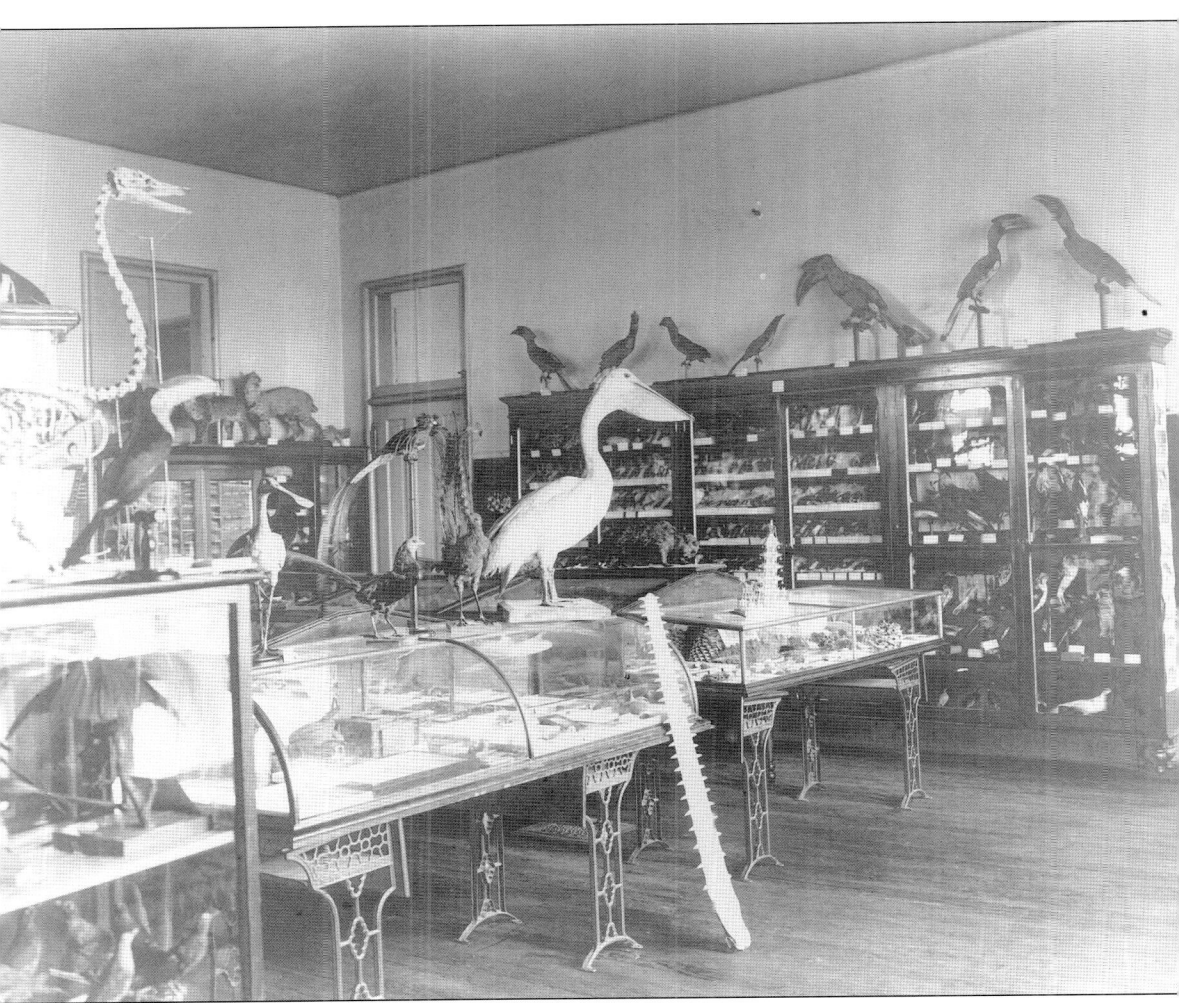

While teaching at the high school, Professor Moseley opened a natural history museum on the third floor of that building. The museum operated in the school from 1891 until 1932. These specimens, collected by Moseley, are displayed in an exhibit room in 1906.

Opposite: Students and teachers of Sandusky High School pose for a graduation photo in 1912. The slender man with the beard in the back row is Edward Lincoln Moseley, renowned scientist and educator. Professor Moseley taught at the high school from 1889 to 1914, when he became the first professor of science at Bowling Green State Normal College (now a university). He published many works in several scientific disciplines, including ornithology, botany, and geology. Popular with students and fellow educators, a building on the Bowling Green campus bears his name.

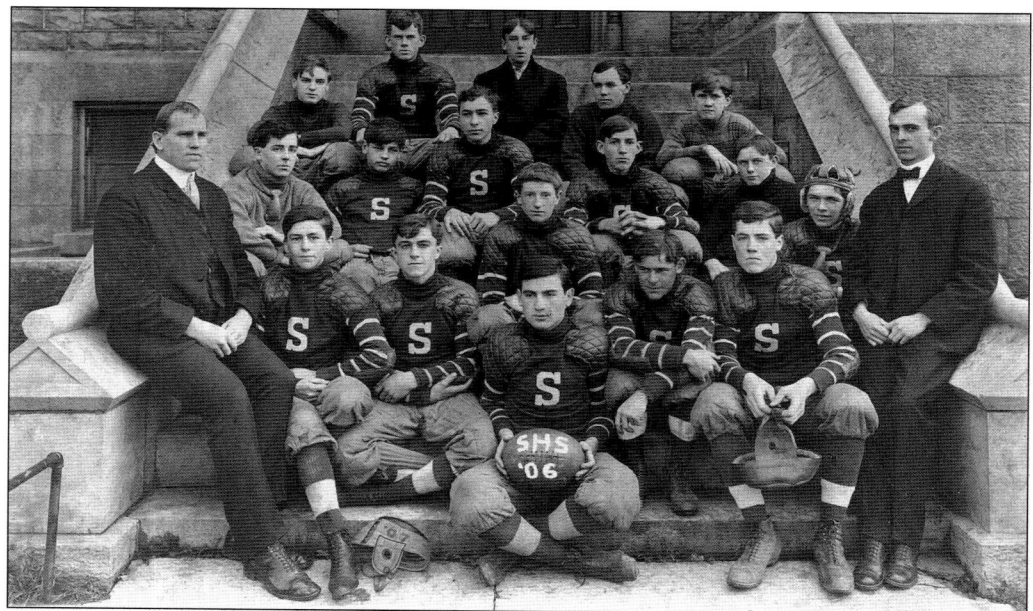

By the 20th century, sports had become a major extracurricular activity in local schools, as was common throughout the nation. The Sandusky High School varsity football program began in 1901. The 1906 football team was one of the best ever at Sandusky High School, winning five games that year by a combined score of 77-0.

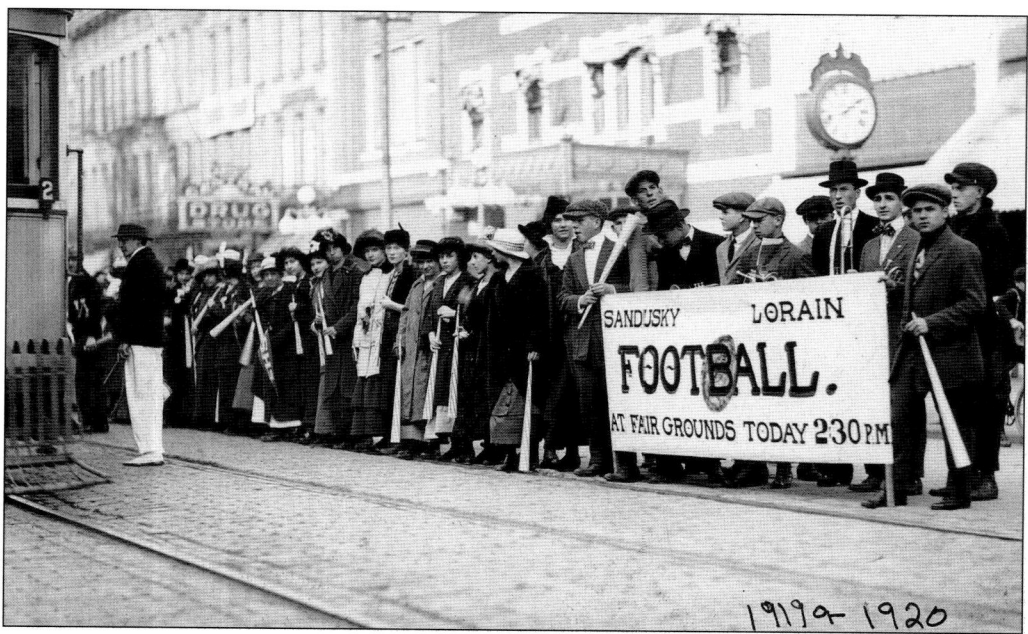

A rally is held for the Sandusky High School football team on Columbus Avenue, 1920. In the hundred-plus years since varsity football was created, the school has produced many successful teams, players, and coaches. Earle Bruce, who later was head coach at Ohio State University, coached the team during the 1960s. Orlando Pace, star in the National Football League, is a graduate of Sandusky High School.

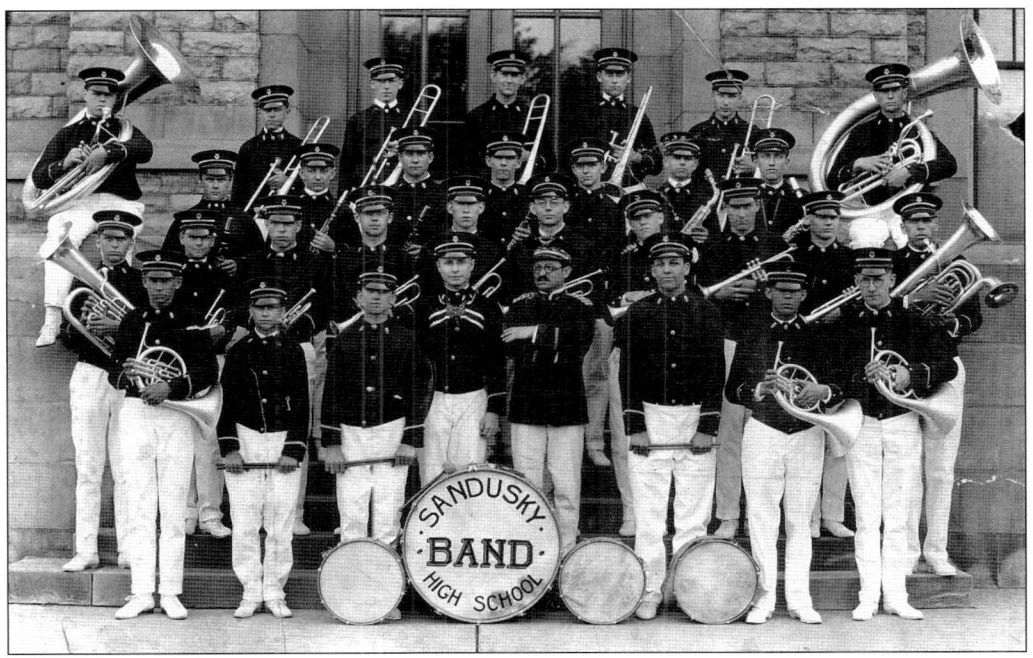

Other extracurricular activities at Sandusky High School originated in the early 20th century. The high school's first band, seen here, was organized in 1923.

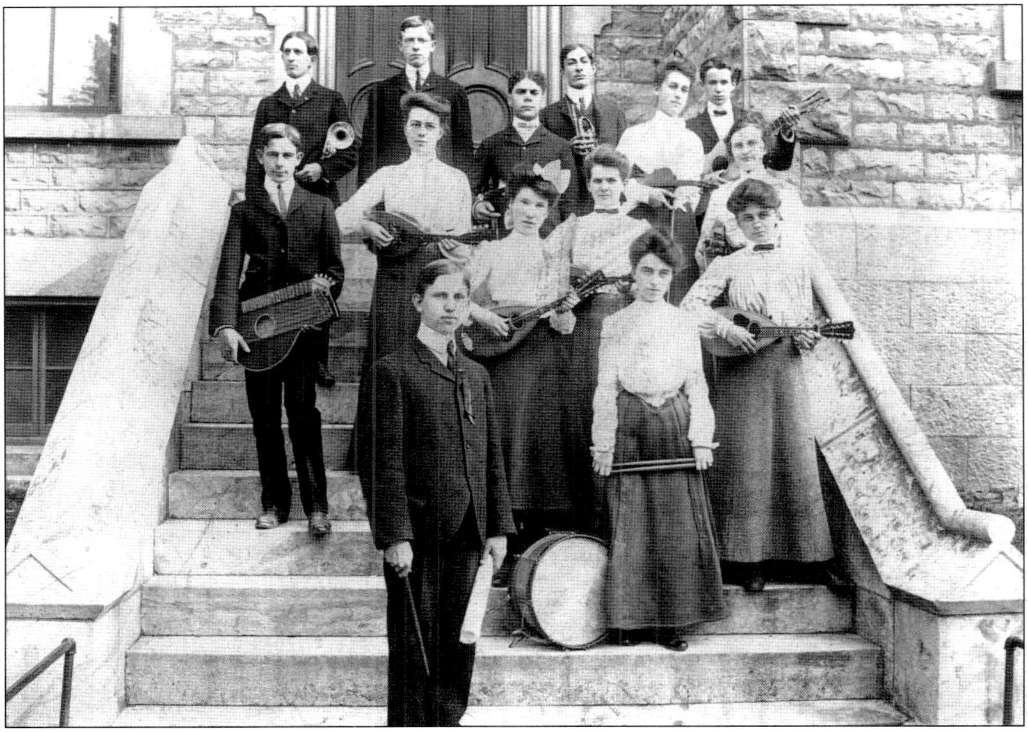

Twenty years earlier, in 1903, the Sandusky High School orchestra performed for the first time, led by Edward Eugene Williams.

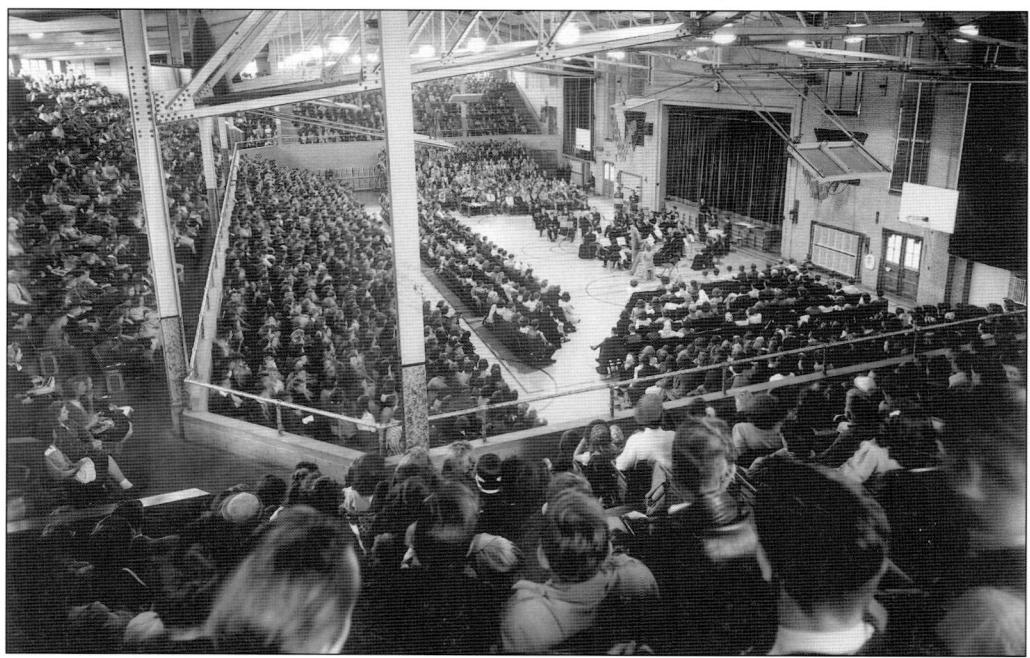

Sandusky Junior High School opened in 1928, with a dedication ceremony on February 26. The school auditorium was designed as a community center for public events. The school's name was changed to Jackson Junior High in 1957, when Adams Junior High School was opened in the former high school building.

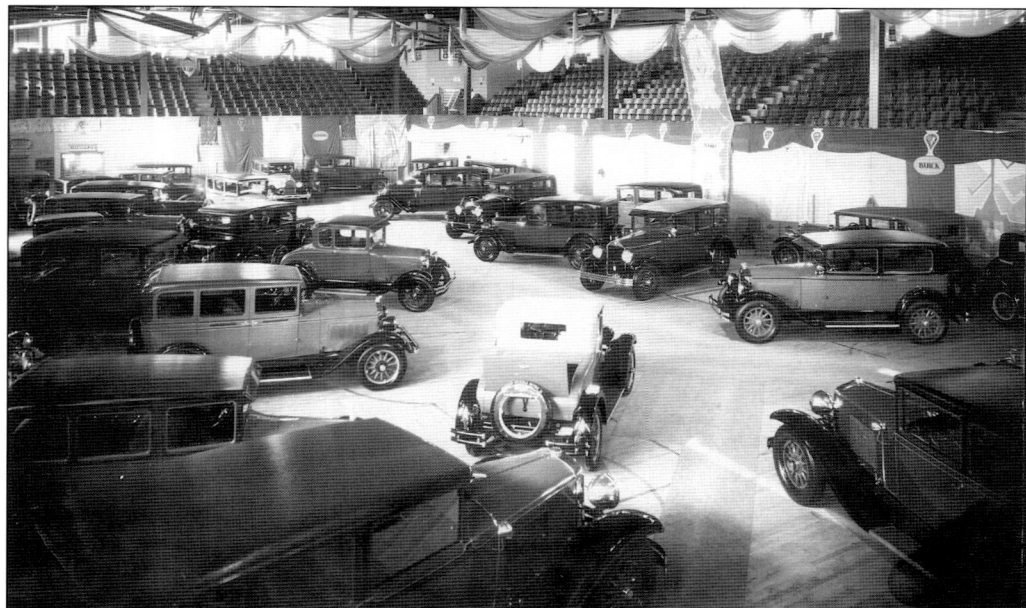

The public events in the junior high auditorium included not only concerts and other performances, but also trade shows and other commercial events. Here we see an auto show in the early 1930s. The doorways of the building were designed specifically to allow large items such as automobiles into the auditorium.

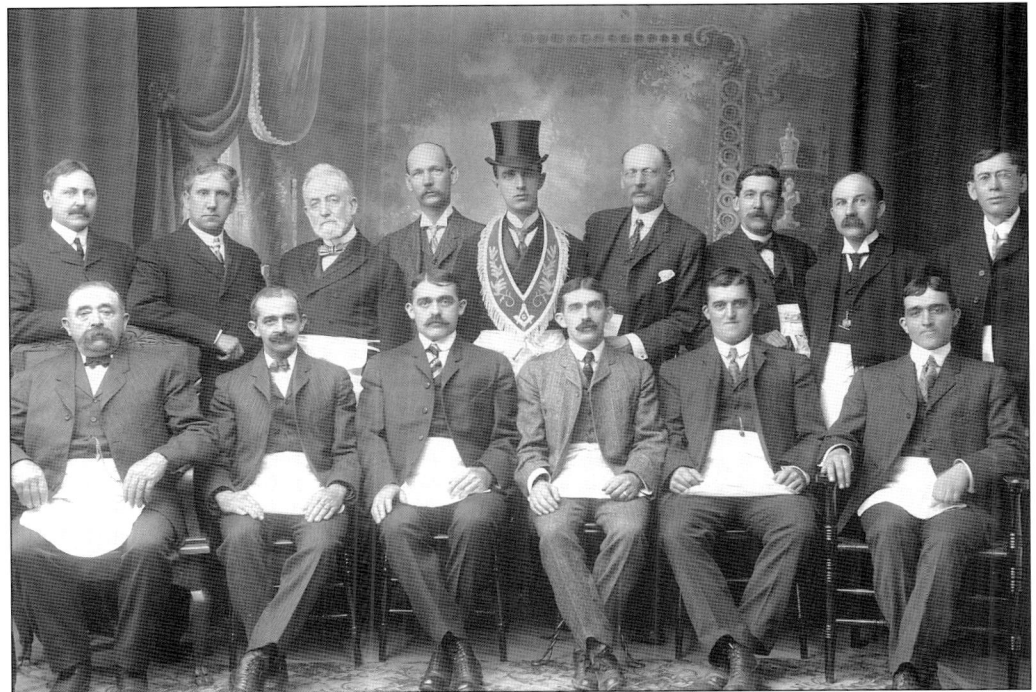

Although many social organizations developed in Sandusky from the earliest days, these community groups flourished throughout much of the 20th century. The first social organization to affect the city (remember the street grid), the Masons continued their prominence many years later. The scene commemorates the induction of five sons of Daniel Hoffman into the Masonic Order in 1904.

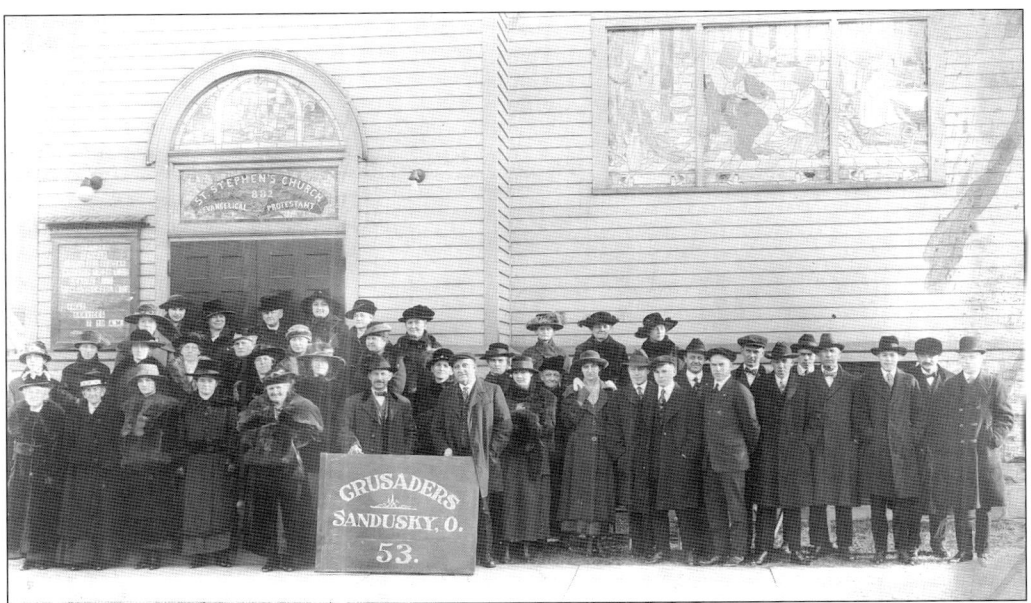

Many of the social clubs in Sandusky were affiliated with local churches. The Crusaders are seen here in front of the original St. Stephen's Church, on Jefferson and Lawrence Streets.

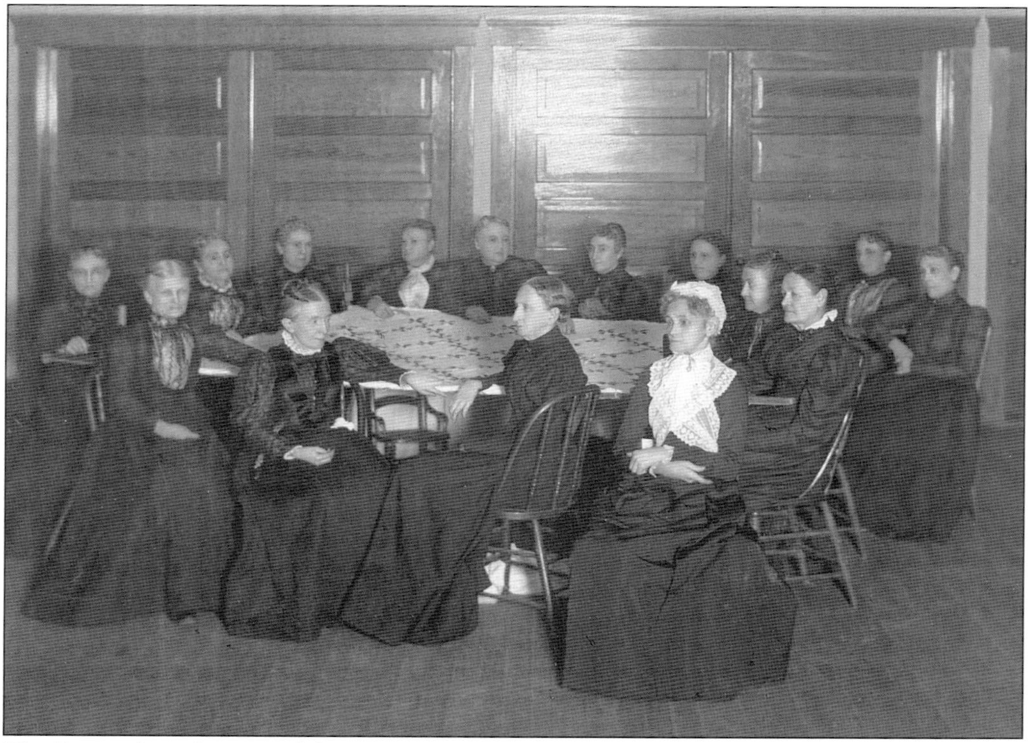

The Benevolent Society of the First Congregational Church appears to be hosting a quilting bee in this image (date unknown).

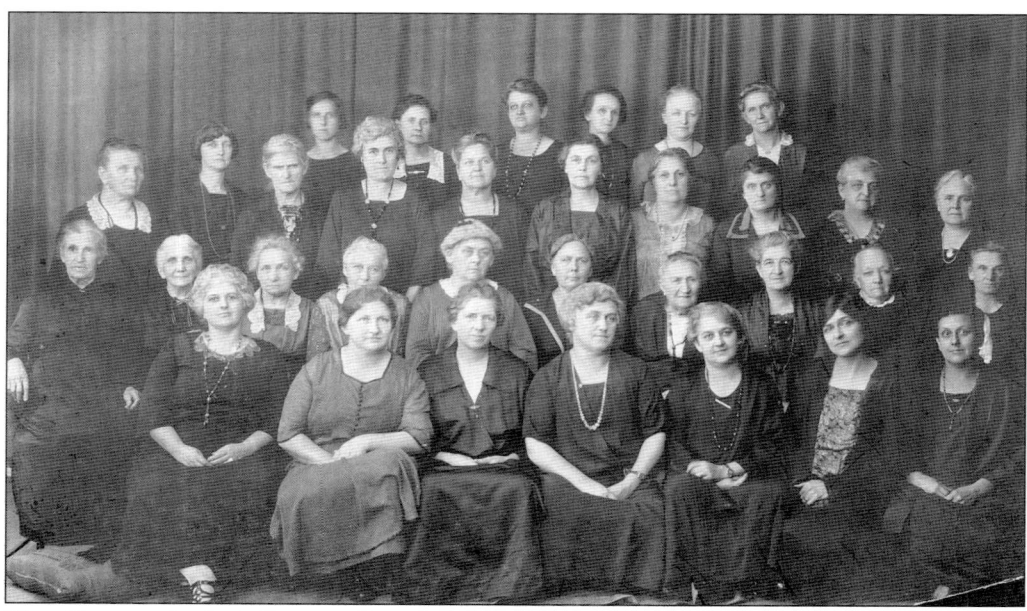

The German Ladies' Sewing Society of the German Reformed Church are seen here (date unknown).

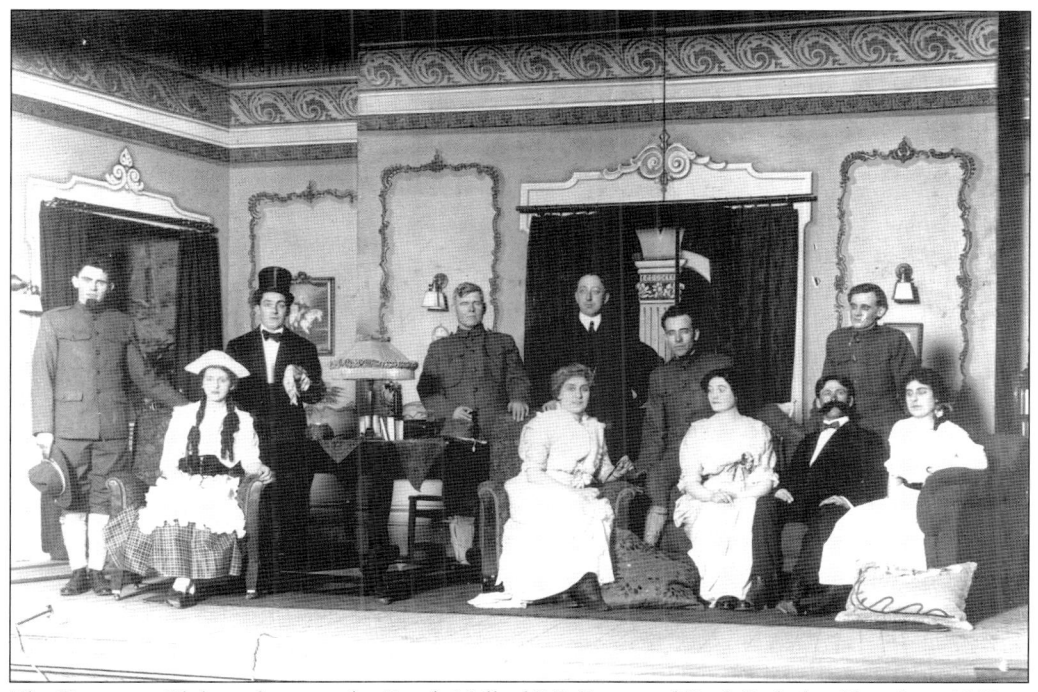

The Dramatic Club performs at the Parish Hall of S.S. Peter and Paul Catholic Church, c. 1920.

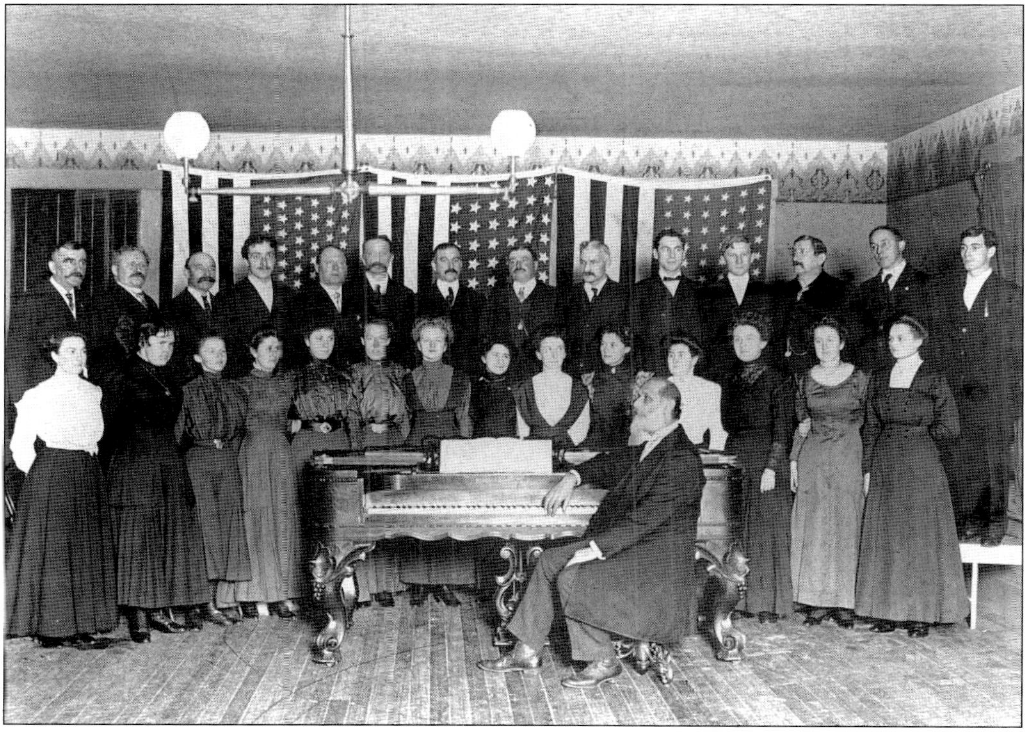

The German Singing Society pictured at Fox's Hall (date unknown).

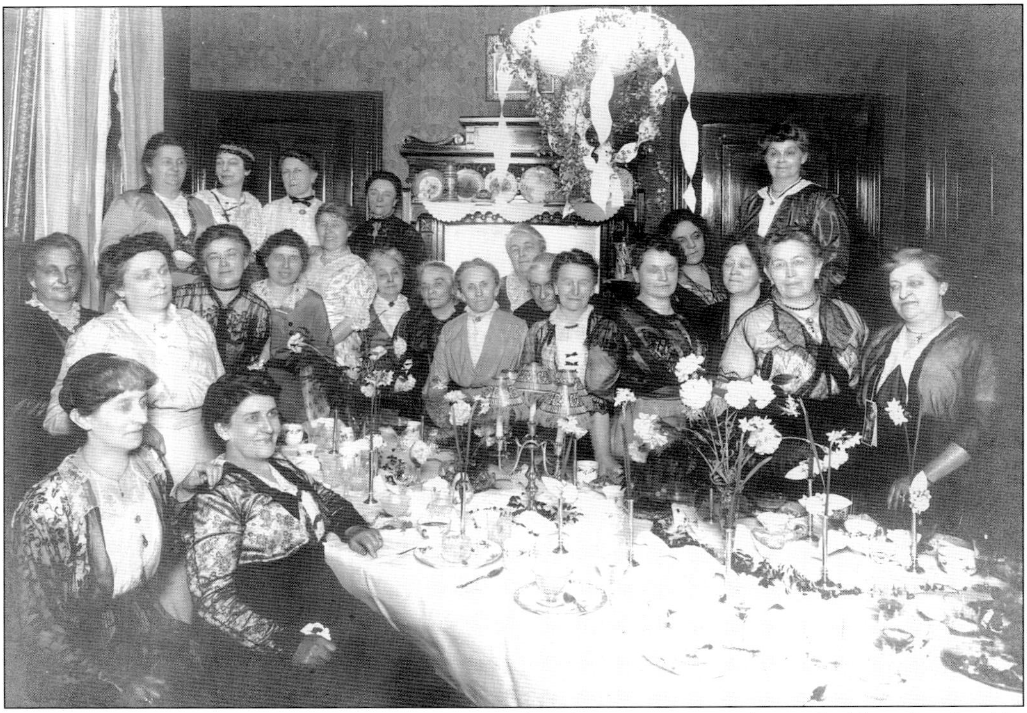

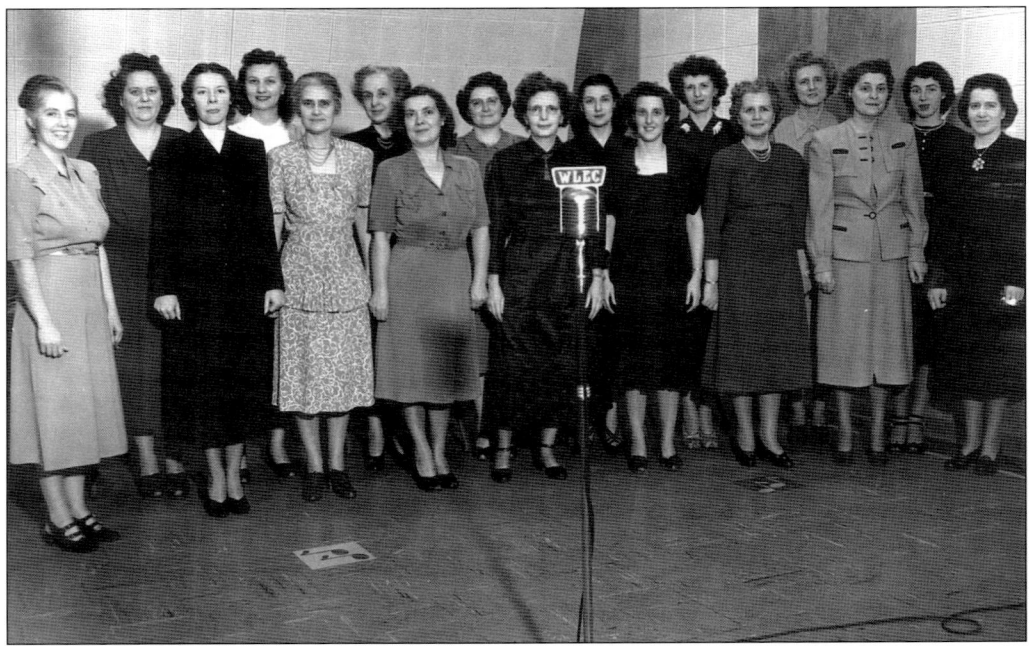

The 25th anniversary celebration for the United Ladies Sewing Circle was held at the Stroble home on Hayes Avenue in 1916. Many women's clubs operated in Sandusky at that time, many of them united under the Sandusky Federation of Women's Organizations.

The College Women's Chorus, pictured here in the late 1940s, was directed by Beverlie Mayer (at far left) for over 35 years. This group later became the Firelands Chorus.

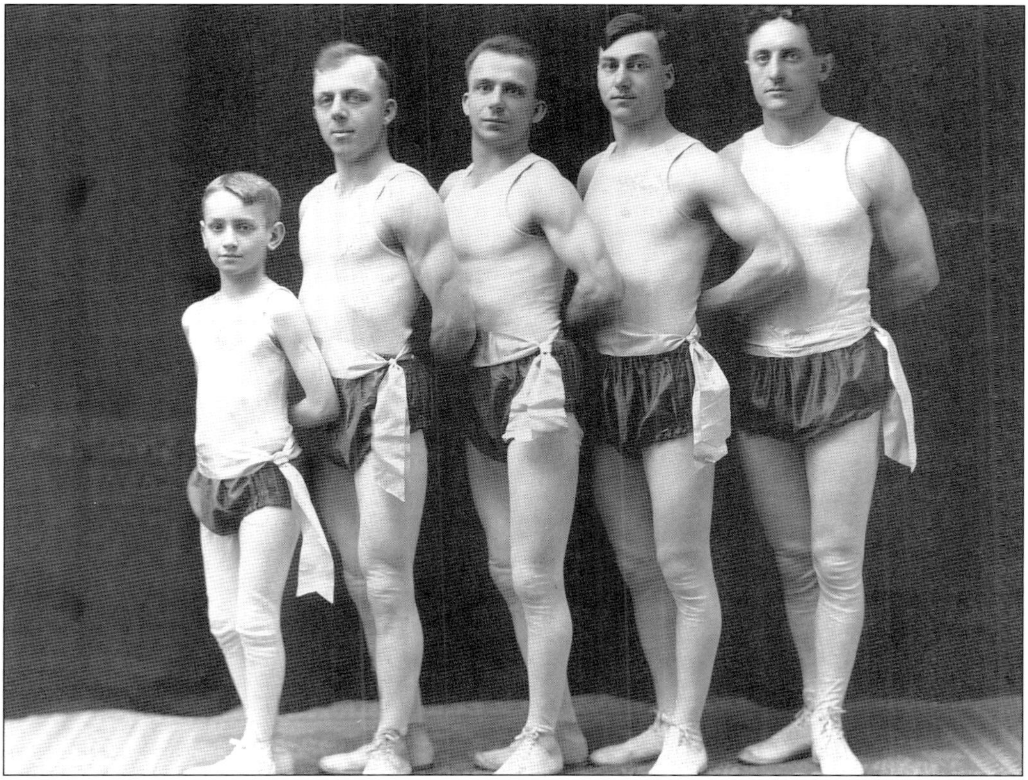

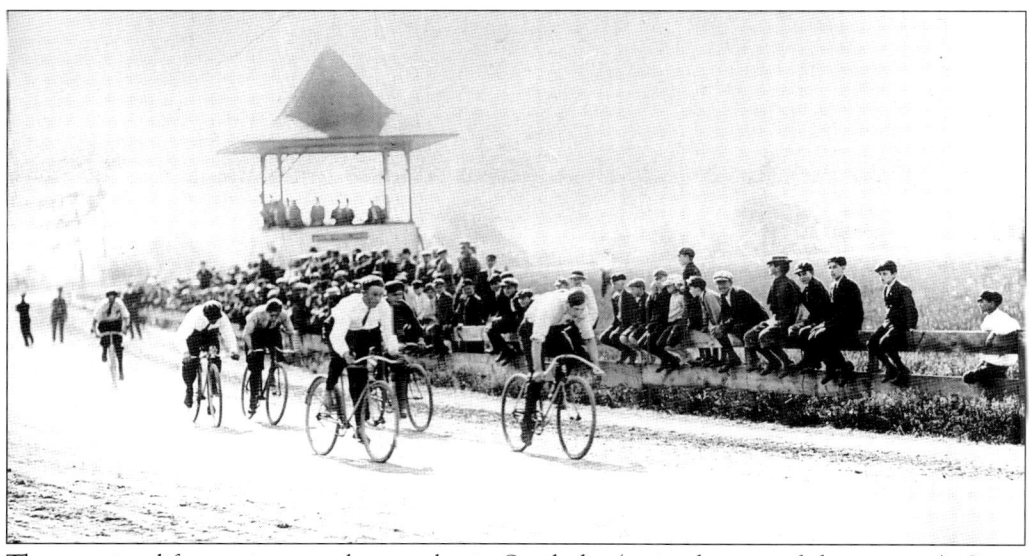

Pictured is the Sandusky Acrobatic Group, c. 1908. The man on the right is William Hommel, manager of the Hommel Wine Company; his son Glenn is the boy on the left.

The sporting life continues to be popular in Sandusky (as in the rest of the country). Some sports, however, are not as popular as they once were. One would be hard pressed to find major bicycle races in Sandusky today. In 1914, bicycle races were held at the fairgrounds, which at that time was at the foot of Wayne Street.

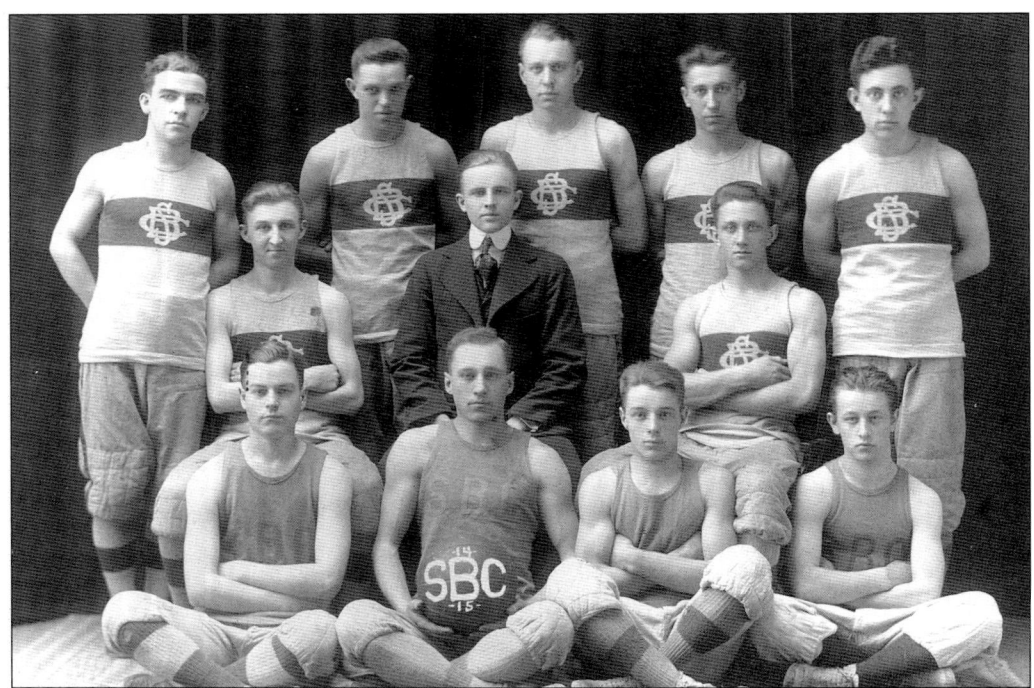

The Sandusky Business College fielded a men's basketball team in the early 20th century. This is the 1914–1915 team. Notice the rather long pants that seem to be padded at the knees.

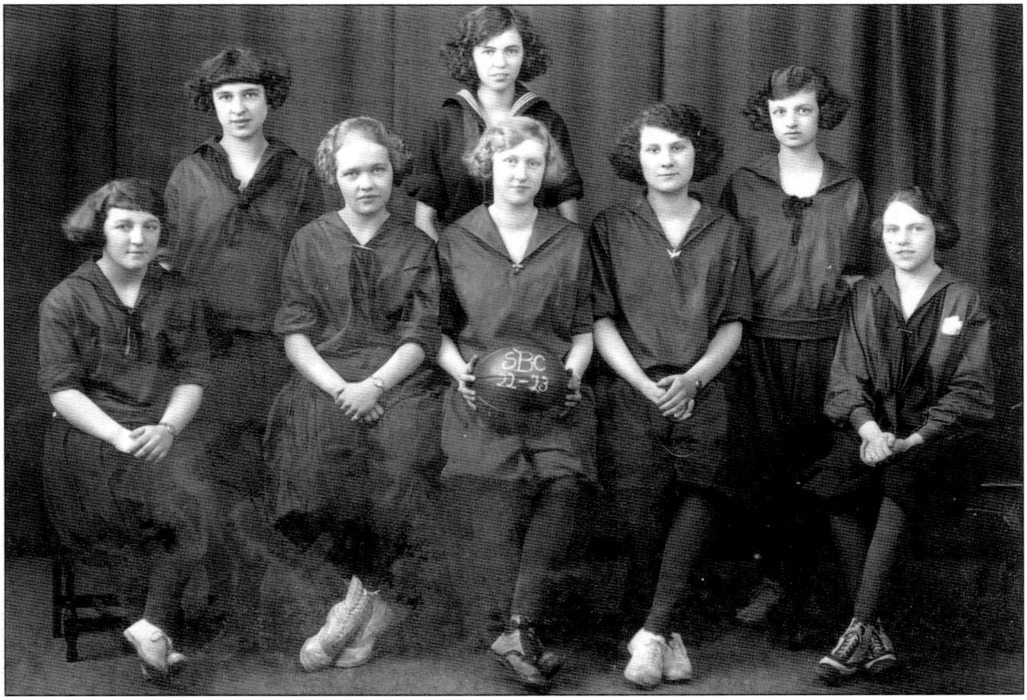

It may be surprising to see a women's varsity team from the 1920s, but here is the Sandusky Business College women's basketball team from 1922 to 1923.

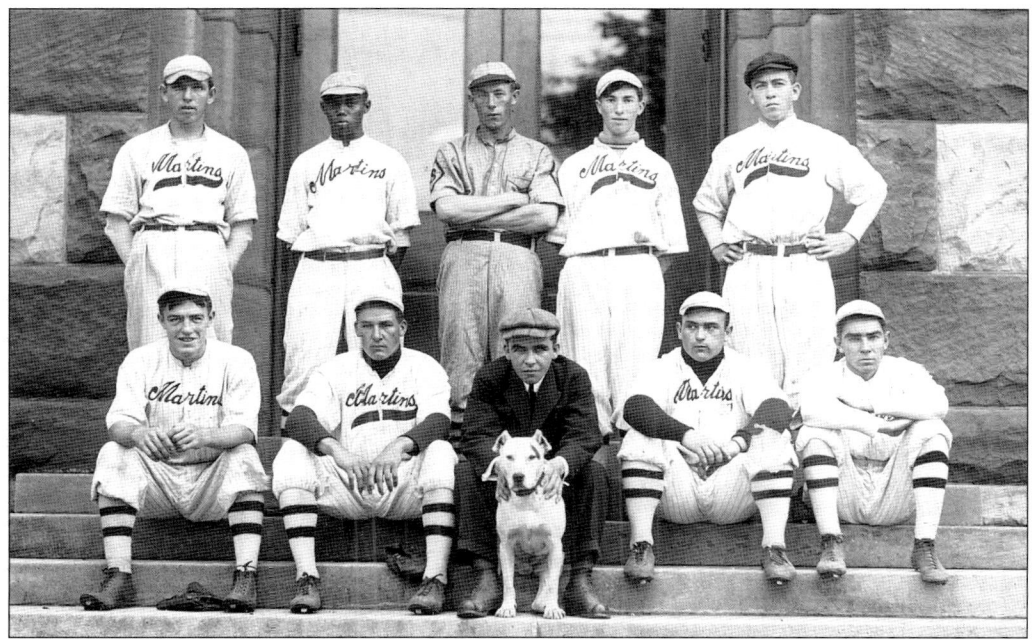

Another pleasantly surprising sight is that of an integrated baseball team in the early half of the 20th century. Little has been discovered about this team, but they appear to be from the 1920s or 1930s, well before the integration of the Major Leagues. The team might have received its name from the Martin's Confectionary, which opened on Columbus Avenue in 1910.

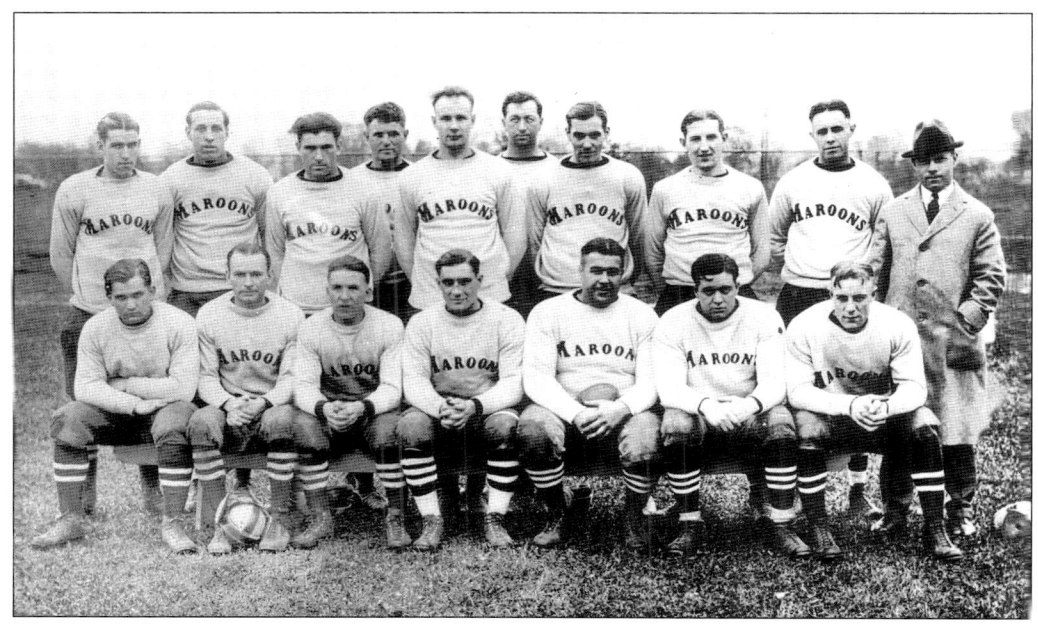

The Sandusky Maroons were a semi-professional football team that played in the 1920s and 1930s. They played their games at Strobel Field. Here we see the 1923 team.

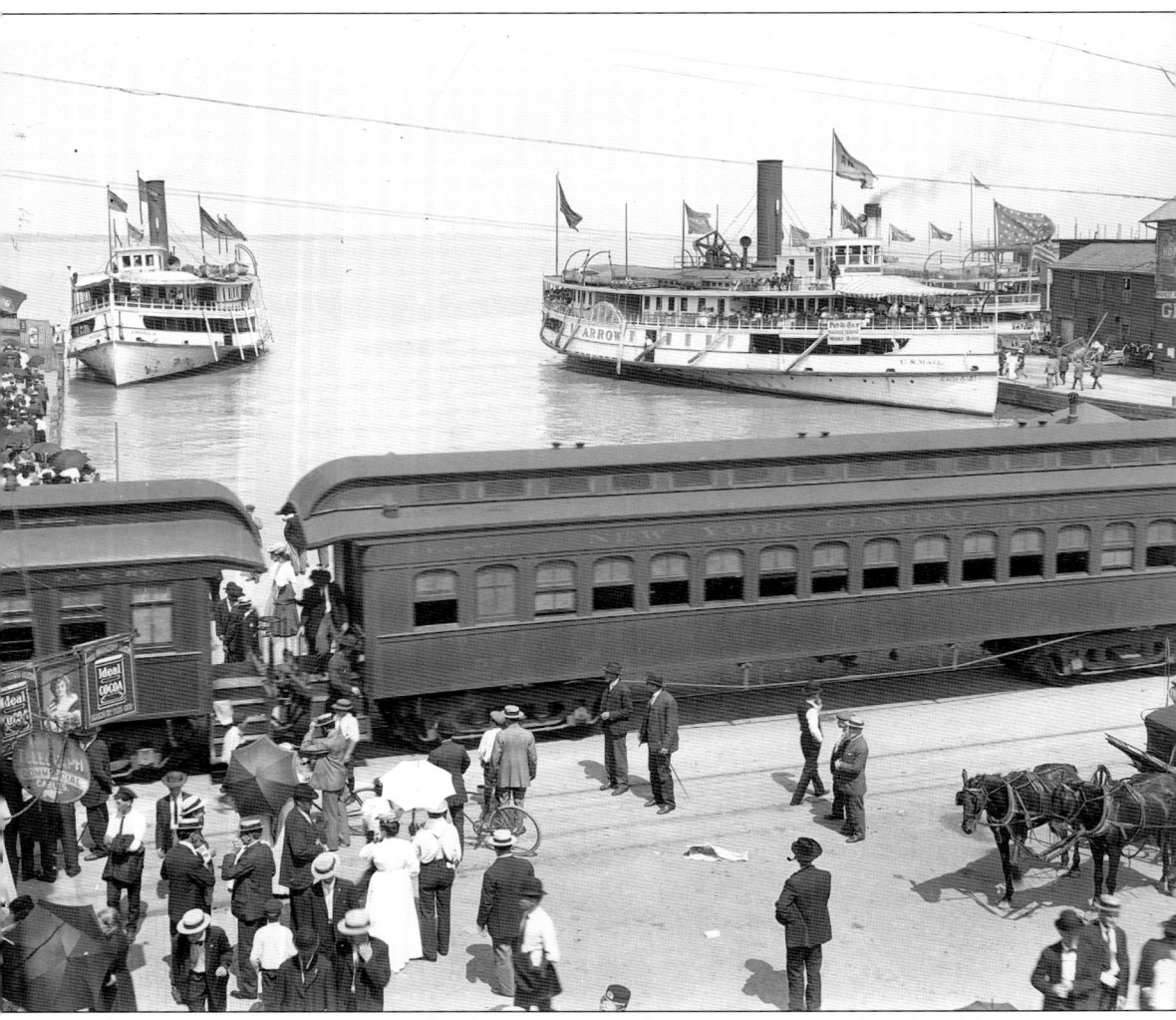

The transportation revolution that began in the 19th century continued in the 20th century—but in radically new directions. The major sources of transportation at the beginning of the 20th century, seen here at the foot of Columbus Avenue, were virtually obsolete by the end of the century. Steamships and passenger rail did not disappear suddenly, but it is fair to say that the horse and wagon did.

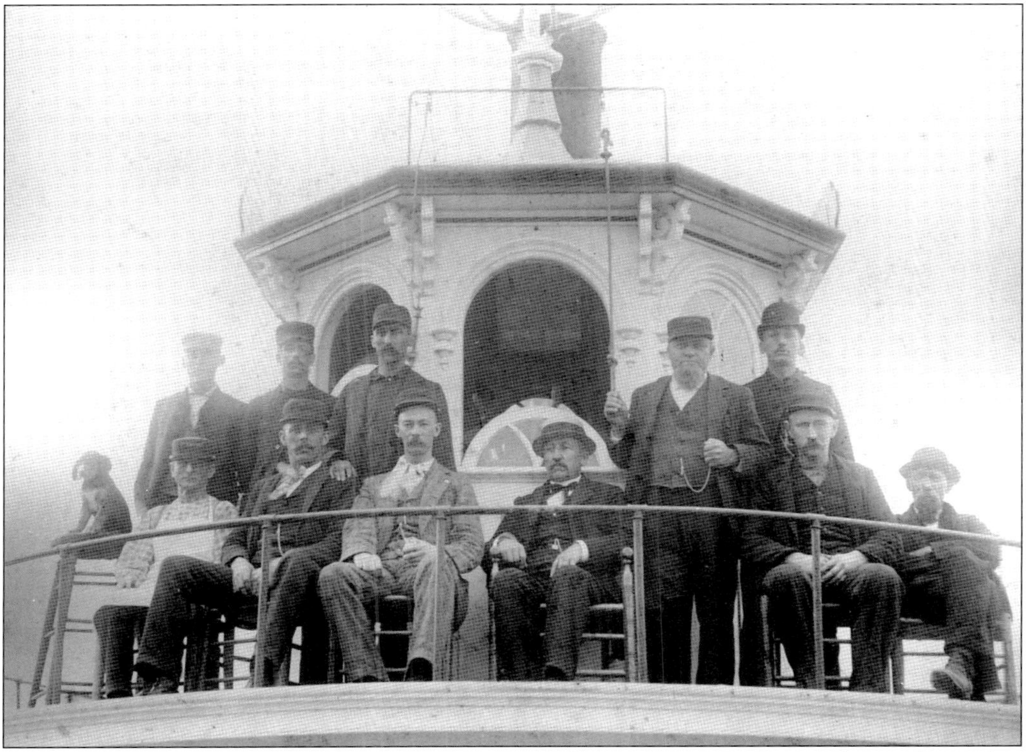

Steamship travel on the Great Lakes continued well into the 20th century, but with steadily decreasing volume. One of the most popular of these 20th-century ships was the steamer G.A. Boeckling, named after George Boeckling, shown in the center of this picture seated on the deck of the R.B. Hayes. Boeckling is best known as the owner of the Cedar Point Amusement Park.

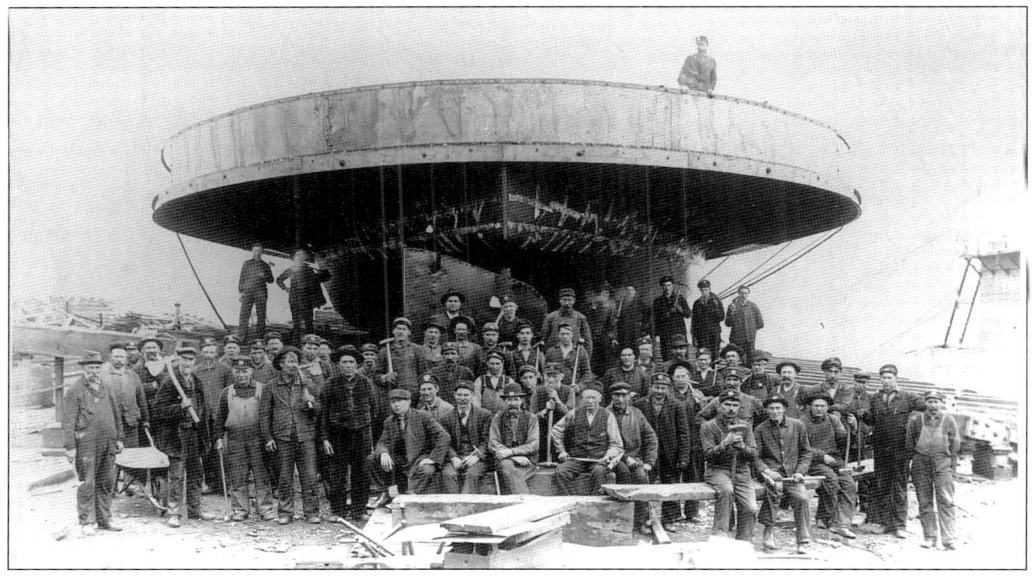

The G.A. Boeckling was built in Ecorse, Michigan, in 1909. Here, the shipyard crew poses in front of the steel hull of the ship as it was being constructed.

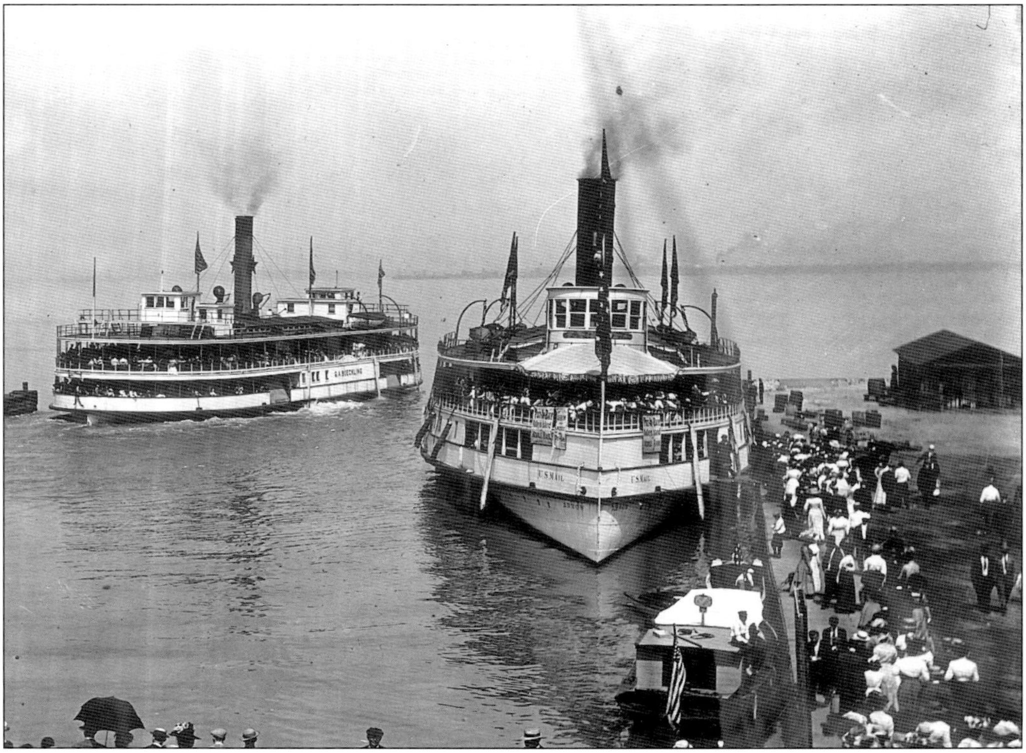

The G.A. *Boeckling* served on the Sandusky to Cedar Point run from 1909 to 1952. Here it is departing the dock at Sandusky, with the *Arrow* docked to the right.

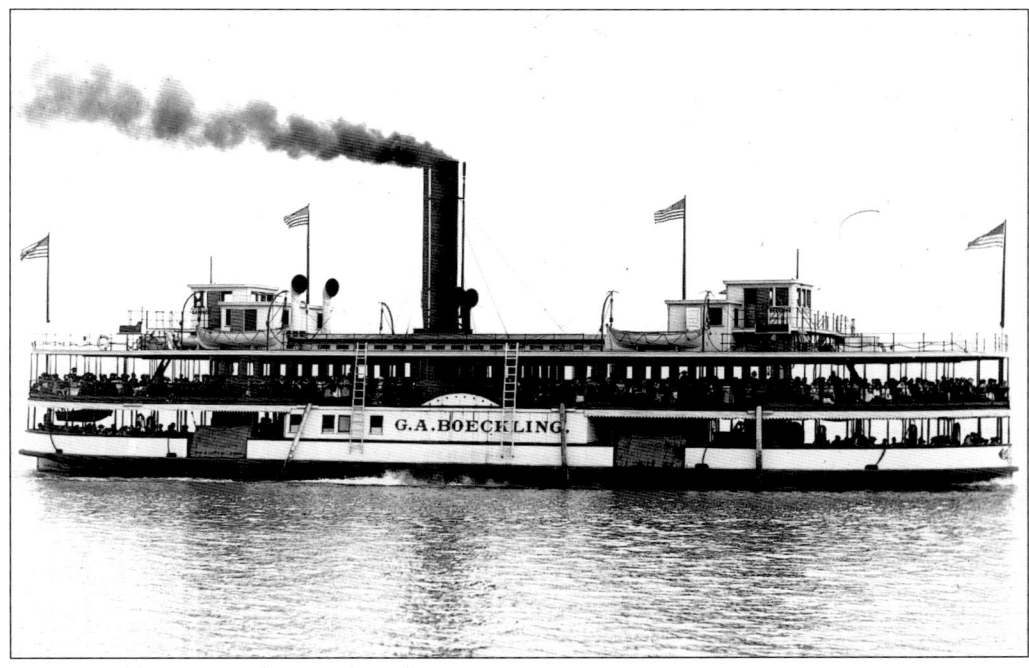

G.A. *Boeckling* pictured in its glory days.

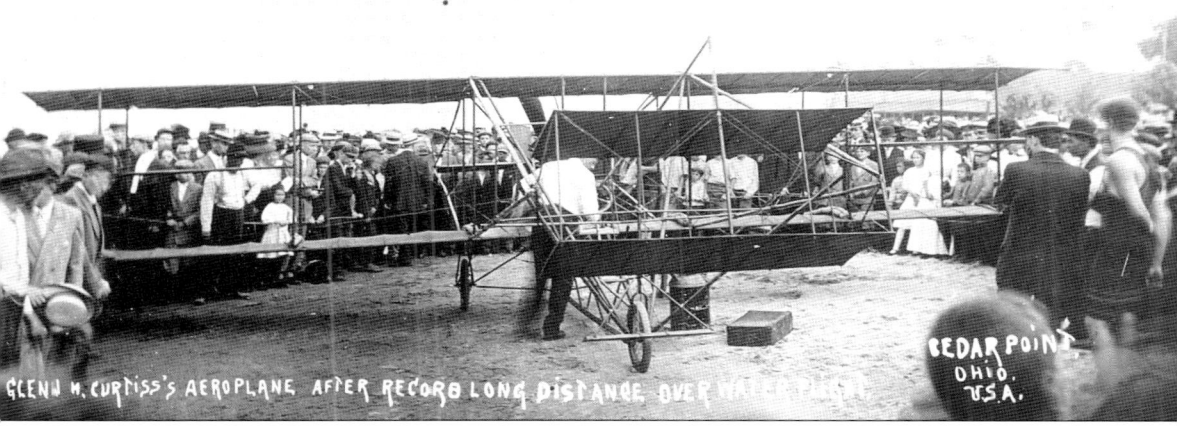

Few people might know that Sandusky played a role in the aviation revolution. At Cedar Point in 1910, pioneer aviator Glenn Curtiss set a record for the first flight over water in an airplane.

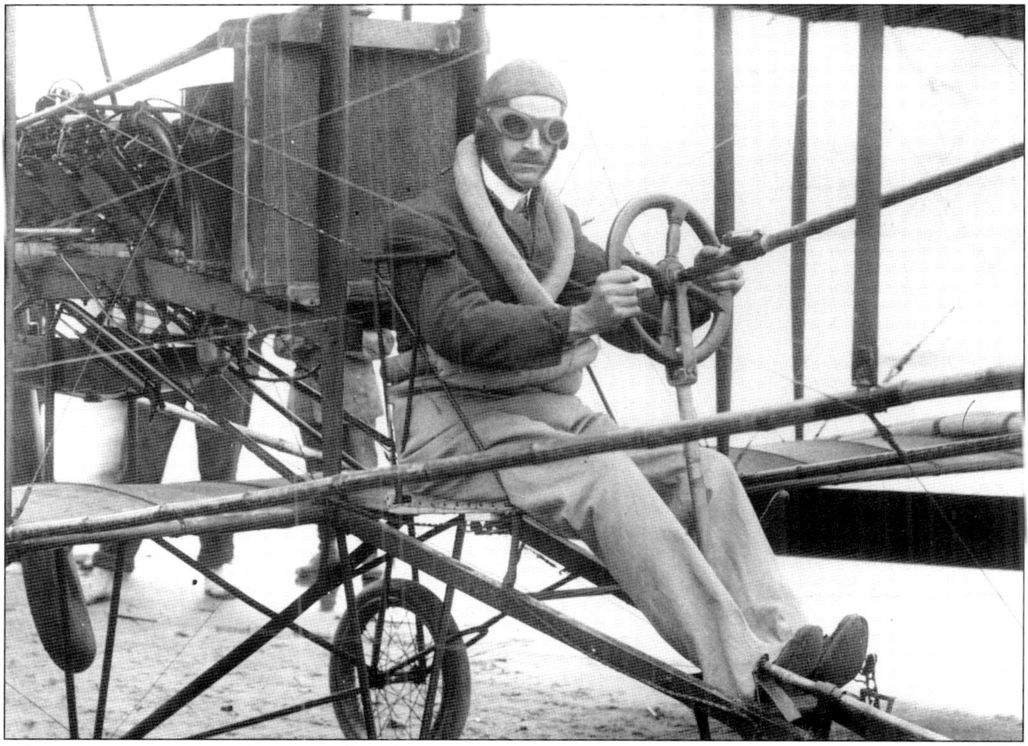

Glenn Curtiss, on Cedar Point beach, is seen just before takeoff, August 31, 1910.

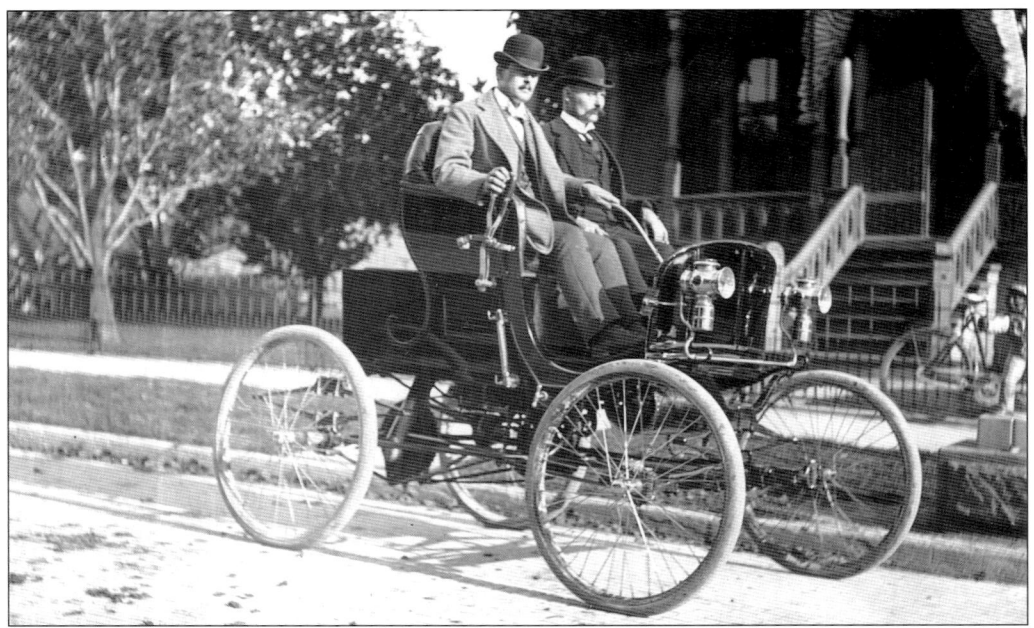

Sandusky also played a pioneering role in the development of the automobile. George Schade owned one of the city's first automobiles, an electric car called "The Sandusky." The Sandusky Automobile Company existed briefly in the first decade of the 20th century.

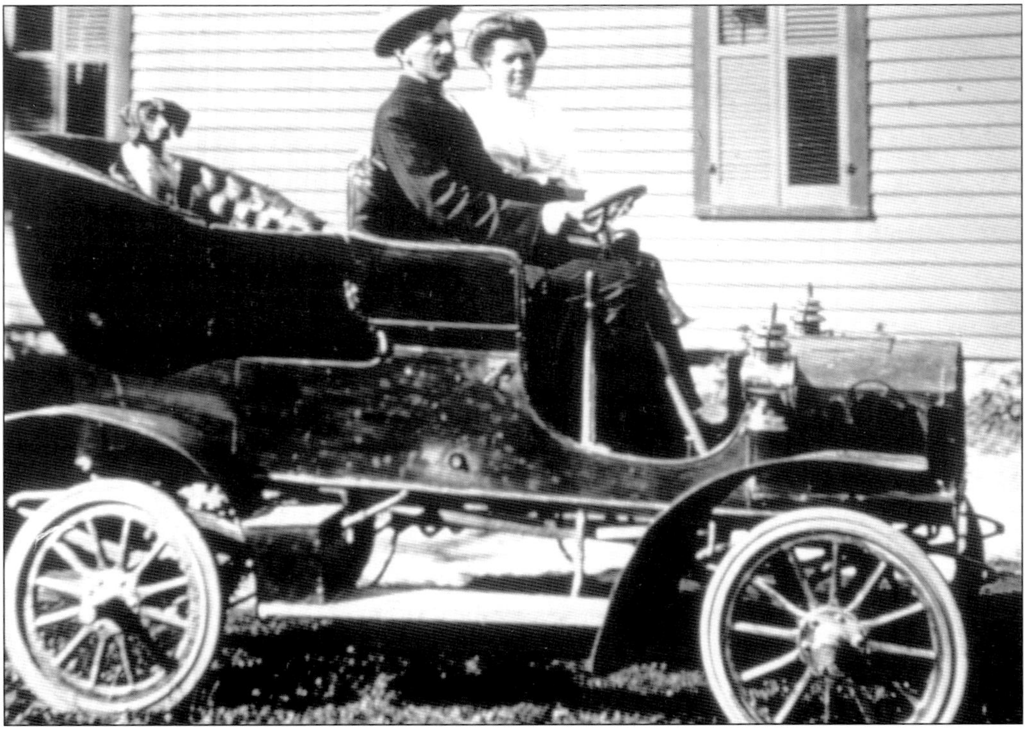

The same company also made the Courier automobile in 1904. The Brown family of Venice, Ohio, is seated in their Courier.

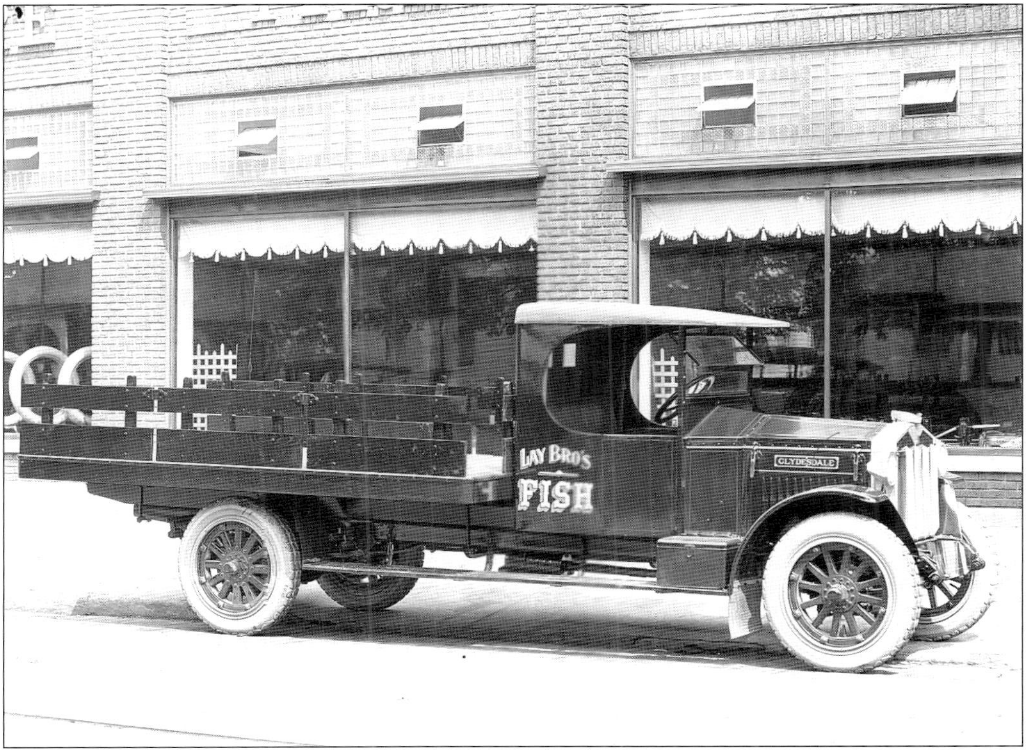

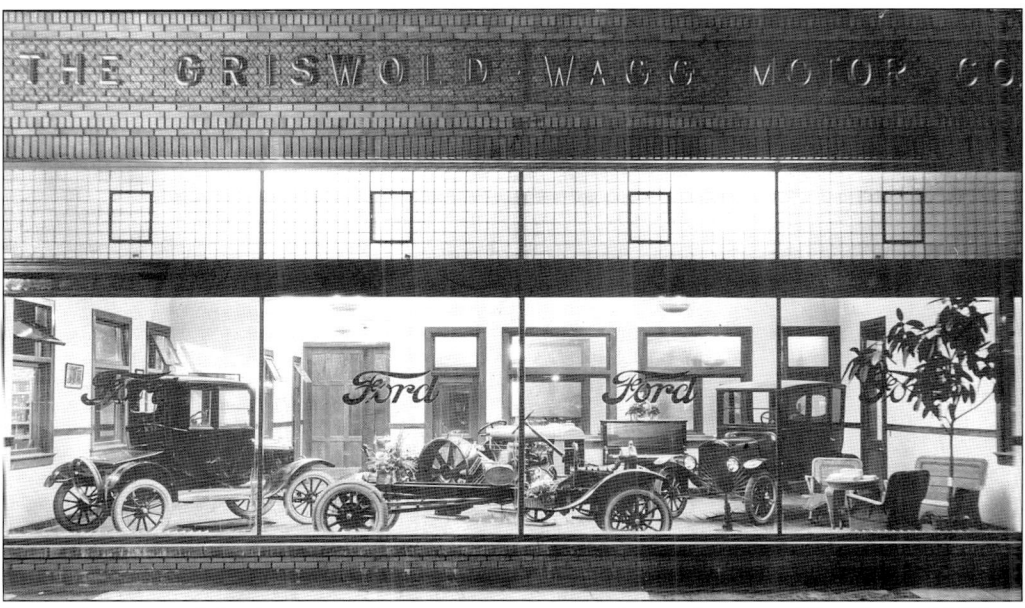

Of course the automobile industry grew rapidly. Motor vehicles soon replaced horse-drawn wagons for business deliveries. The Lay Brothers' Fisheries shows off its new Clydesdale truck, made in nearby Clyde, Ohio.

Soon the automobile showroom became a common sight in America. The Griswold Wagg Motor Company opened a showroom on East Washington Row in 1919.

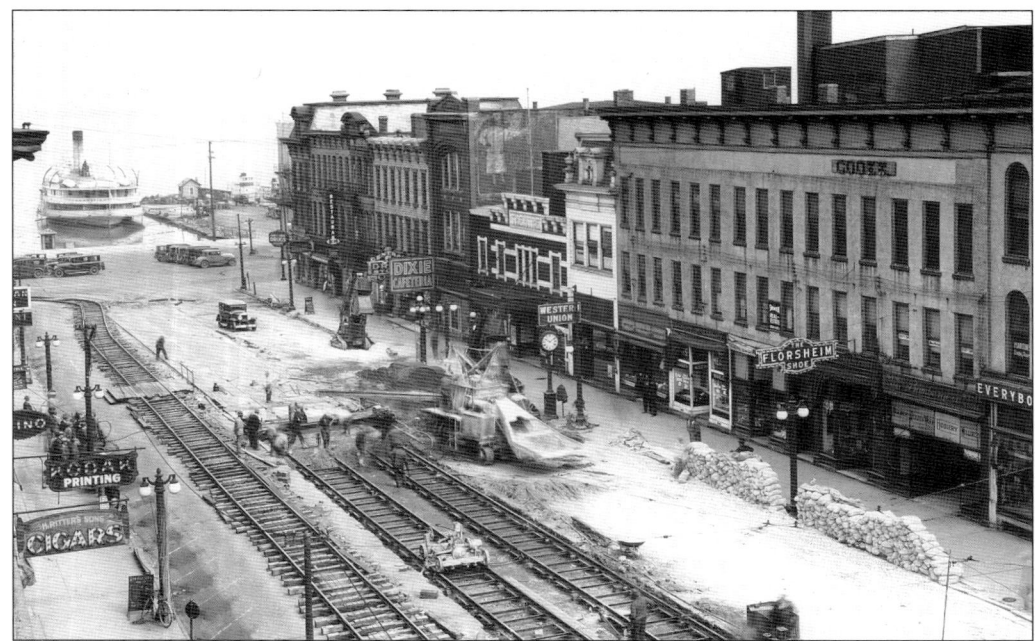

As the popularity of the automobile increased, the decline of the interurban system became inevitable. Although the tracks on Columbus Avenue originally laid in 1883 for the first horse-drawn trolleys were replaced in 1925, the trains that rode on these tracks did not survive much longer.

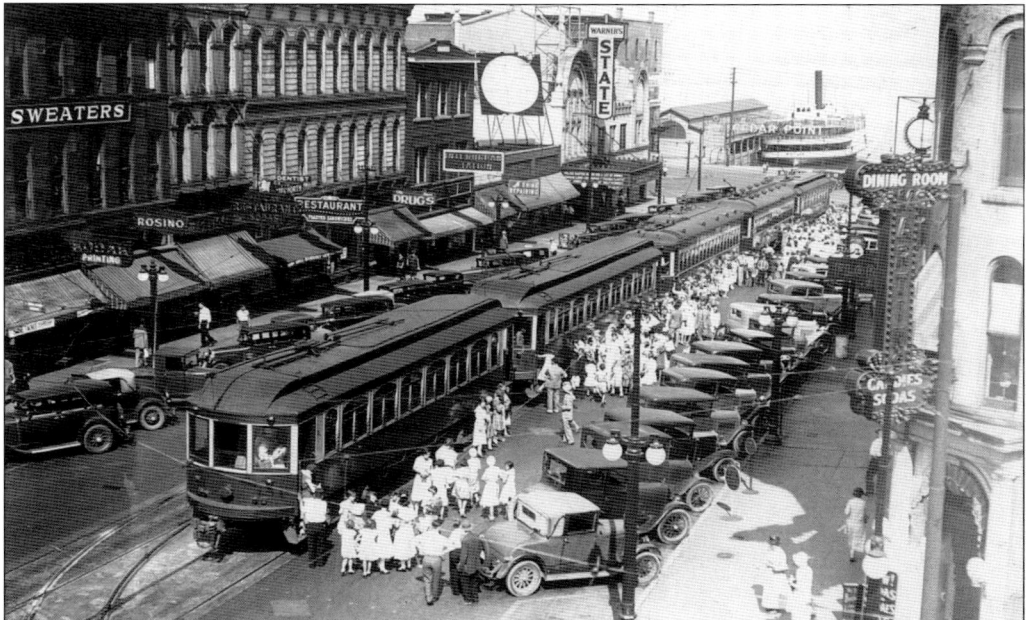

One of the last gasps for interurban service: A 4-H club excursion to Kelleys Island, September 12, 1931. The passengers are getting off the Lake Shore Interurban cars and preparing to board the steamer *Chippewa* in the background. In only a couple more decades, both the interurbans and the large steamships would be just memories.

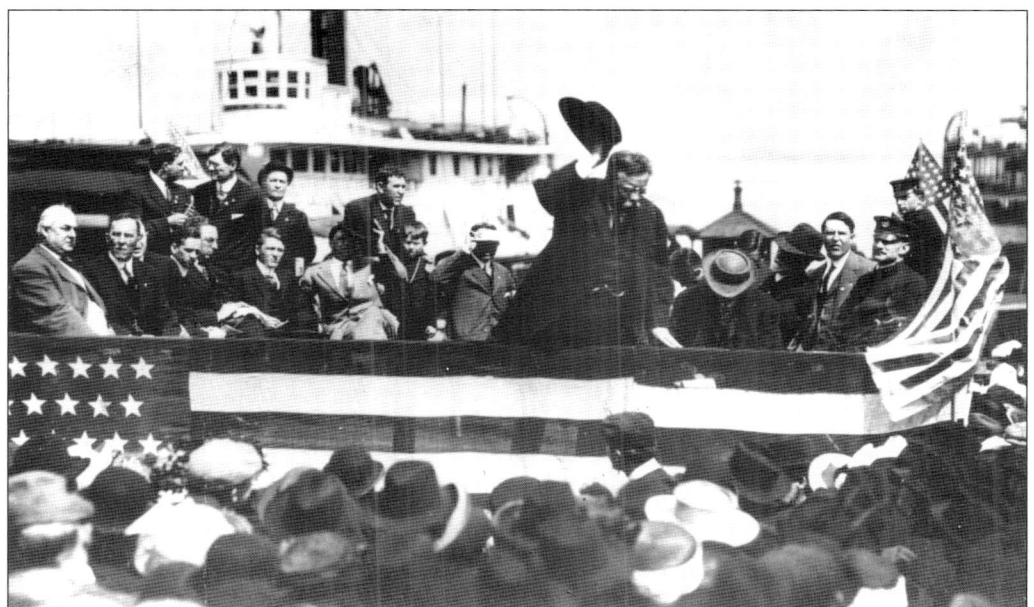

Sandusky has been long perceived as a "typical" Middle American city. This probably explains the number of political candidates who have made campaign appearances in the city. One of the biggest political events was when Theodore Roosevelt passed through town during the 1912 presidential campaign. He spoke at a rally at the foot of Columbus Avenue on May 15. Sandusky Mayor George T. Lehrer is at the far left.

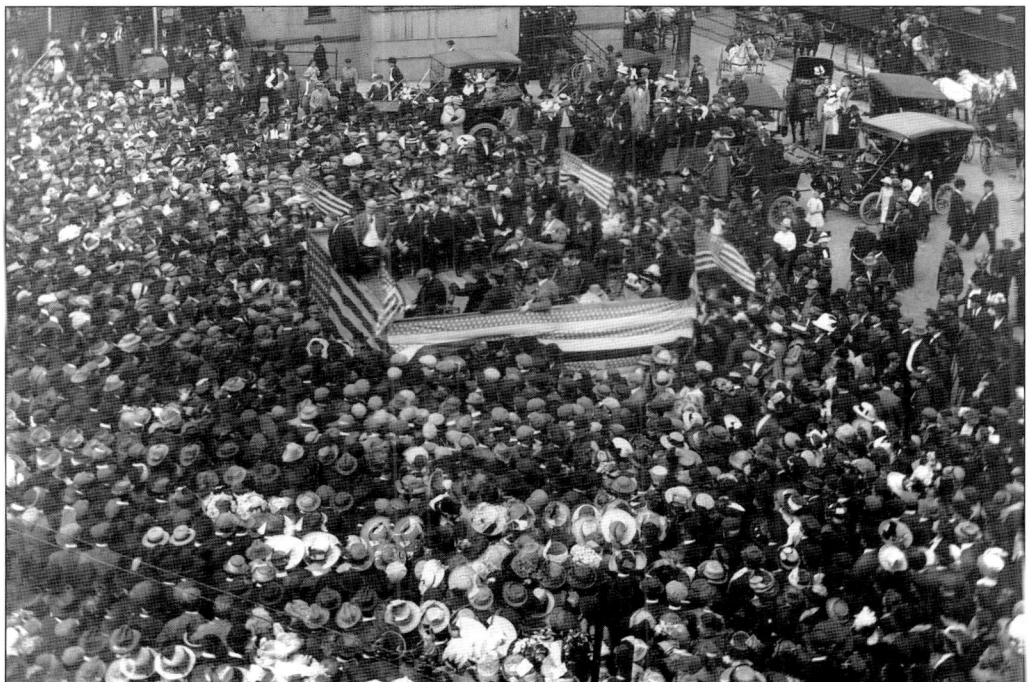

Roosevelt arrived on a special train, which can be seen in the background, to give his speech to a large crowd, of which apparently none forgot to wear a hat that day.

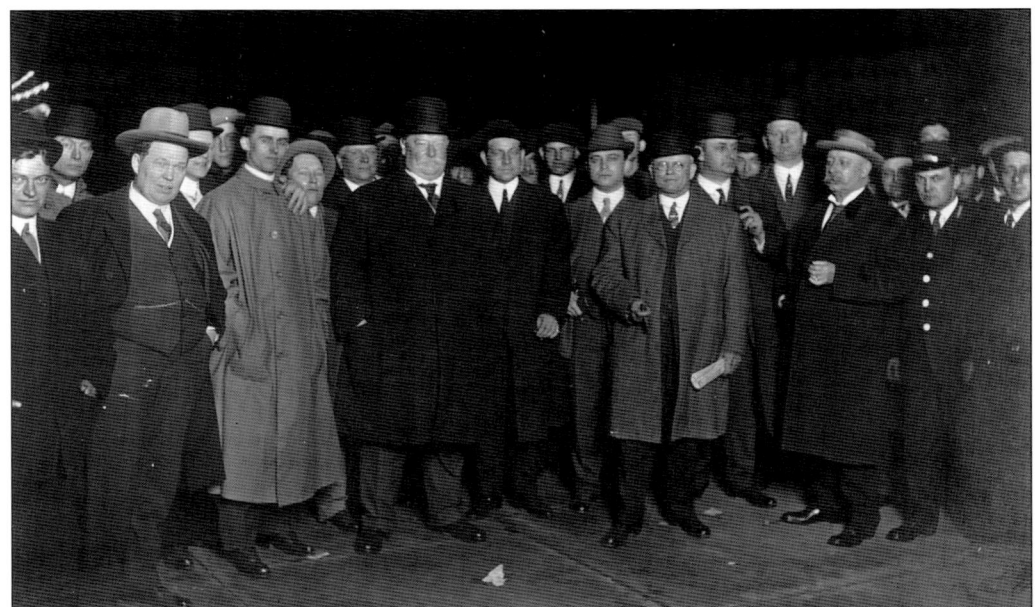

William Howard Taft visited the area several times for personal reasons—a close friend, Edward H. Marsh, lived on Washington Street—but also made political appearances, as in this gathering during the 1908 presidential campaign. During that visit, he gave a speech at the Soldier's Home.

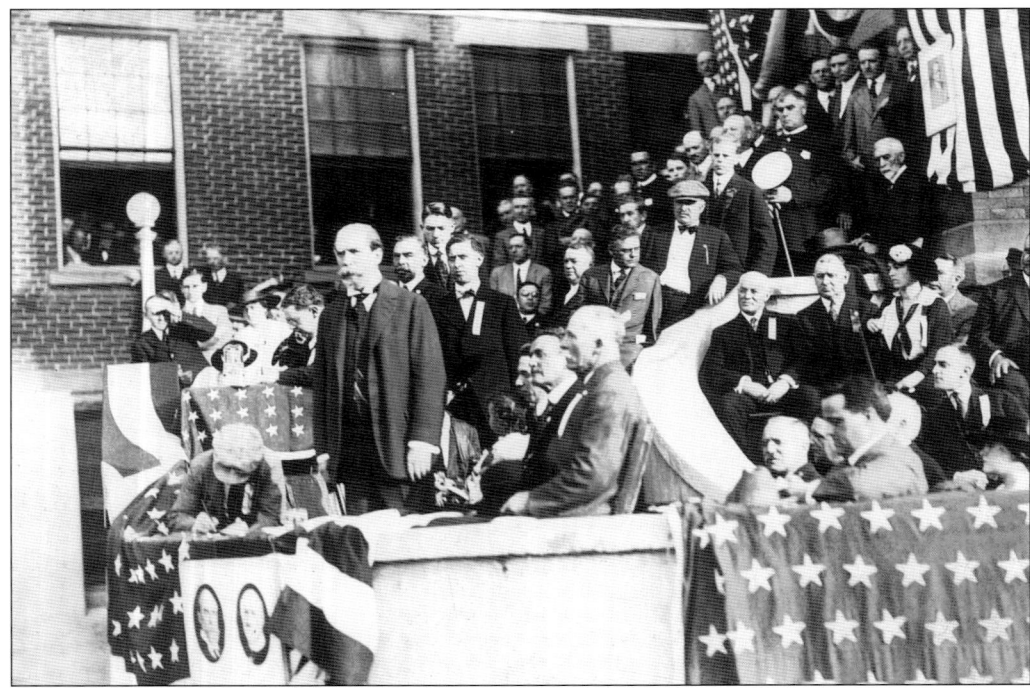

In 1916, Charles Evans Hughes made an appearance in Sandusky during his unsuccessful campaign against Woodrow Wilson. He spoke at a rally outside the American Crayon Company building on September 26.

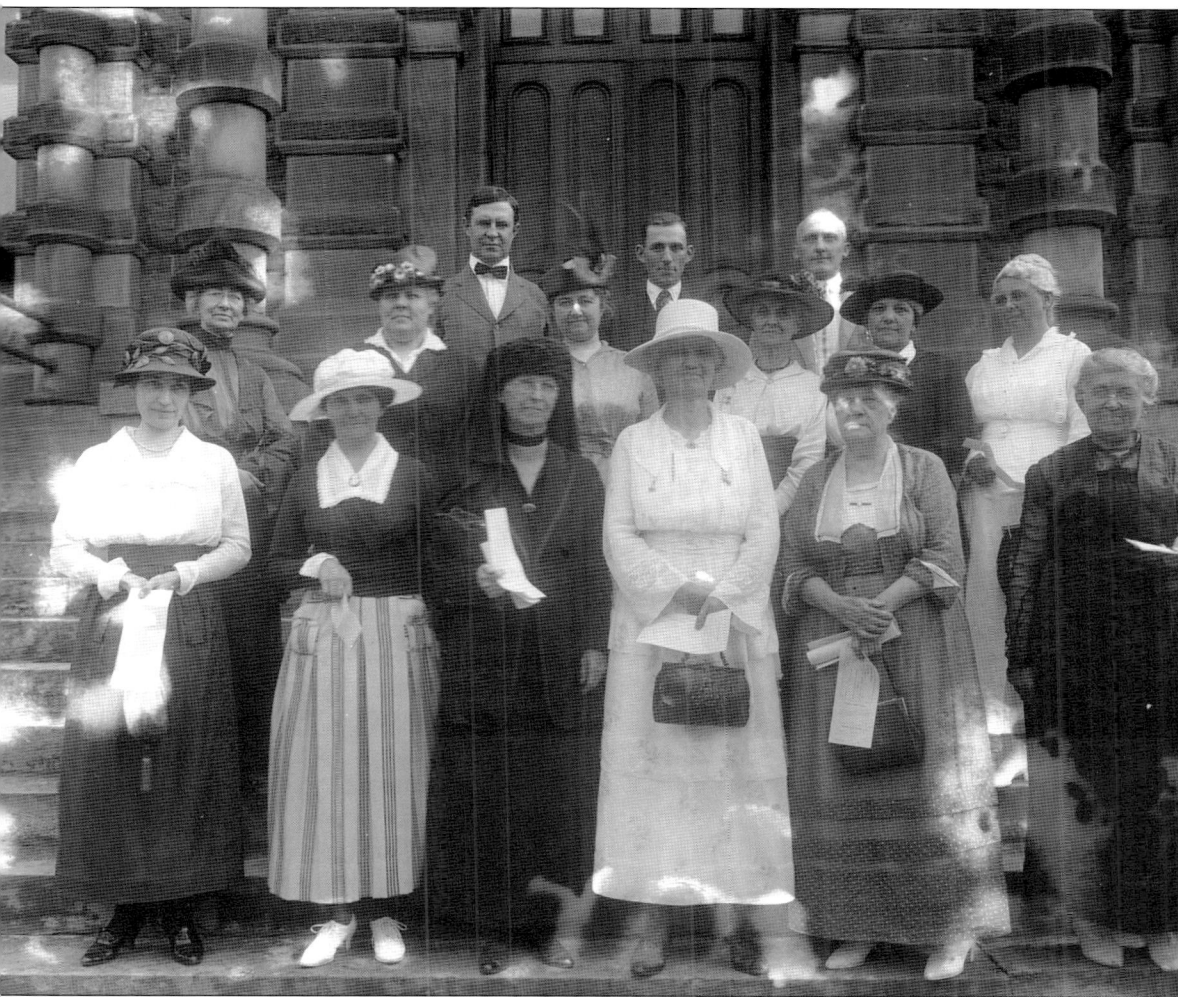

Some might forget that women were not allowed to vote for those candidates who visited Sandusky, as woman were not granted the right to vote in the United States until 1920. Consequently, women were not eligible to serve on juries until then. The first jury in Erie County that included women was composed entirely of women, on August 26, 1920. In the back row is Judge Roy H. Williams and the attorneys in the case.

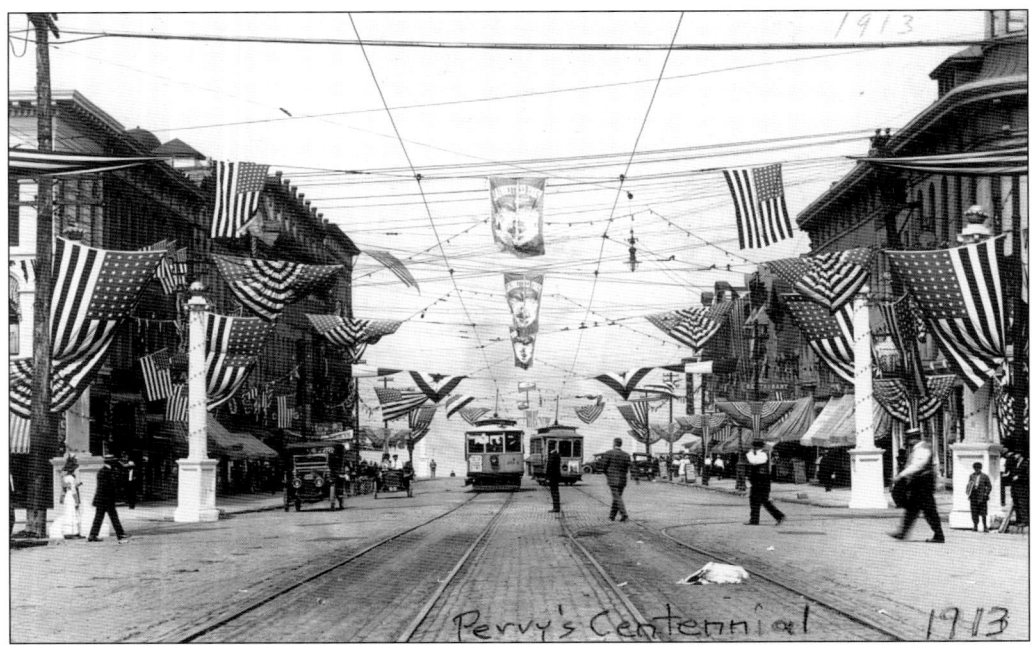

Community celebrations were even more popular in the 20th century. Among the more popular events were the city centennial in 1924, the Grape Festival in the 1930s, winter carnivals, and the Perry's Victory centennial celebration in 1913. The city was decked out to commemorate Commodore Perry's victory over the British Fleet in the War of 1812. The Battle of Lake Erie was fought in the waters around Put-in-Bay, near Sandusky.

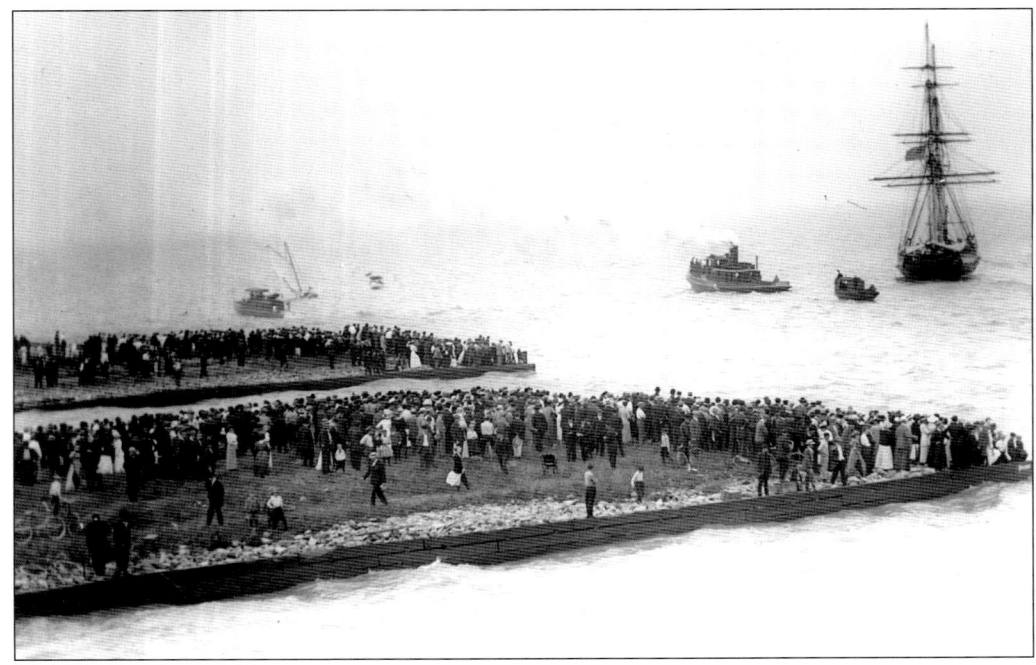

One of the biggest events in the Perry's Centennial was the arrival of the restored ship *Niagara*, used by Perry in the battle. Crowds gathered at the Jackson Street slip awaiting the ship's arrival.

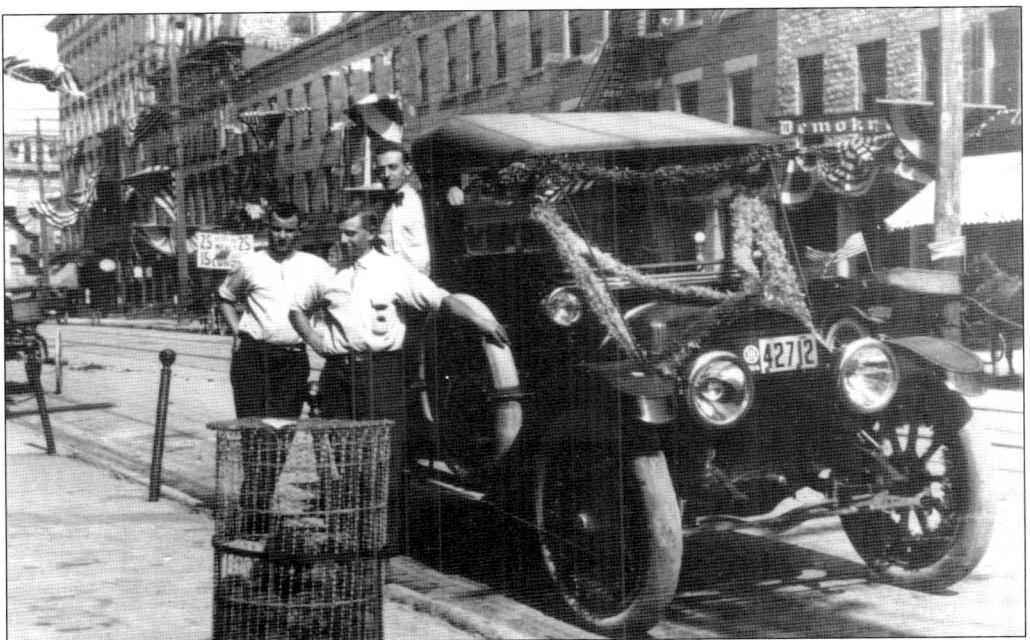

As with most public celebrations of the time, a parade was the highlight event. This truck, owned by the Donahue Hardware store, is decorated for the Perry's Victory parade in downtown Sandusky.

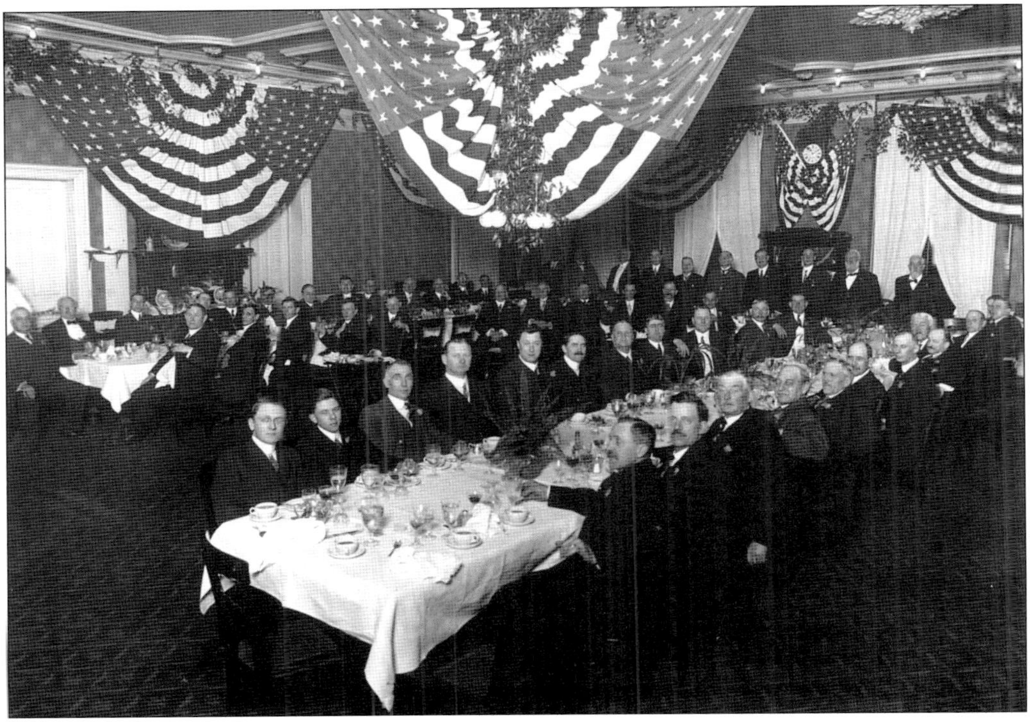

Preparation for the Perry celebration was elaborate. The Inter-City Perry's Centennial Commission helped to coordinate events, and hosted a banquet at the Sloane House hotel on January 14, 1913.

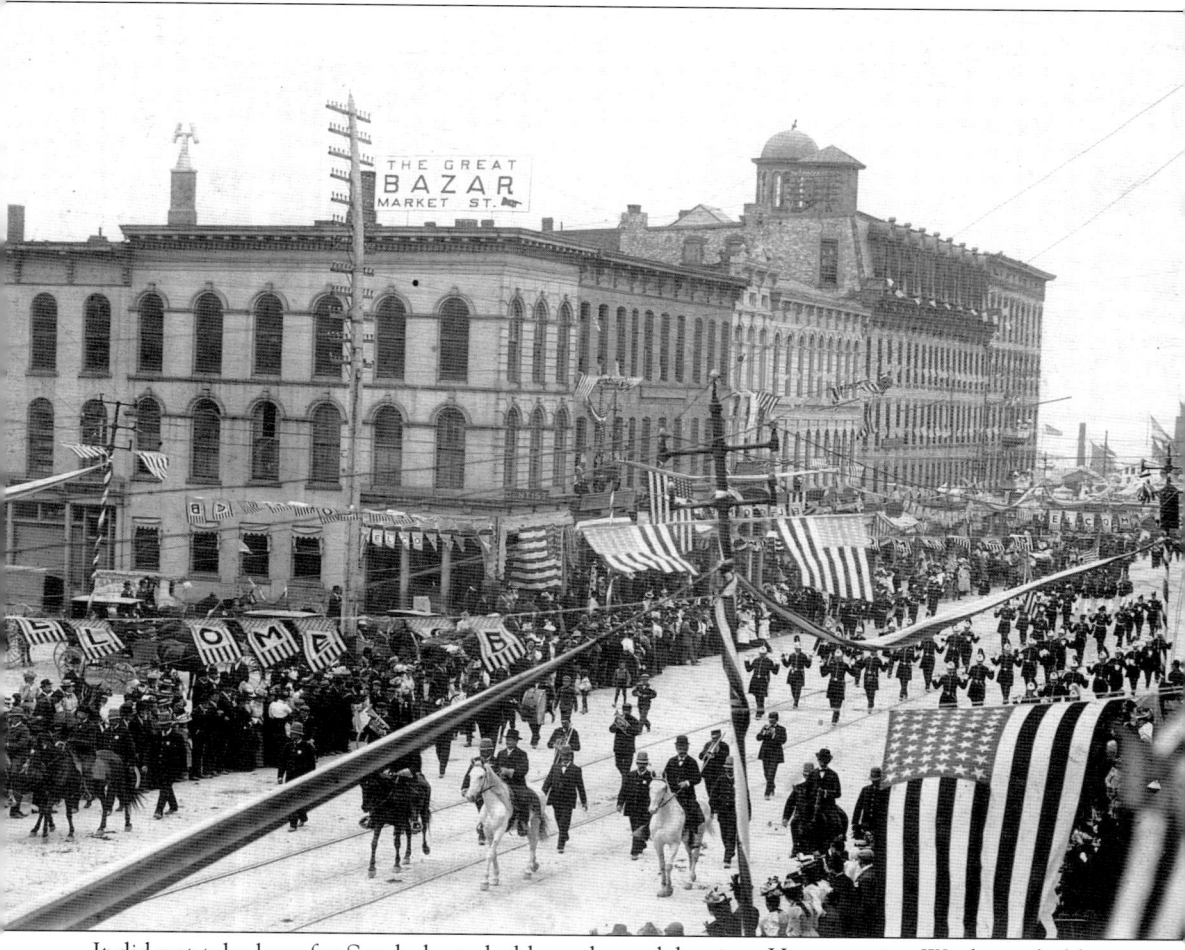

It did not take long for Sandusky to hold another celebration. Homecoming Week was held in July 1914 in honor of former Sanduskians. It was estimated that thousands of persons traveled to Sandusky to take part in the festivities. And of course, one of the biggest events of the week was a parade down Columbus Avenue, with welcoming banners draped over the street.

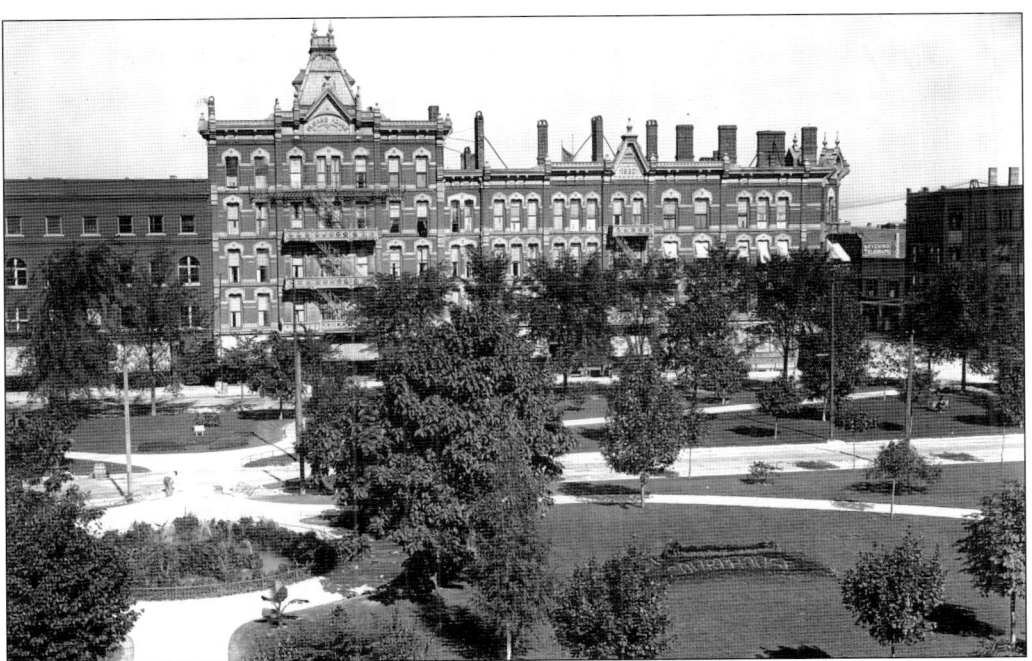

Many Sanduskians are especially proud of their parks system, with its green spaces and attractive landscaping. Washington Park, seen here at the turn of the century, is particularly noteworthy for its landscaping and landmarks. This view is from the county courthouse, with the Sloane House in the background.

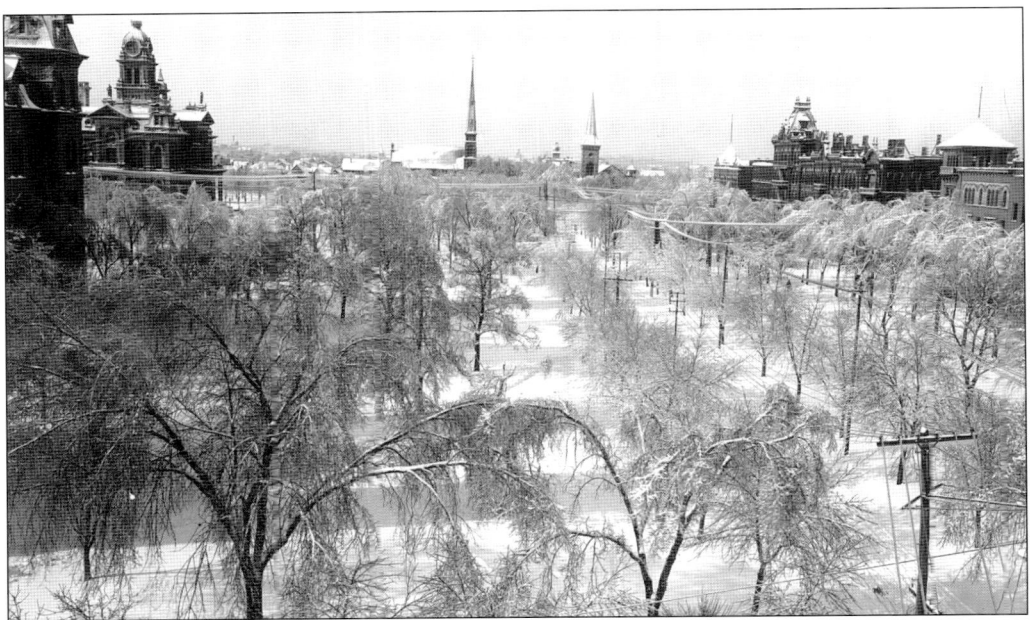

Here is another view of Washington Park, after the sleet storm of February 14, 1909. A portion of the old high school is visible at the extreme left, with the courthouse (before it was remodeled) beyond it. The storm created beautiful scenes, but did significant damage in the city. Many power lines were toppled and some buildings were damaged.

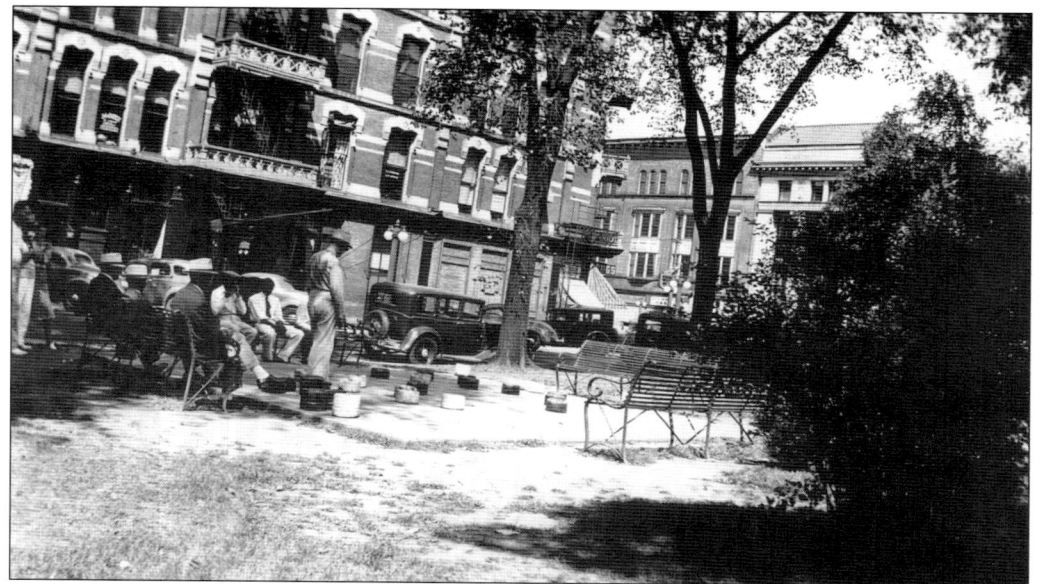

A large checkerboard in Washington Park, c. 1940, was popular with many residents.

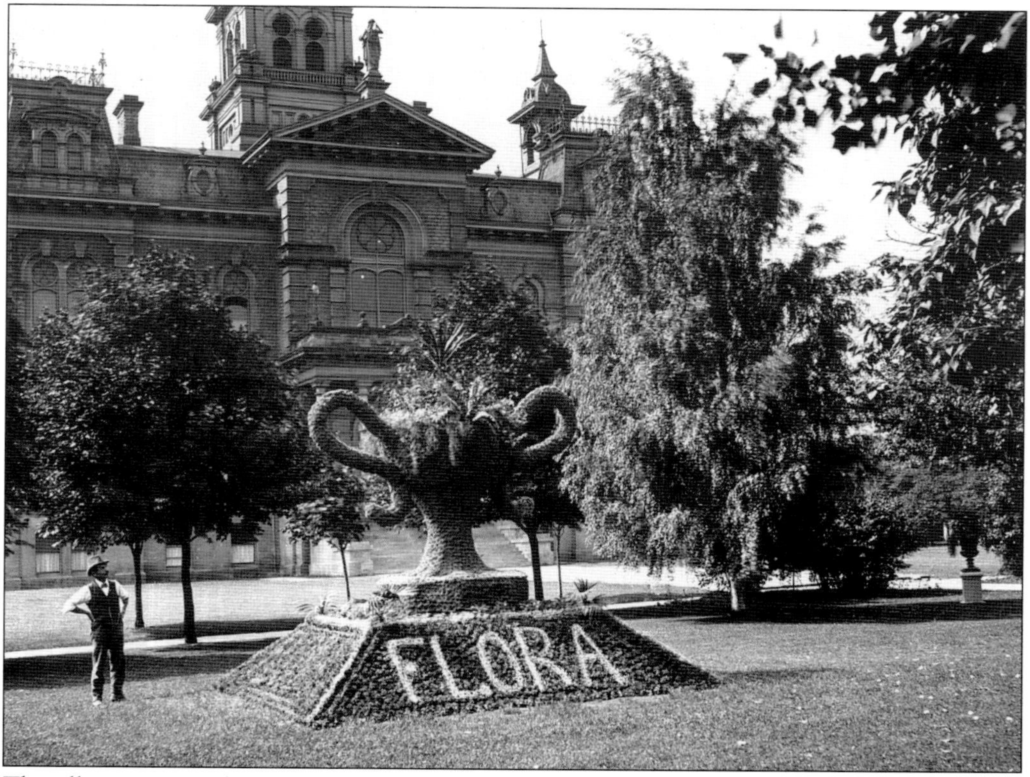

This illustration spells out what is perhaps most popular about Washington Park. The floral displays are often elaborate—sometimes decorated in mounds to commemorate special events, organizations, or citizens of achievement. This mound, c. 1910, simply celebrates the plants that give the park its beauty.

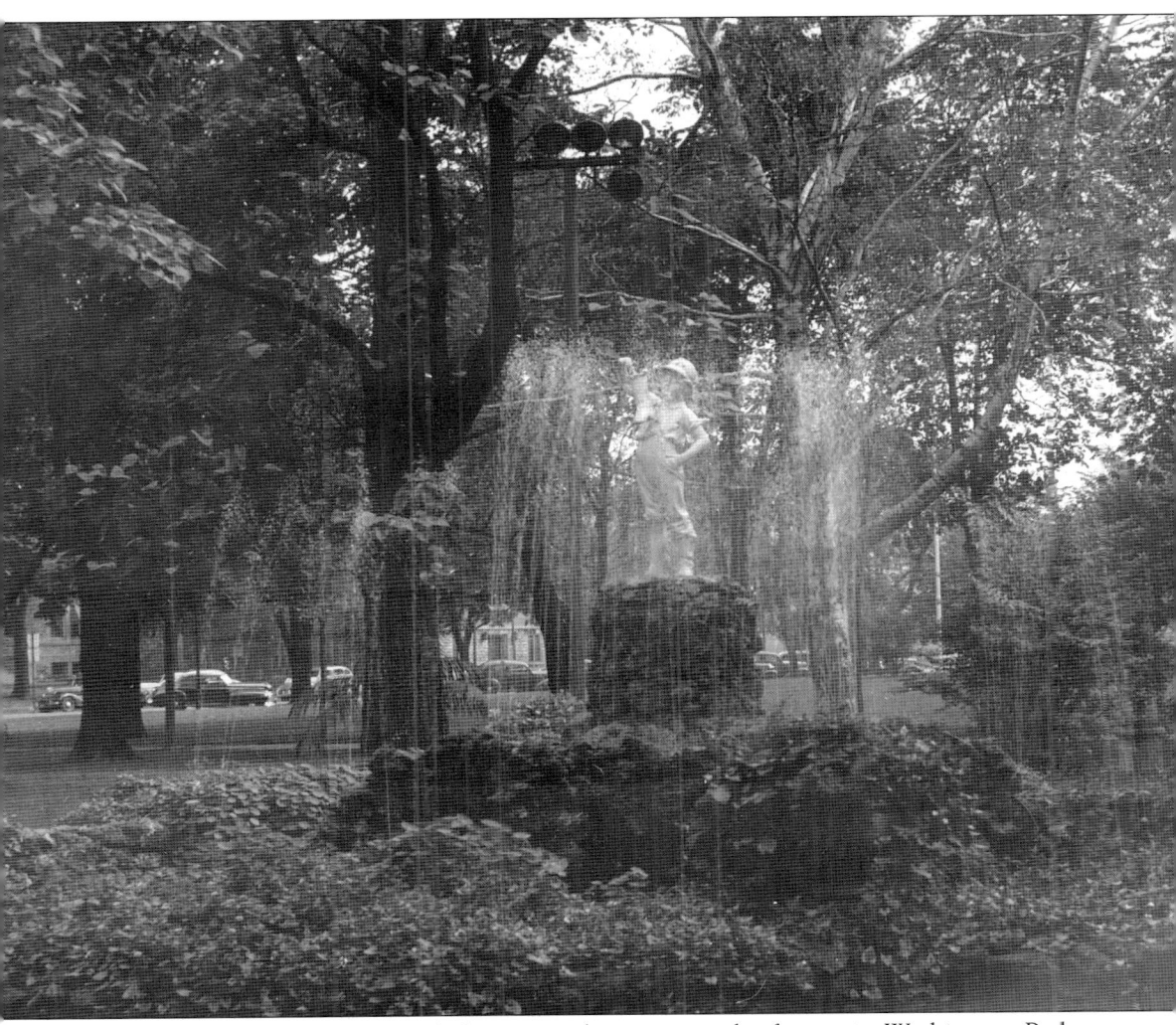

Some may argue that the *Boy with the Boot* is the most popular feature in Washington Park. Brought to Sandusky by Voltaire Scott in 1895, the *Boy* has been an interesting fixture in front of the courthouse since the 1930s.

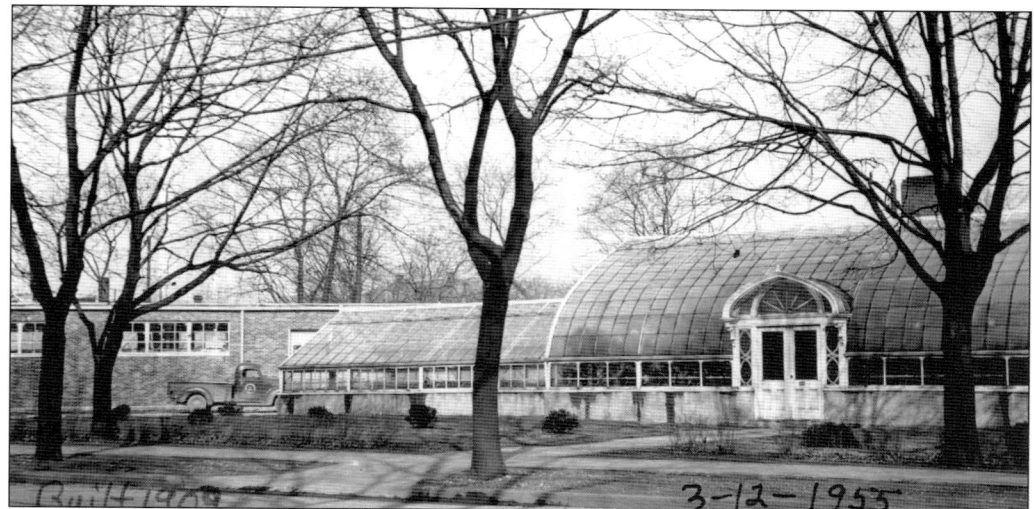

The City of Sandusky Greenhouse on East Monroe Street is the primary source for the beauty of the parks. City workers cultivate the plants for the park decorations in the greenhouse, which was built in 1909.

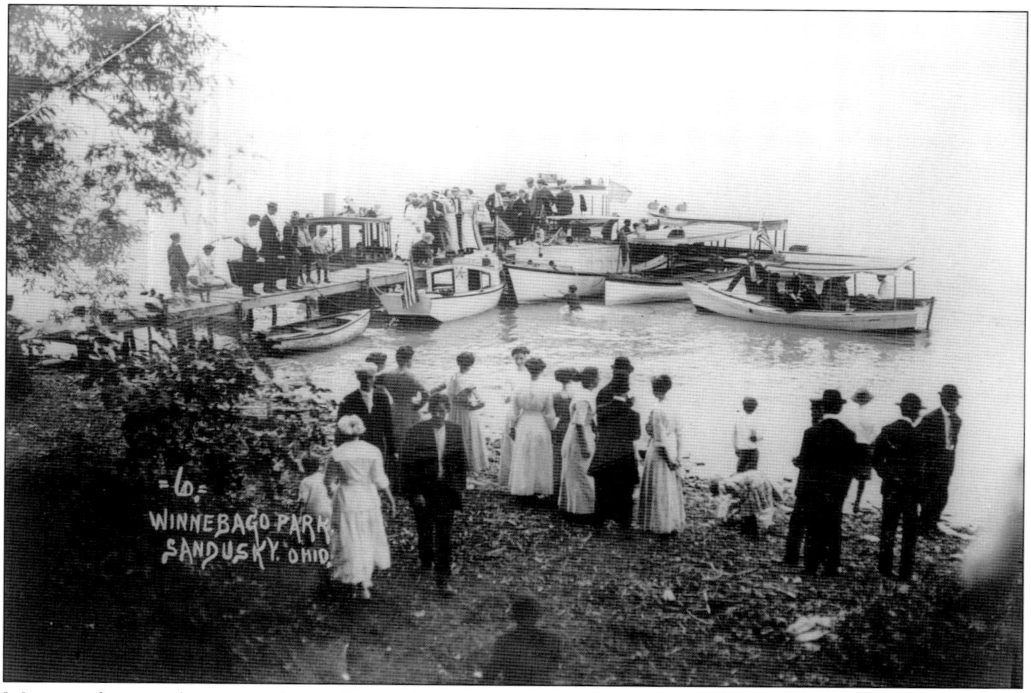

Many other parks exist throughout the city, with the parks along the bay shore among the most popular. This is a scene from Winnebago Park, c. 1910, when it was a private park. It was renamed Lions Park in 1927, after the Lions Club donated the park (given to them by George Eger) to the city.

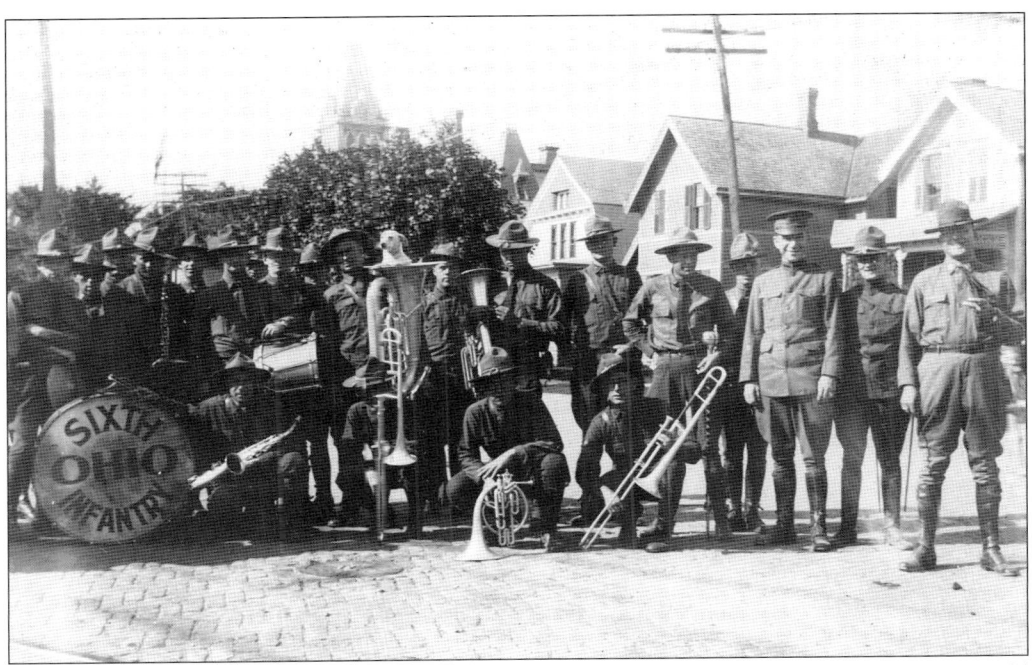

As with the rest of the country, Sandusky did its part in service to the nation during the world wars. Here we see the band of the Sixth Ohio Infantry in Sandusky during World War I.

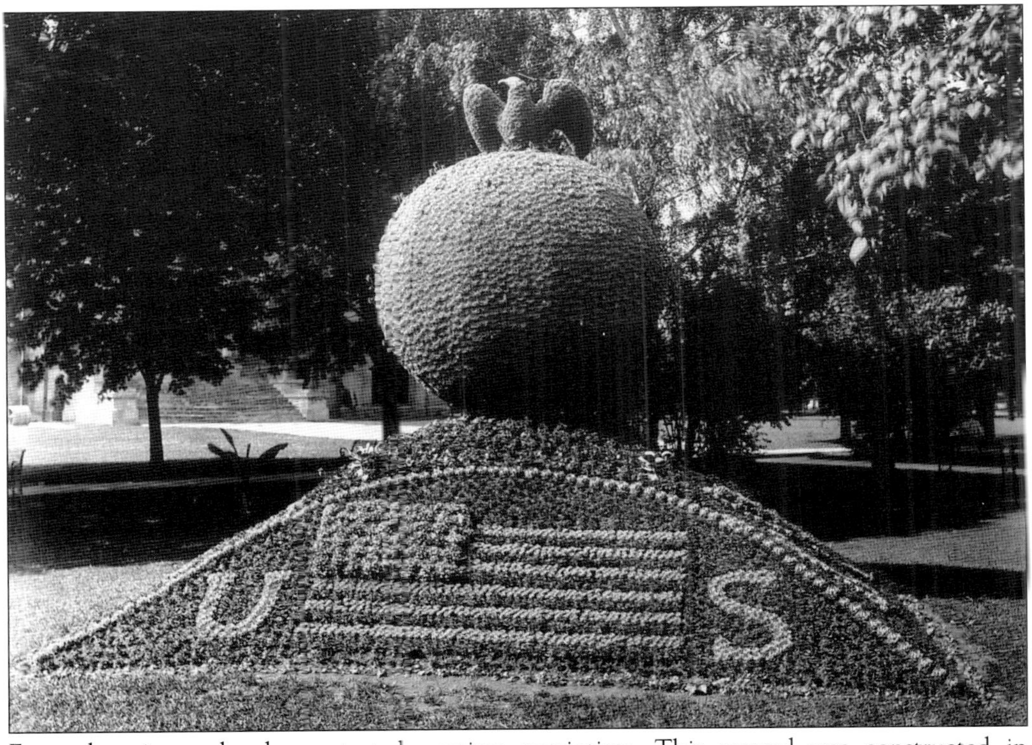

Even the city parks demonstrated wartime patriotism. This mound was constructed in Washington Park in 1917.

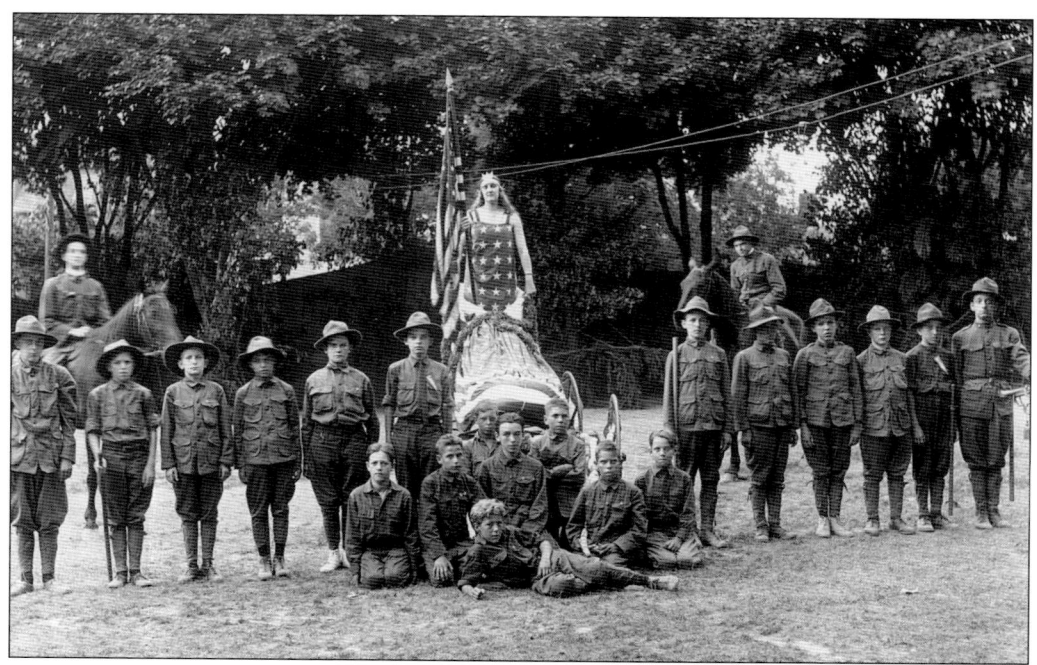

Although the United States did not enter World War I until 1917, preparation for war began much earlier. This scene of Boy Scouts in Washington Park in 1916 suggests the future that was in store for the people of Sandusky and the patriotism that was aroused by world events.

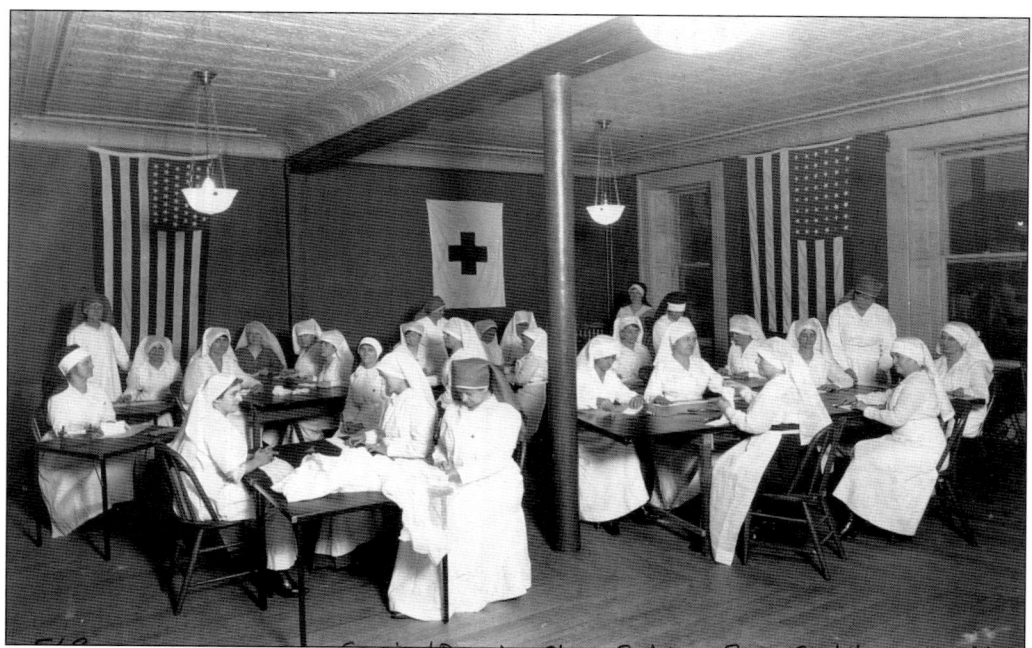

As in all wars, home front contributions are important. Here women are in a surgical dressing class sponsored by the Red Cross and held in the Roct House at the corner of Adams and Hancock Streets.

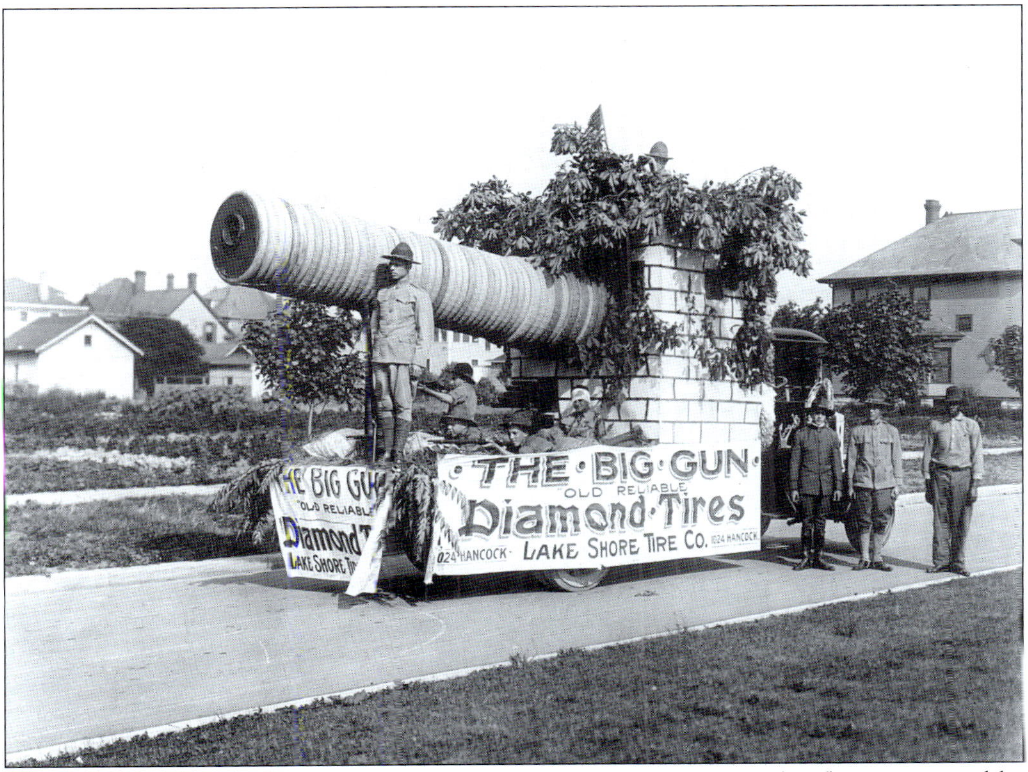

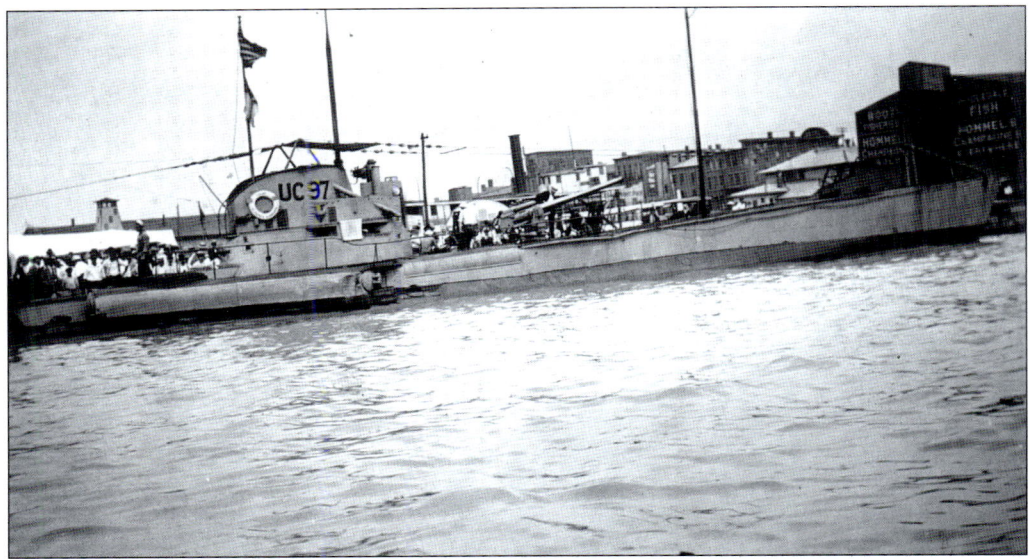

Business also did its part to promote wartime patriotism. Presumably, this float, sponsored by the Lake Shore Tire Company, was in a Fourth of July parade in 1918.

After World War I, a German submarine that the allies had taken as part of their war reparations visited Sandusky, landing briefly at the Jackson Street dock. The U-boat *UC 97* toured Great Lakes ports during the summer of 1919 as a promotional tool for a Victory Bond drive.

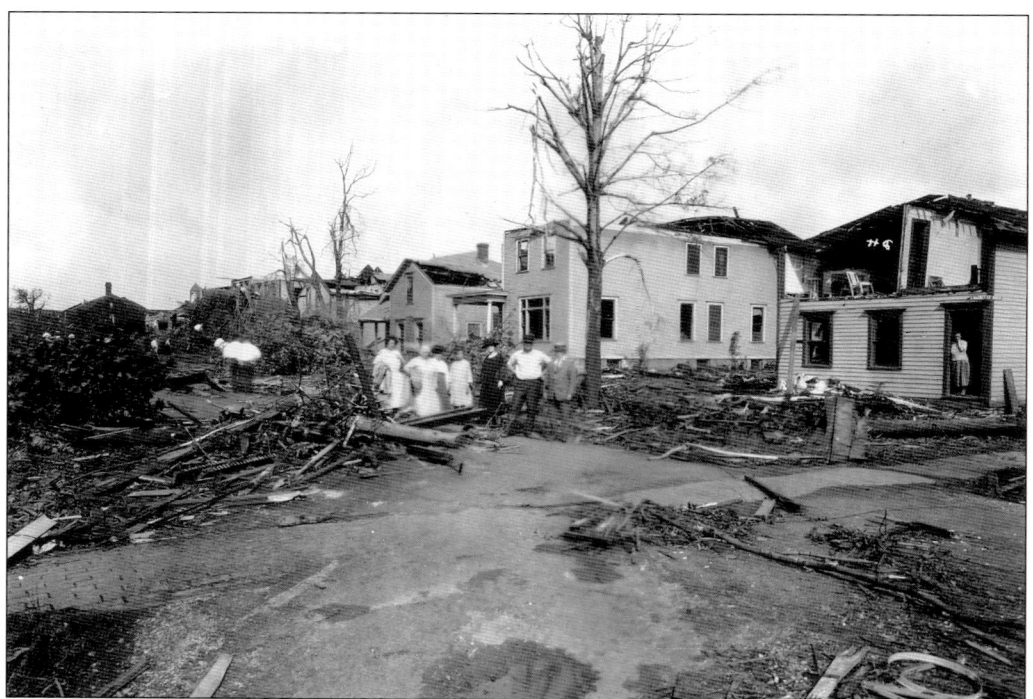

In the afternoon of June 28, 1924, one of the largest tornadoes in United States history destroyed a substantial portion of downtown Sandusky along the bay shore, killing eight people. Incredibly, the same tornado system traveled nearly 30 miles east to Lorain, where more than 70 were killed. This scene of the devastation is at East Market and Meigs Streets.

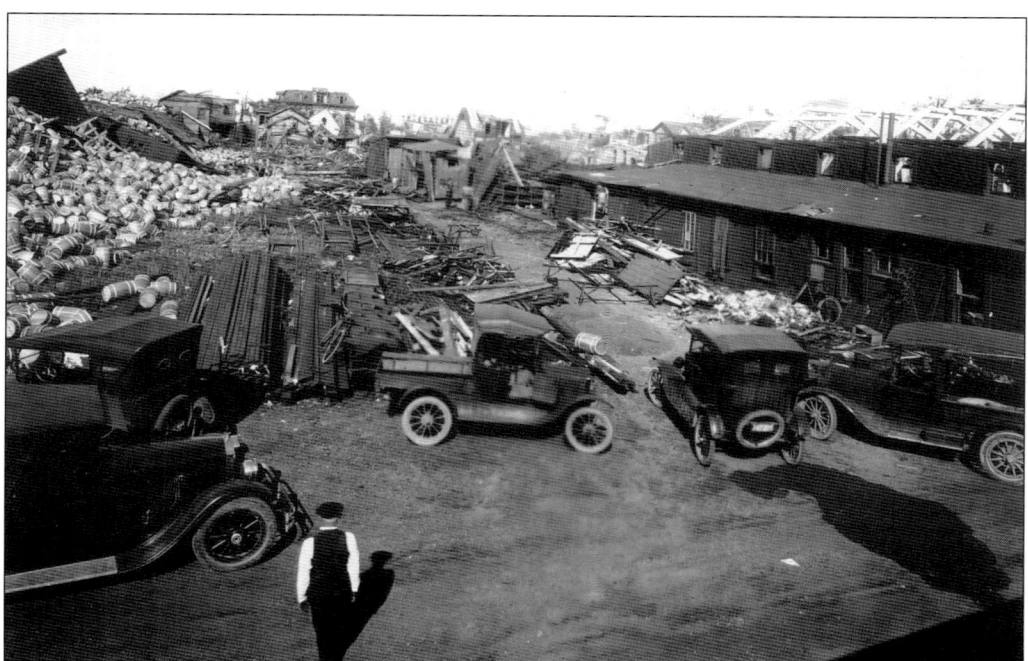

The wreckage of the Kilbourn Cooperage on Water Street illustrates the extent of the damage.

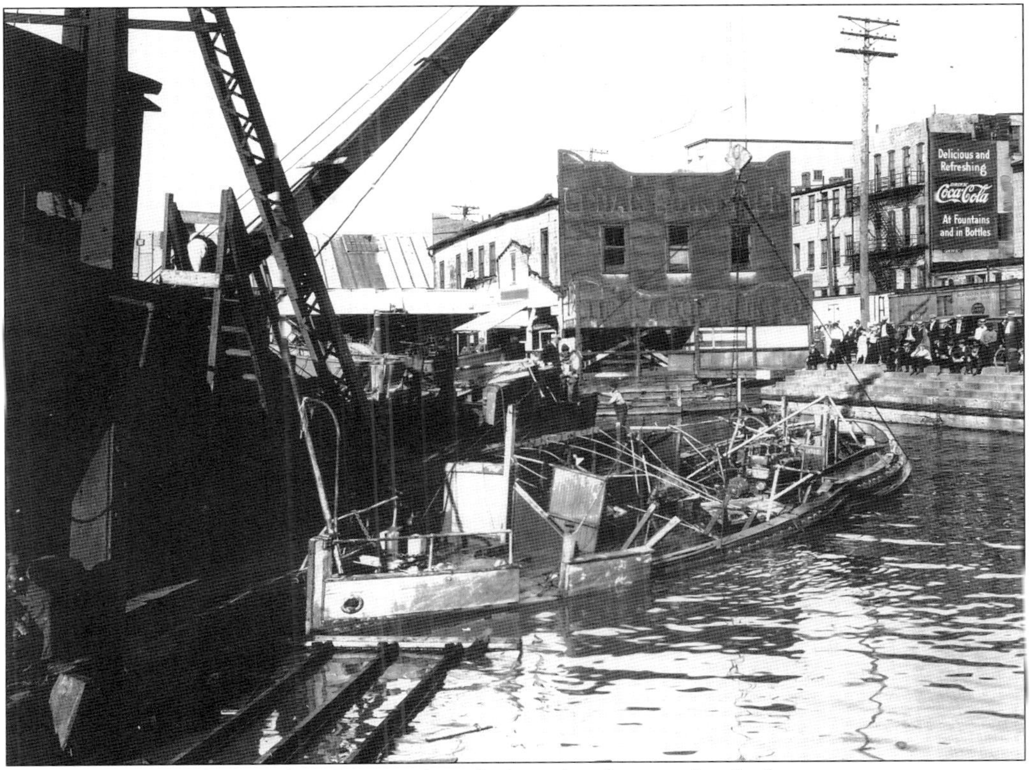

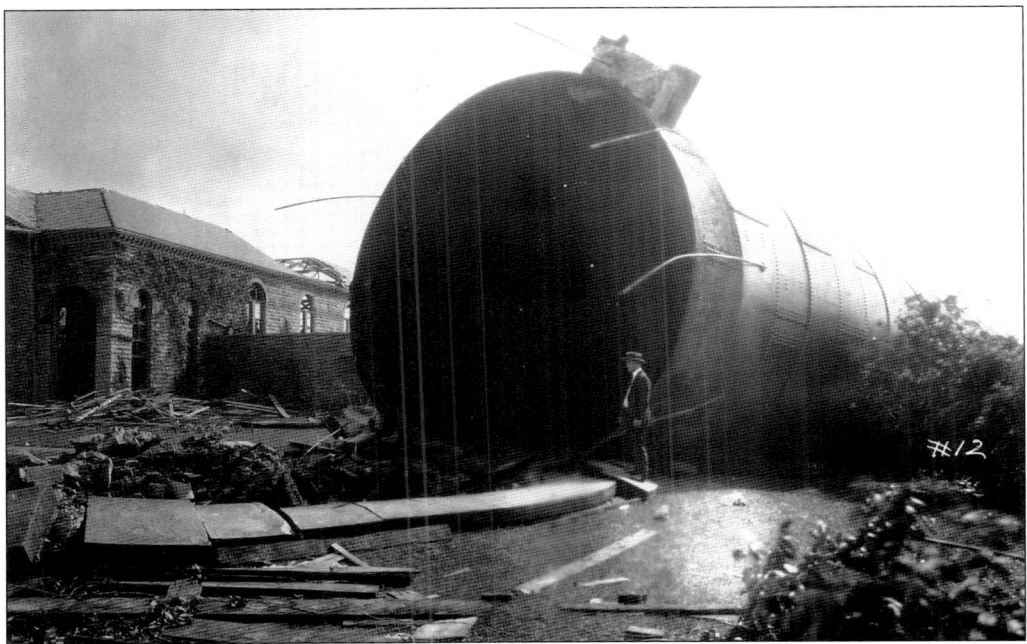

Many boats were damaged or destroyed, including this ferry at the dock.

The standpipe of the Sandusky Water Works on Meigs Street toppled from the force of the tornado.

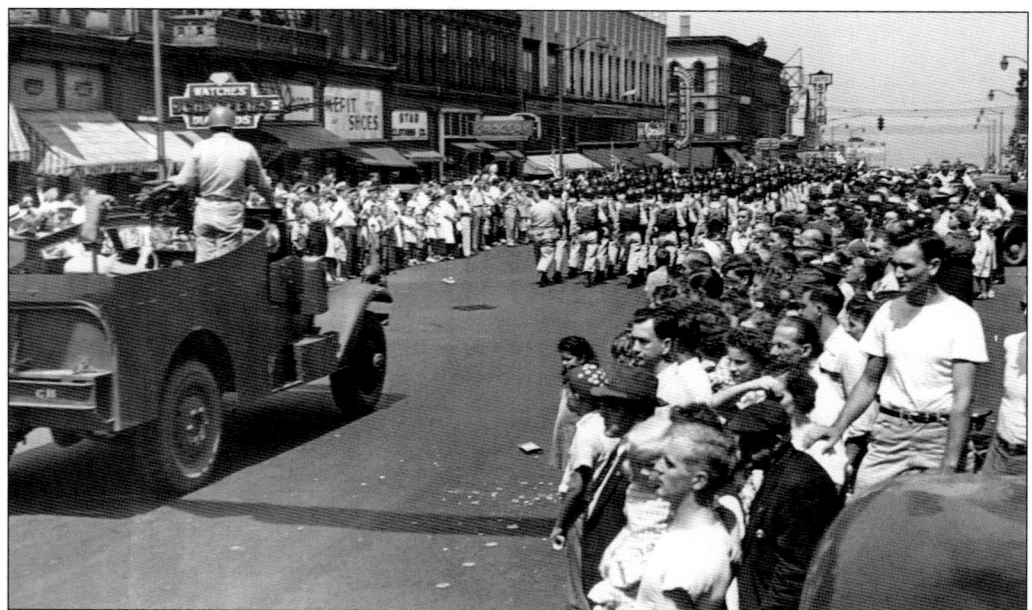

The recurring theme of Sandusky's history is one of resilience in conquering adversity. This resilience was reflected nationally in the victory of World War II. As expected, Sandusky contributed its part in the war effort and shared in the joy of victory. The All-Ohio Veterans Day Parade marched down Columbus Avenue on August 3, 1946.

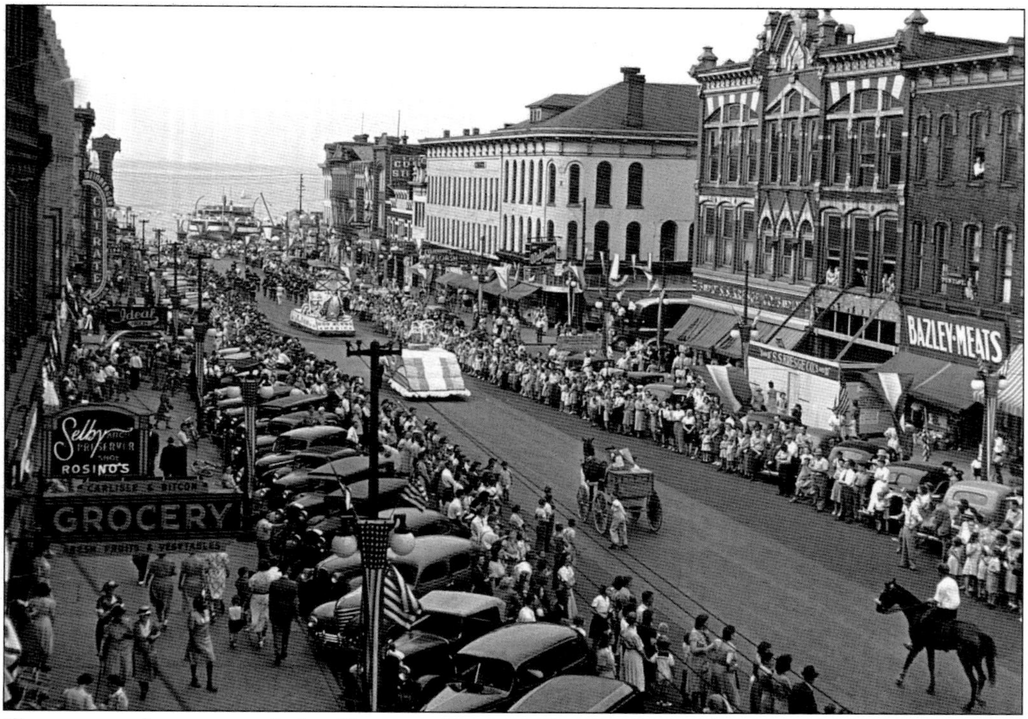

Here is another view of the Veterans Day parade. Sandusky Bay is visible at the foot of Columbus Avenue.

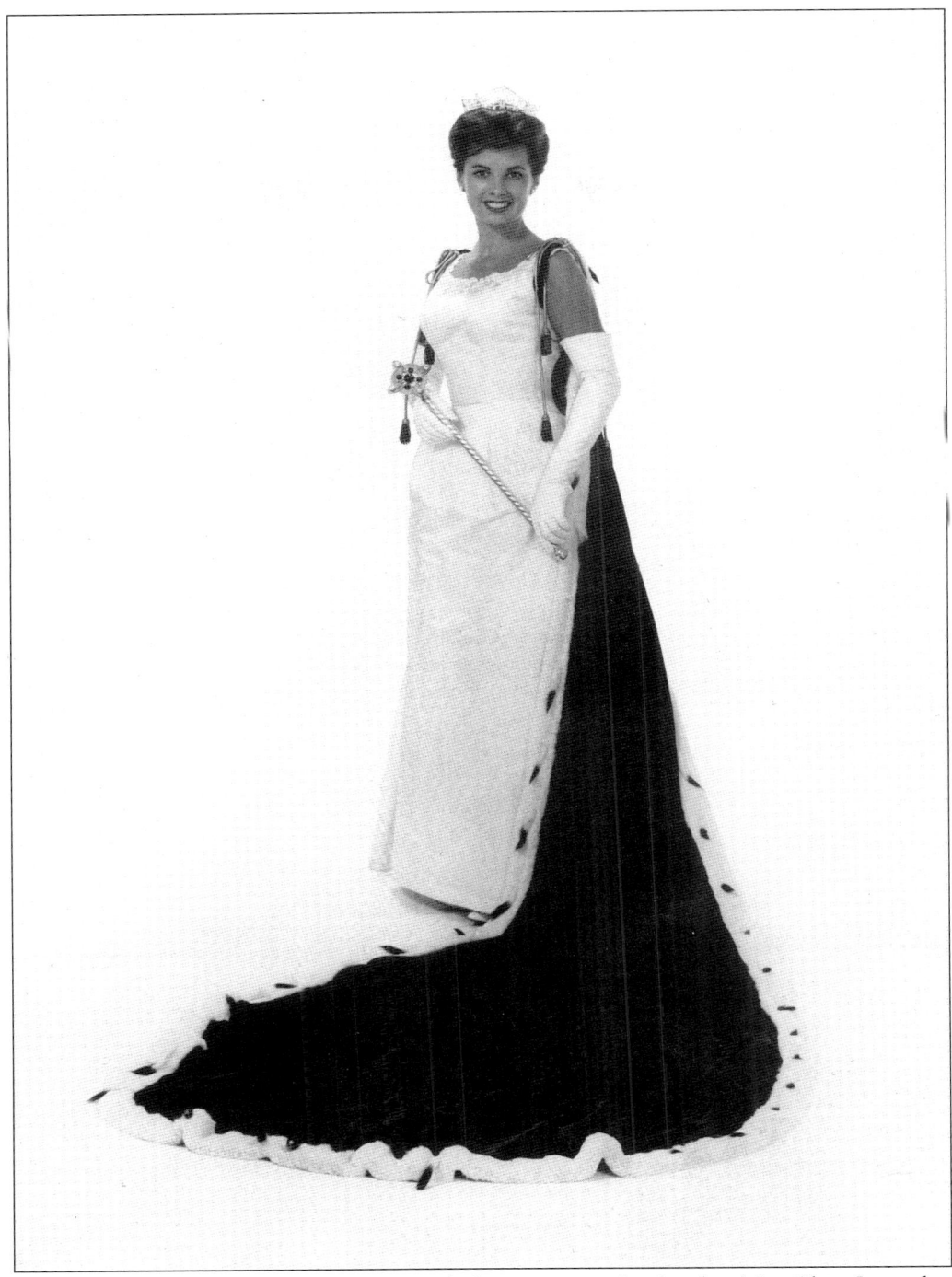

September 8, 1962, was a great day for Sanduskians—it was the day that Miss Ohio, Jacquelyn Mayer of Sandusky, was crowned Miss America 1963.

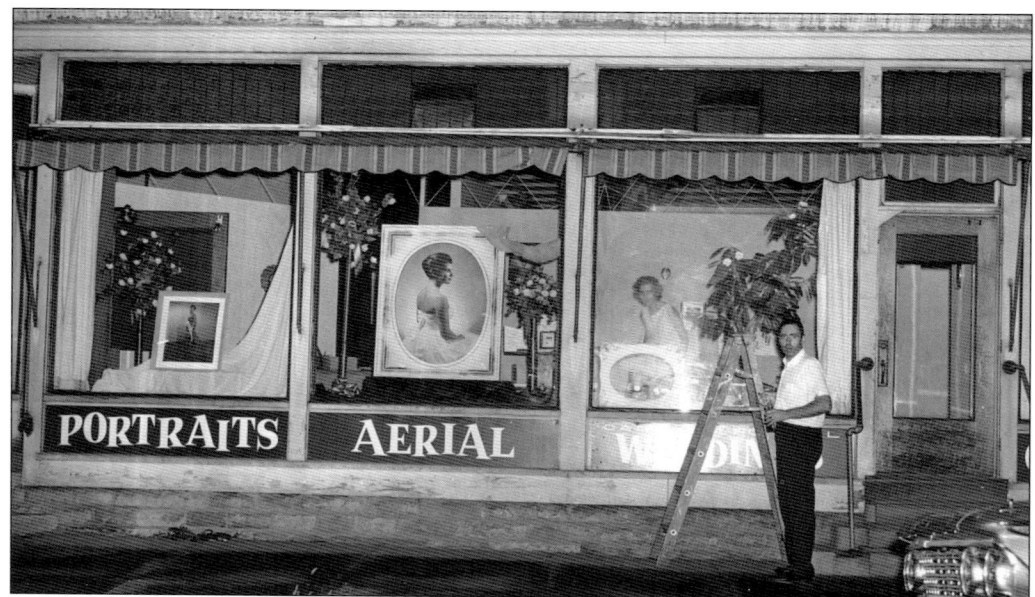

Sanduskians were rightfully proud of Jackie Mayer's achievement, and set out almost immediately upon hearing the news to express their happiness for the new Miss America. Al and Ginny Wintersteller of the Alden Photography Studio on Campbell Street were out at 1:30 a.m. on the night of the pageant to decorate their studio in celebration of Miss America's crowning.

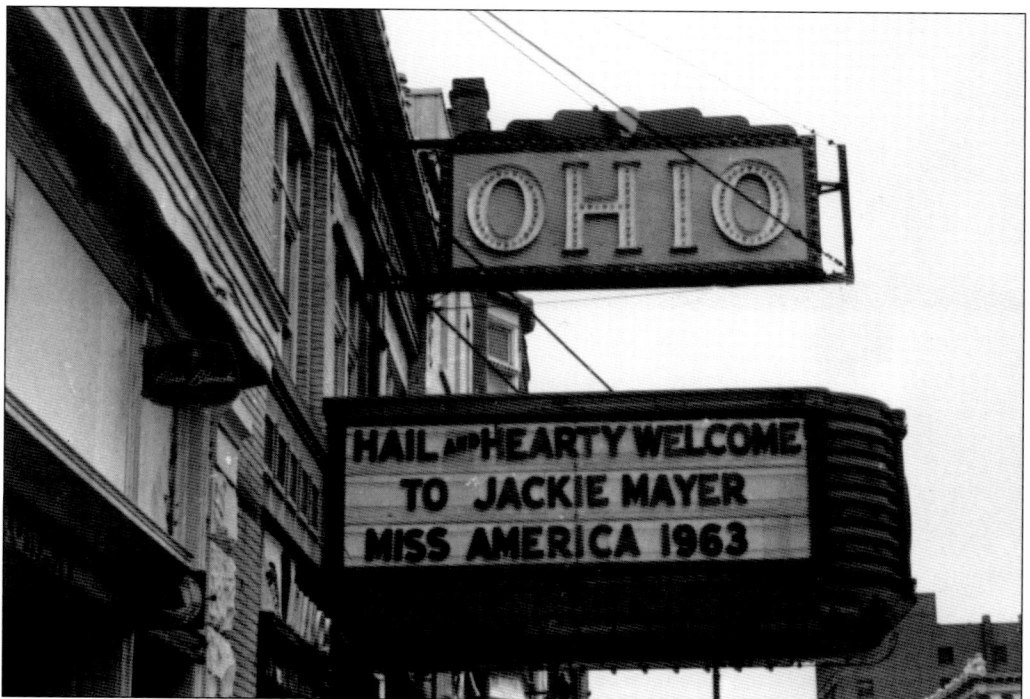

The Miss America Homecoming celebration on November 14, 1962, became another great celebration in Sandusky's history. The downtown parade attracted thousands of people to express their pride in a member of their community.

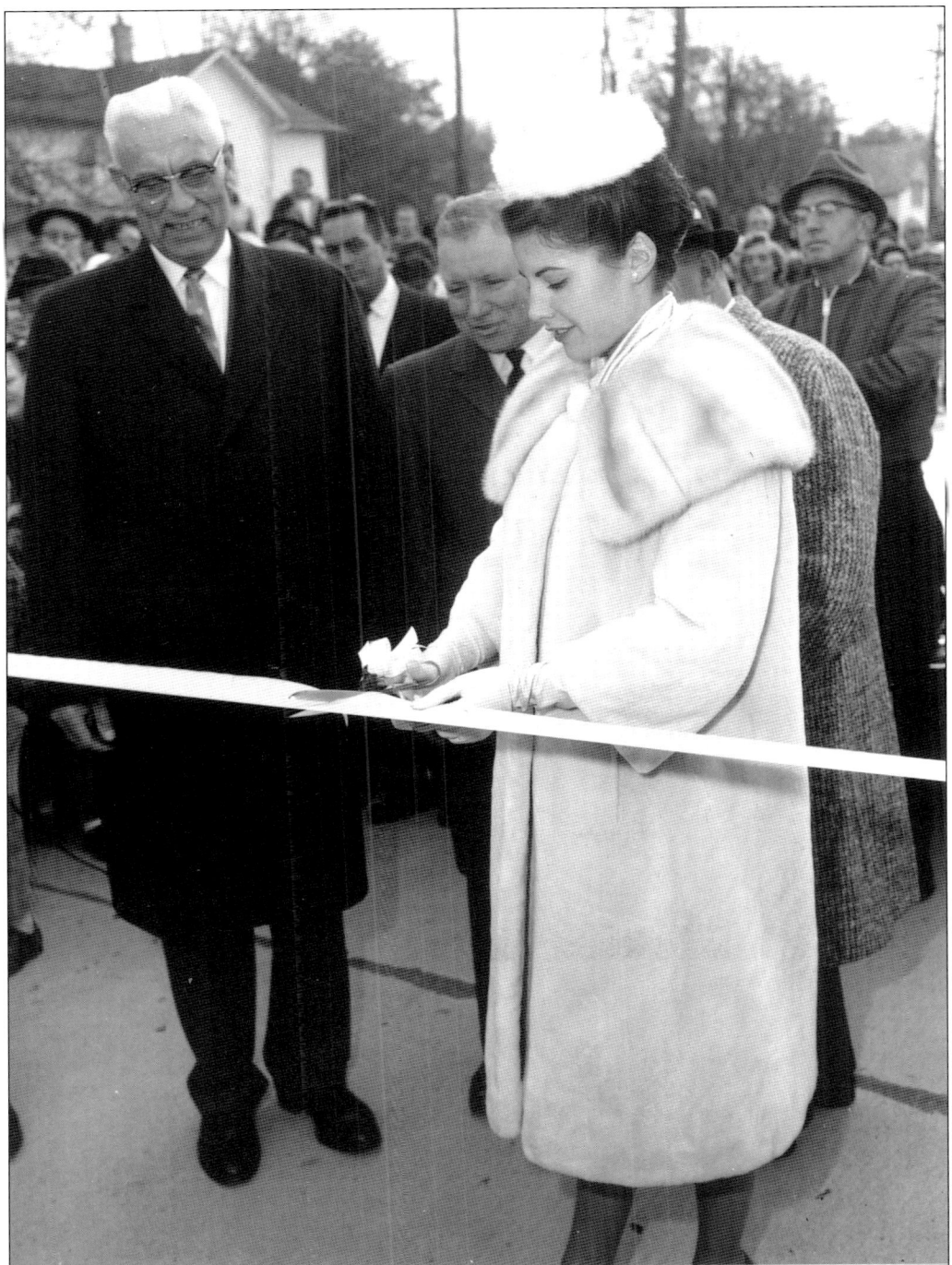
The ribbon cutting ceremony for the "Jackie Mayer Highway" on Route 2 in Huron drew a large crowd of admirers. Governor Michael DiSalle looks on as Miss America cuts the ribbon.

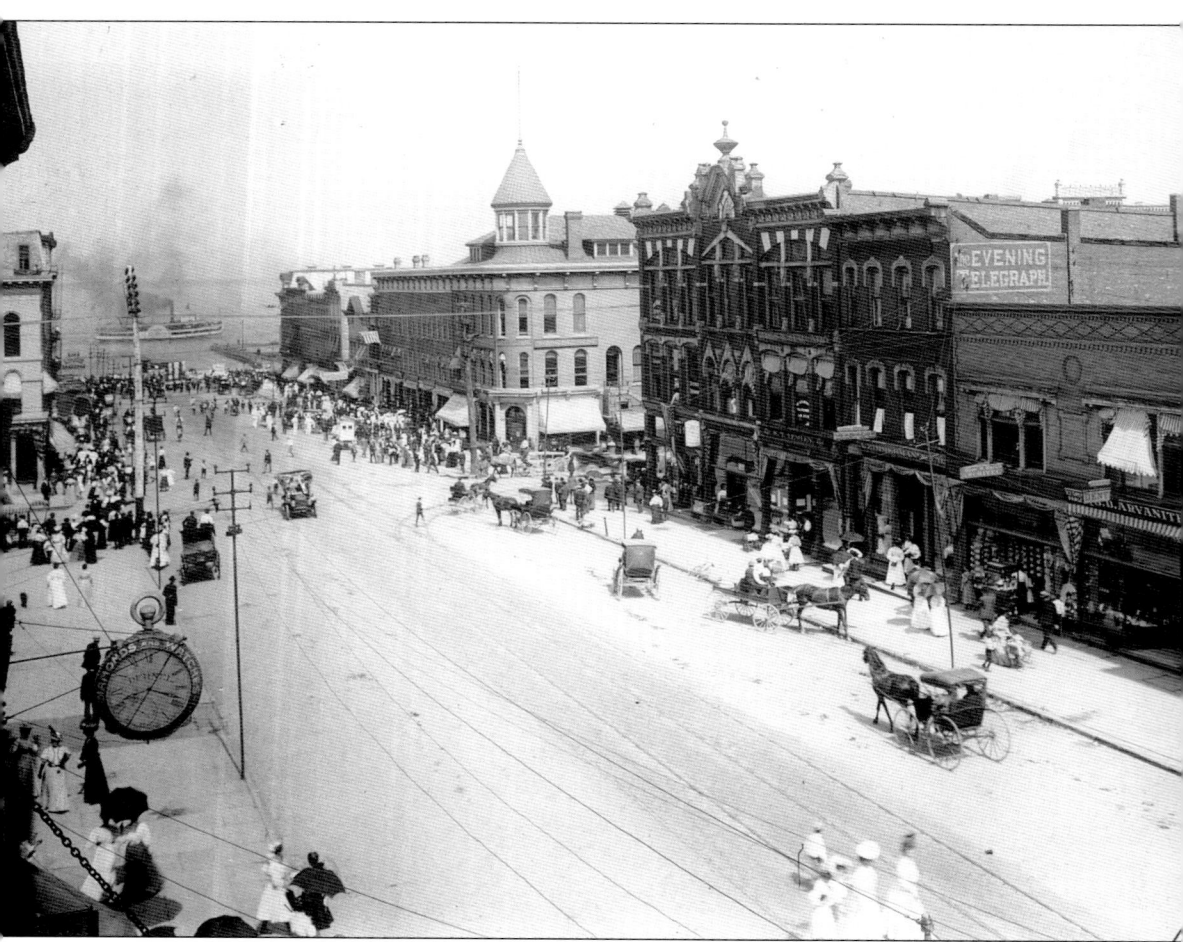

Although the scenes in the city may change, the heart of the community remains essentially the same.